"*Body Shots* is a wake-up call to girls and women everywhere. Fox-Kales' savvy analysis of filmic and other media representations of the female body in contemporary culture is riveting and utterly persuasive. Every woman, whether suffering from a disordered body image or not, will be compelled to reexamine the way she views her own body and her satisfaction or dissatisfaction with it in the light of this powerful and life-changing book."

uthor of
n Memoir

"In this   t culture
run amo   america's
unhealthy   , in film
after film   the spell
of pencil   nces are
disastrous   and cultural stud   ied with
teenagers

g Movies

"*Body Shot*   nnection
between I   culture
that is der   ertise in
the treatm

D, ScD,
School

"Emily Fo: of the
film indust   a great
resource t   images
impact our

service
ciation

D0205751

"With rising rates of obesity, we tend to overlook an equally important weight crisis—the fear of fat that can lead to anorexia, bulimia, bingeing, and other eating disorders. Fox-Kales applies her expertise as a clinical psychologist specializing in disordered eating to diagnose the celebrity culture's influence on normalizing an unhealthy ideal body standard. Her analysis is a must-read—well-researched, insightful, and engaging, filled with teachable moments to help deconstruct messages that encourage us to diet and exercise, even undergo plastic surgery, to attain the distorted body image reflected in Hollywood movies."

— Bobbie Eisenstock, Co-Director,
The Body Media Image (BMI) Project,
California State University, Northridge

"*Body Shots* offers a penetrating look at ways Hollywood films and related TV and advertising products perpetuate a profoundly destructive culture of eating disorders in the United States and beyond. Informed by her many years experience as a scholar, professor, and therapist, Fox-Kales zeros in on this meeting place of fantasy and actuality, where life-threatening ideals masquerade as desirable goals within the reach of women, teens, and tweens. The sweep of materials covered, supported by analysis and experiential testimony, yields a compelling, informative, dismaying, but also empathetic and highly readable book of significance to both professionals and the general public."

— Linda Dittmar, coauthor of
Multiple Voices in Feminist Film Criticism

"Psychologist Emily Fox-Kales' *Body Shots* is a compelling and uniquely interdisciplinary analysis of the impact of popular media on the lives of girls and women. Weaving vivid personal accounts from her clinical practice with insightful readings of contemporary films, television, and interactive media, Fox-Kales demonstrates the ways girls and women struggle to define themselves and their bodies against the damaging ideals fostered by popular culture. Wide-ranging and immensely readable, *Body Shots* brings feminist theory to life."

— Kathleen Rowe Karlyn, University of Oregon

BODY SHOTS

BODY SHOTS

Hollywood and the Culture of Eating Disorders

EMILY FOX-KALES

excelsior editions

State University of New York Press
Albany, New York

Published by State University of New York Press, Albany

For information, contact State University of New York Press, Albany, NY
www.sunypress.edu

Excelsior Editions is an imprint of State University of New York Press

Production by Eileen Meehan
Marketing by Fran Keneston

Library of Congress Cataloging-in-Publication Data

Fox-Kales, Emily
   Body shots : Hollywood and the culture of eating disorders / Emily Fox-Kales.
        p. cm.
   Includes bibliographical references and index.
   ISBN 978-1-4384-3529-9 (hardcover : alk. paper)
   ISBN 978-1-4384-3528-2 (pbk. : alk. paper)
   1. Human body in motion pictures.   2. Body image in motion pictures.
3. Motion pictures—Influence.   4. Motion pictures and women.   5. Women
in motion pictures.   I. Title.

   PN1995.9.B62F69 2011
   791.43'6561—dc2   2010031821

10 9 8 7 6 5 4 3 2 1

Contents

List of Illustrations   vii

Acknowledgments   ix

Introduction: Screen Bodies and Eating Disorders   1

CHAPTER ONE
Body Identifications: The Movie Screen and the Mirror   19

CHAPTER TWO
Celebrity Bodies   35

CHAPTER THREE
Body Mastery and the Ideology of Fitness   53

CHAPTER FOUR
Body Transformation: Ugly Ducklings, Swans, and
Movie Makeovers   73

CHAPTER FIVE
Body Stigmatization: Fat Suits and Big Mamas   95

CHAPTER SIX
Teen Bodies: Valley Girls and Middle School Vamps 119

CHAPTER SEVEN
Alternative Visions 141

Glossary of Terms 155

Notes 159

Bibliography 177

Index 187

List of Illustrations

Figure 1.1.   Borrowing an identity in *Mulholland Drive*   21

Figure 1.2.   A bevy of Veronica Lakes wait to dance in *The Major and the Minor*   29

Figure 1.3.   LAPD detectives mistake the "real" Lana Turner for a call girl in *L.A. Confidential*   30

Figure 1.4.   Call girl masquerading as Veronica Lake foregrounded against screen image of the "real" Veronica Lake in *This Gun for Hire* (1942)   31

Figure 2.1.   Oprah's triumph over fat (Courtesy Paul Natkin)   45

Figure 3.1.   Fashionable assassin Elle Driver waits for her victim to die in *Kill Bill 2*   60

Figure 3.2.   Beatrix Kiddo battles her enemies in Tokyo   62

Figure 3.3.   Beatrix checks for signs of pregnancy   66

Figure 3.4.   Maggie in the ring as her trainer watches from the ropes in *Million Dollar Baby*   69

Figure 3.5.   Maggie takes a blow to the face   69

Figure 4.1.   Hotel maid Marisa and her new admirer in Central Park in *Maid in Manhattan*   82

Figure 4.2.   Preparing for the ball   83

Figure 4.3.   The transformation completed   84

Figure 4.4.	Agent Gracie Hart has one more for the road in *Miss Congenialty*	90
Figure 4.5.	Miss New Jersey takes center stage	93
Figure 5.1.	The bride carries her groom over the threshold in *Shallow Hal*	105
Figure 5.2.	Hal rushes to the aid of his date	107
Figure 5.3.	Together at last in the same frame	107
Figure 5.4./5.5.	The mystery of the giant underpants	109
Figure 5.6.	Fiona defends her man in *Shrek 2*	113
Figure 5.7.	Death struggle with a pig in *Misery*	116
Figure 6.1.	A trio of Barbie dolls in *Never Been Kissed*	122
Figure 6.2.	Cher as the object of the male gaze in *Clueless*	124
Figure 6.3.	Regina struggles with her Prom dress in *Mean Girls*	127
Figure 6.4.	Lunchtime at the Plastics' table	128
Figure 6.5.	The anorexic Miss Teen takes a bow in *Drop Dead Gorgeous*	129
Figure 6.6.	Courtney's clique makes their entrance in *Jawbreaker*	131
Figure 6.7.	Courtney seduces her high school boyfriend in her bedroom	132
Figure 6.8.	Jim and Nadia "live" in his bedroom in *American Pie* . . .	133
Figure 6.9.	. . . and online	133
Figure 6.10.	Happy hour with *Mean Girls'* cool mom	139
Figure 7.1.	Elizabeth stands for her body assessment in *Lovely and Amazing*	144
Figure 7.2.	Annie contemplates her image	146
Figure 7.3.	Ana and her mother battle over dessert in *Real Women Have Curves*	149
Figure 7.4.	Letting it all hang out at the dress factory	151

Acknowledgments

I wish to express my gratitude to the many individuals who helped bring *Body Shots* into being. Given the nature of the project, I was fortunate to receive the collective wisdom of colleagues across a wide range of disciplines. They include faculty members of the Cinema Studies program at Northeastern University, especially Inez Hedges and the late Kathy Howlett, whose friendship and support helped me build the bridge from psychology to film studies, as well as many other colleagues at the Northeastern Women's Studies Program and the Graduate Women's Studies Consortium who have provided lively conversations in cultural and gender studies. I am also grateful for the support of the Department of Psychology and Gerald Herman of The Center for Interdisciplinary Studies who generously allowed me not only the opportunity to create the courses and research from which the idea for this book emerged but also the precious gift of time to move the project along during the academic year. I am equally indebted to the Society for Cinema and Media Studies as well as the Institute for Psychological Study of the Arts whose conferences provided an engaging forum in which to present my work on many of the themes that made their way into *Body Shots*. I am particularly grateful to the individuals who so generously took time to read earlier drafts of specific chapters in the book, including Kathleen Rowe Karlyn, Suzanne Leonard, Kim Michelson, and Kim Rice Whittemore, all of whose comments were consistently sharp and insightful. I also greatly appreciated the input from peer reviewers who remain anonymous to me but whose careful readings of the manuscript proved truly helpful in formulating its central arguments. Above all, I wish to thank the wonderful staff at SUNY Press, most especially my editor Larin McLaughlin, who from the very start was an abiding source of support and guidance and the individual most central to the "birthing" of the book.

It is impossible to imagine the possibility of *Body Shots* without all those individuals with whom I have been so privileged to work throughout my clinical career. The courage and honesty of the many women and girls who have shared their struggles with body image and eating problems, including my patients at McLean Hospital, participants in the Feeding Ourselves program and my psychotherapy clients, as well as the enthusiasm of the students in my courses who so energetically investigated the relationship between popular cultural images and eating disordered behavior, provided the motivation to write this book and I am deeply indebted to each and every one of them for the inspiration.

Many others have provided invaluable "behind the scenes" expertise, which helped make the process of writing *Body Shots* far more pleasant and efficient than I could have ever imagined. I especially want to thank my tireless research assistant Danielle Khalife, generous technical advisors Terry Beadle and Jim Gokhale, and ever-cheerful and competent administrator Eileen Stack. Deep appreciation goes also to my agent Janice Pieroni for her unfailing encouragement and thoughtful counsel. Moments of rest and relaxation were freely provided by loving—and understanding—friends and family members, especially Matthew, Michelle, Eli, and Annabel Kales, and Norma Fox Moxley, throughout the many months during which I was absorbed in the project. This book is dedicated to my husband David Kales, who with steadfast good humor and patience watched more Hollywood movies with me over the years than he ever signed on for.

Introduction

Screen Bodies and Eating Disorders

The genesis of this book lies at the intersection of three paths I have traveled in my personal and professional life: the first as a clinical psychologist specializing in the treatment of eating disorders and body image disturbance, the second as a university professor of cultural studies and psychology, and the third as a passionate moviegoer. But it grows even more deeply out of lifetime membership in the diverse community of women who come of age in what I call "the culture of eating disorders"—a world in which food has become more taboo than sex ever was and the bathroom scale more challenging a confrontation than the confessional booth. If fitness is the new religion and slenderness represents spiritual perfection then surely food abstinence is both piety and purity, reviving the asceticism of fasting medieval girl-saints and pioneering health faddists such as Sylvester Graham who exhorted American mothers to protect their families from gluttony, wanton sexuality, and moral depravity by making his legendary bran cracker "the centerpiece of a stark but flavorful life."[1] Renunciation has replaced indulgence in the sinful pleasure of eating while vigilance is the rule of the table; the dollop of whipped cream on a cup of cappuccino is removed as gingerly as if it were a time bomb, while the bowl of peanuts is pushed to the other side of the table to ensure a safe distance from temptation. The age-old sisterhood of trading recipes and exchanging food traditions and tastes has been replaced by a different bond: what women in a weight-obsessed culture share most of all is a fear of food and its dreaded outcome—fat.

For more than thirty years I have counseled women and girls whose eating and weight problems are the all too vivid manifestations of a diet culture run amok. Many of my most memorable cases have been dramatic and tragic—from the sixty-five-pound anorexic girl hooked up to naso-gastric feeding tubes who stashed her meal tray in the hospital ceiling tiles over her bed to the 350-pound binge eater driven to demolish her children's snack packs in the pantry at three in the morning and the fifty-two-year-old life-long bulimic woman who never divulged her shameful secret to her family. Countless others have shared stories less sensational but just as telling. These are the thousands of women, college students, teens, and tweens I have seen in therapy or taught in courses or met with in small groups around the country and overseas who get up each morning touching their abdomens to see if they are sufficiently flat, who quiet growling bellies with *venti* black coffees and endless diet energy drinks while holding out until evening to devour their daily allowance of steamed vegetables and sugar free/ fat free ice cream, who count calories instead of sheep as they drift off to sleep. Such food and body anxieties echo far beyond the eating disorder hospital and the therapist's office to the gym, the fitting room at the mall, and the office cafeteria where women inhabit a calorie conscious territory bounded by "legal" and "forbidden" rations or worry their way through daily workouts convinced their thighs are jiggling with dreaded cellulite while calculating how much they can go into debt for corrective liposuction surgery. Ashamed and demoralized at gaining weight they skip college reunions and weddings or avoid the beach on the hottest of days, while others just as fiercely maintain dangerously low weights because everyone tells them they "look good."

While each woman's story is uniquely her own, it shares one common and implacable theme: a troubled relationship to the body's "look"—its size and shape, sexual attractiveness, its exposure both dressed and undressed—in a consumer beauty culture where the body has become inextricably linked to personal identity and self-worth. Surface has replaced core; internal character virtues such as integrity and courage are subordinated to external manifestations of bodily control and discipline while self-concept is synonymous with body image.[2] Today the toned body represents strength of character: it signifies the "will power" to abstain from overeating as well as a praiseworthy dedication to shape the unshapely form through devotion to exercise and investment of personal capital in its physical rehabilitation.

Even more poignantly than their stories of body hatred and shame, what women and girls talk about how is they *want* to look— their fantasies of transformation into their "dream bodies." The most powerful visions, which drive them to starve on a raw vegetable diet or save their money for tummy tucks, are found not in the mirror but in the movies. As film scholar Richard Dyer reminds us: "Your ideas about who you are don't just come from inside you; they come from the culture. And in this culture they come especially from the movies. We learn from the movies what it means to be a man or a woman." Put still more succinctly by actor Tony Curtis: "The movies is where we learn about life."[3]

It is in this sense that all visual media productions "teach" viewers about femininity and male desire, power, and love, through their circulation of images that literally *embody* popular cultural meanings and values. But no other medium, even in the face of a vast array of new media technologies, constructs images with such extraordinary immediacy as the cinema—and it is the image of the screen body that most compels our attention. We may soon forget the dialogue we hear in the screenplay of a film but we take away indelible visual memories of how the characters dressed, moved, and revealed their bodies both to the camera and our own gaze. And because of the market realities confronting the corporate entertainment industry today, Hollywood movies rely on visual impact more than ever before. Escalating production costs mean fewer movies are being released; to ensure profits studios demand higher budgets for marketing and "big name" stars to churn out blockbusters targeted for international distribution. To win the broadest audience appeal worldwide, big studio films focus not only on the dazzling technical special effects of spectacular action blockbusters but also on the bodies of those movie stars universally recognized for their stylized beauty and glamour—bodies that are remarkably the same: "As a commercial entertainment that is produced with mass audiences and greatest box office in mind," notes film scholar Philippa Gates, "Hollywood film presents mainstream rather than radical or controversial attitudes. This uniformity of mores and values in the fictional Hollywood world creates a consistency in representation across the films it produces."[4] Not surprisingly, such globally marketed films are designed to emphasize the surface rather than the depth of the images they construct, and Hollywood is loathe to trouble them with either complexity or critique of a contemporary consumer culture that is equally dedicated to the cultivation of the body's outward appearance.

Hollywood images of bodily perfection and slenderness do not simply *reflect* cultural ideals of femininity and fitness; they can actively influence the way the female moviegoer engages with her own body image and eating behavior. One reason that cinema can exert this kind of impact is that it has the capacity to elicit processes of screen identification within the spectator that contribute to the body dissatisfaction and appearance anxiety found by clinical research to be a highly potent risk factor for developing eating disorders.[5] The complex pathway that leads from the construction of the Hollywood movie to the female viewer's personal relationship to food and her body is the subject of this book. In it I will trace how popular movies, movie stars, and celebrity media help propagate the values of an "eating disordered culture" which promotes constant self-scrutiny and body vigilance, denial of appetite, and overcontrol of weight—a culture, in short, that naturalizes and even idealizes pathological behaviors and beliefs in the compulsive pursuit of an eternally elusive body ideal so powerful that many women and girls feed on a collective screen dream instead of the food they crave—but are afraid to eat.

In order to trace exactly how Hollywood productions contribute to those social risk factors that can lead to subclinical and clinical eating problems among vulnerable moviegoers, *Body Shots* reads the texts of recent popular films as visual representations of those social forces discussed in each of the book's chapters. These include the medicalization of consumer beauty practices, the fitness movement's ideologies of discipline, and discourses of celebrity body maintenance. My larger goal is to demonstrate not only how popular film narratives and cinematic conventions reflect contemporary body culture but even more crucially to engage the reader in a media literacy project to critically interrogate both the screen images and the gendered assumptions they perpetuate about women and girls.

Endless pursuit of the perfected screen body can help push the most vulnerable viewers over the razor-thin line that separates what has become the "new normal" of nagging weight worries on the one side from destructive dieting and eating behavior on the other, just as it informs the imagery here of the fifteen-year-old girl I met with on a hospital eating disorder unit. She had recently lost thirty pounds during weeks on a semi-starvation diet. Her hair thinning and falling out, anemic and shivering on a hot summer day, she was nonetheless exultant: "You don't know how hard I've worked to finally get thin. I'm not *ordinary* anymore; everyone says I look just like some hot Hollywood starlet!" But that "look" this young movie fan is desperately trying to emulate—hipless, belly-less, and above all "thin"—is biologically beyond the reach of 95 percent of American women.[6] Put in statistical terms, it is the "outliers" who dictate the norm for what women and girls think is acceptable and ideal, in large part because the images of superslender movie stars and celebrities can so dazzle us that we lose sight of the fact that their bodies represent the exception rather than the rule of women's natural shape and size.[7] And while their glamorous and seductive images provide immediate visual pleasure for both male and female viewers they can also create a deep frustration in susceptible individuals that inspires them to go to dangerous lengths to squeeze their bodies into sizes they are not naturally designed to be unless overexercised, undernourished, and literally "whipped into shape."

In this way Hollywood media and beauty culture has become a prominent element of what I call the "Eating Disorder Formula": the wider the gap between the culturally constructed ideal body a woman internalizes and that of her own biological template, the more driven she is to impose harsh regimens of body discipline and dietary restraint to close that gap. And though today's moviegoers are certainly savvy about digital morphing, body doubles, and the artifice behind flawless Hollywood movie images, after two hours of gazing at female bodies that are impossibly leggy and lean, toned and ageless, it is not surprising that many viewers suspend their critical faculties and surrender to the feeling that in comparison their own bodies are "ordinary" or terribly wrong—and may be inspired to take drastic steps to make them right.[8] Hollywood's fantasies can be so seductive that we may even forget our initial skepticism that these glamorized and sexualized bodies are cast in everyday roles such as a police detective or stay-at-home mom yet somehow mysteriously manage to glide through their "average" workaday lives with the practiced grace of a supermodel. Film scholar Laura Mulvey points to this visual contradiction in her famous essay on cinematic pleasure and female movie stars, who "act out a complex process of likeness and difference [in which] . . . the glamorous impersonates the ordinary."[9]

This book does not argue that movies *cause* anorexia or bulimia. (And certainly throughout the history of Hollywood millions of moviegoing women and girls have managed to delight in the gorgeous illusions on the screen without harmful side effects!) First of all, it is crucial to note that a host of other factors—biological, familial, psychological—contribute to individual resilience or susceptibility to developing these illnesses, so many in fact that attributing anorexia or bulimia or binge eating disorder to any single cause has long since proven both inadequate and inaccurate. Both researchers and clinicians have come to understand the impossibility of reducing such complex disorders which involve both psyche and soma—including nutritional status, eating and exercise habits, and cognitions—to one simple etiology. For well over a century, depending on historical, political, scientific, and sociocultural trends, which influenced methodology and diagnosis,[10] the symptoms of eating disorders have been attributed to everything from unresolved sexual conflicts and obsessive personality styles to absentee fathers and dieting mothers and more recently to neurochemical and genetic predispositions.[11] And since the diagnoses historically have fallen disproportionately upon among women, feminist researchers have focused on issues of gender and institutional power as key contributing factors.[12]

Secondly, we need to bear in mind that each media consumer brings her or his own unique story—personal history, memories, cultural identities—which affects how media images are interpreted from one viewer to the next. This is why many social scientists and communications theorists are skeptical about the validity of *any* actual effects of media on human behavior.[13] These critics point out that any individual viewer's behavior is motivated by far too many variables, ranging from biological to sociocultural, to assume a uniform effect of "mass" media on audiences; instead they posit a complex interaction between an actively engaged viewer who interprets media images in an infinite number of ways. Nonetheless, even such a harsh critic as scholar David Gauntlett (who dismissed "media effects" research as "rubbish") admits that "this is not to say that media does not have an *influence* on the thoughts and perceptions of its viewers, and their attitudes to life, and relationships, and their expectations about the world."[14] Put another way, while it is simplistic to blame a monolithic big bad Hollywood system for causing the explosion of eating disorders around the world, its active participation in the circulation of ideals, beliefs, and attitudes about the body should not be underestimated. According to the "cultivation theory" formulated by communication scholars, media both reflects and reinforces cultural norms as it constantly interacts with culture to shape our understanding of the world. And when it comes to body image and the body ideal, media psychologists see culture and media as still more inextricably linked: "Indeed," observes David Giles, "this is one of the few areas in psychology in which culture and media are treated as synonymous."[15]

Throughout the book I will demonstrate how Hollywood movies are particularly powerful in reinforcing the cultural beliefs echoed in other popular media texts, all the while resonating with cumulative impact as they help construct what we recognize as "mainstream" beauty culture. For example, the "makeover movies" I discuss in the chapter "Body Transformation" reflect current trends in celebrity body culture, social media networking, consumer marketing, and the democratization of aesthetic surgery, as well as the credo of the fitness movement—all of which are reinforced in turn by the circulation in television, film, print, and electronic media of images of perfected and "reformed" bodies. The net result of all these developments is that Hollywood's screen visions of body transformation resonate with more impact than ever before on the behavior and beliefs of moviegoers who seek to perfect their own bodily imperfections. In this way Hollywood films actively participate in a dynamic threefold process: They initially amplify contemporary body and beauty ideals, which are subsequently reinforced via supportive celebrity media and marketing, thereby gathering increasing resonance and ultimately go on to affect viewers already primed to aspire to those same ideals—the target audience of girls, adolescents, and young women who consume Hollywood movies and their spin-off products and productions.

In recent decades researchers and clinicians searching for causes of eating disorders have focused more intently on mass-marketed images of the body in popular media, largely in response to the marked increase of problematic eating and weight control practices in ever wider populations both at home and abroad. While the prevalence of the most devastating eating disorders—anorexia, bulimia, and binge eating disorder—is relatively small and stable with nationwide rates of .05-1 percent for AN and 1.5 percent for bulimia and 3.5 percent for binge eating disorder, the rate of what we call "subclinical eating disorders"—troubled patterns of rigid dieting, binge eating, and excessive exercising that fail to meet the diagnostic criteria for acute psychiatric illness—has continued to show ominous growth across all age groups, ethnicities, and genders.[16] While no stranger to college campuses where body disturbances and abnormal eating behaviors have been rampant for years,[17] problems among high school and middle school students are skyrocketing with reports showing more than 50 percent of adolescent girls engaging in unhealthy weight control behaviors, including purging and laxative abuse, diet pill dependence, and just about every type of crash diet imaginable.[18] Still more worrisome is the transmission of these problems to even younger American girls, with oft-cited studies finding 81 percent of ten-year-olds to be seasoned dieters[19] and nearly one-quarter of eight-year-olds afraid to eat lest they get fat.[20] It is no longer unusual for parents to see their preschoolers frowning at their "fat tummies" in the mirror as increasingly children mimic the fasting and exercise rituals of their mothers and grandmothers in a multigenerational panic at gaining weight. Nor is body obsession strictly gendered; while the ratio of female to male eating disorders is still heavily weighted toward women[21] as many as one million males suffer from some form of eating disorder, particularly a variant known as muscle dysmorphia—commonly dubbed "reverse anorexia"—where men and boys spend hours bodybuilding in the gym only to see themselves as impossibly scrawny in the distorted mirror of their self-perception.[22]

Once considered the exclusive malaise of privileged white females, body image disturbances and disordered eating now affect all ethnic and racial groups, including those that had previously been thought to be protected by communities sharing more diverse or traditional body ideals. Today that cultural protection has eroded, in large part due to the proliferation of mass media images which circulate a uniform "look" that cuts across socioeconomic, racial, and ethnic body diversities. Thus, it is not surprising that in a large study of more than 4,500 Hispanic, Asian American, Caucasian, and African American teens in a Midwestern school system researchers found virtually no difference in the rates of body dissatisfaction and extreme weight control methods among female students; in fact on several measures the Hispanic and Asian American subjects were even more troubled than their white counterparts about their weight.[23]

Still more striking is research showing that since the turn of the twenty-first century eating disorders have indeed gone global. Hefty percentages of high school girls in Mexico now use laxatives and diuretics to lose weight,[24] a large subset of teen girls in the United Arab Emirates test high on the risk scale for anorexia,[25] while an alarming number of young women in Tanzania report binge eating and purging.[26] Many researchers have been quick to attribute the recent increases in disturbed eating behavior to the fact that access to Western television and other popular media extends to remote corners of an increasingly "wired" world. If the adolescent girl in East Africa can now conjure the images of supermodel actresses at the Academy Awards on her cell phone it is no wonder that when she looks in the mirror it is with disapproving eyes at a reflection that tells her she falls short of the feminine body ideal that has become universally coded for success, power, and sexual desirability. In fact, world marketing of Hollywood productions would seem to include at no extra charge a lifetime supply of body anxiety and dissatisfaction. Notes commentator Ellen Goodman: "The biggest success story of the entertainment industry is our ability to export insecurity: We can make any woman anywhere feel perfectly rotten about her shape."[27]

In search of the source of this near-universal body discontent a host of social scientists and media psychologists have examined the effects of popular media exposure on girls and women. Among the best-known studies is a cross-cultural research project conducted in the Fiji Islands. Before the advent of television in 1995 Fijian girls believed that "going thin" was a bad sign and that gaining weight was healthy. Three years after their exposure to American television as many as 74 percent of the girls reported feeling "too big," 62 percent were dieting, and 15 percent were purging. The most avid viewers showed the highest risk for eating disorders; among their favorite were shows like *Melrose Place* and *Beverly Hills 09210* that featured hypersexualized or pencil-thin female actresses.[28] More typically, studies have been conducted in an experimental laboratory where subjects are presented with images from print and television media displaying slender bodies and models. Their emotional and cognitive reactions are then compared with those after the same subjects are exposed instead to general news media or "non-body" product advertisements. While these studies report some variability in their outcomes, with some showing stronger exposure effects than others, they trend in the same direction: the more the research subjects were exposed to high fashion magazines, advertisements, music videos, and television shows featuring slender models and performers, the more they were likely to report feeling unhappy with their own bodies and express an increased determination to get thinner. The studies also confirm that after viewing glamorized bodies young adult women and girls were particularly vulnerable to internalizing the "thin ideal" and to valuing slenderness as a primary source of meaning and self-worth.

Impressive validation of these findings comes from a "meta-analysis" of seventy-seven experimental media exposure studies conducted between

1975–2007 which analyzed data from standardized psychological tests measuring body esteem, figure rating, body attitudes, and body satisfaction, as well as a variety of diagnostic scales for disordered eating cognitions. It concluded: "These findings suggest that, overall, thin-ideal media exposure is related to higher levels of body dissatisfaction, stronger internalization of the thin ideal, and more frequent bulimic and anorexic attitudes and behaviors." Still more striking in terms of the general proliferation of body disturbances worldwide was the finding that internalization of the thin ideal appeared stronger since the turn of the twenty-first century, suggesting that the more women were saturated with slender body images the more profound the impact. But perhaps most troubling of all was the finding that repeated exposure persuaded these media consumers to endorse behaviors such as severe food restriction and purging as normal and acceptable methods necessary to embody the media ideals they so deeply admired.[29]

At the same time it is important to qualify such compelling research data with questions about methodology and research design. We might ask, for example, exactly how long do these media effects last? Are they transient or really enduring? Were the research studies experimental or correlational? Each has their methodological drawbacks: experimental studies are conducted in the laboratory under tightly controlled research conditions but only capture short term effects, while correlational studies, which can follow viewers' exposure over time, are dependent on individual self-reporting; such subjective findings are harder to quantify. We might also question if these studies were sensitive to ethnic and cultural differences among research subjects.[30] And in view of new and constantly changing viewing habits of media consumers we must wonder exactly *how* the material is being watched: On a smartphone while dashing to work? On a television monitor buzzing in the background of an airport terminal? Or in a quick mashup on You Tube or music video on Hulu? In an environment in which we are increasingly media "multitasking " it might be a combination of all of the above![31]

Most importantly we must ask exactly *who* are the subjects of these media exposure studies? The majority have tested adolescent and college age females, the age group most susceptible to peer influence and role modeling at that fragile developmental stage where it has been said "our sense of self is balanced precariously on the threshold of adulthood."[32] Moreover, since within this demographic there is a subgroup who respond far more dramatically than their peers to the media images they were exposed to in the studies, we are left with yet another question: Are women and girls who already suffer from troubled body images more likely to be drawn to television shows and fashion magazines that feature their slender ideal, catching us in a chicken-and-egg dilemma? Both clinical and media researchers often point to the fact that eating-disordered individuals who have a distorted body image and thus may be more profoundly impacted by images of superslender celebrity bodies also tend to negatively compare themselves to others, whether it is the girl in the next gym locker or the model in a fashion magazine. In a strangely vicious cycle, then, it is these very individuals who suffer the most insidious effects of exposure to media yet are its most frequent consumers![33]

Despite these and other questions that emerge from the difficulty of proving a direct cause and effect mechanism, taken collectively over so many studies and years the data is sufficiently compelling to point to media exposure as a potent influence on the eating behavior and body image of susceptible viewers. Most media exposure research, however, has focused on the effects of television, magazines, and advertisements, leaving the impact of popular film largely unexamined. And while from the perspective of cultivation theory we cannot separate out the influence of movies from the surrounding cultural matrix, more than any of the other forms of popular media previously studied Hollywood films are constructed to maximize their potential to affect moviegoers' beliefs about the body as a source of desire, love, success, and power.

Movies, known from their earliest days as the products of Hollywood's "dream factory," exert a particularly strong influence because they work upon both unconscious as well as conscious processes of seeing. Film scholars long ago noted the similarities between the cinema and the dream state: we sit quiet and motionless in the dark theatre, suspending our own consciousness as we enter an illusory world created by the succession of fleeting images projected on the blank screen. For two hours we enjoy a kind of "out of body experience," uninterrupted by intrusions from the outside "real" world or television commercials, enveloped by larger than life figures and the magical weave of motion, color, sound, and light, which combine to create the spectacle of the cinema. Other film theorists who went on to apply psychoanalytic models to cinema spectatorship were quick to identify in the cinema such unconscious dream processes as wish fulfillment and displacement, leading critic Parker Tyler to conclude: "The movie theater is the psychoanalytic clinic of the average worker's daylight dream."[34] As a famous movie star, actress Susan Sarandon understands only too well the awesome power of Hollywood dreams on the moviegoer: "Movies are important and they're dangerous because we're the keeper of the dreams. You go into a little dark room and become incredibly vulnerable. . . . It can encourage you to be the protagonists in your own life. On the other hand it can completely misshape you."[35]

At the same time that movies may evoke our own personal "daylight dream" they also visualize a collective dream that we share with the rest of the spectators in the theater audience. That is because Hollywood movies are quick to absorb the cultural *Zeitgeist*—our generational anxieties, traumas, and deeply held beliefs, our unspoken fears and desires—and reflect them back as screen visions of a social dream or nightmare. In a post 9/11 world for example, global fears of terrorism become visually embedded in a superhero blockbuster such as *Dark Knight* (2008) with its explosive images of a crime-ridden metropolis in a chaotic society symbolized by the irrational malevolence of the "mad" Joker. Equally resonant with current conflicts from identity politics to climate change and world destabilization is James Cameron's 2009 futuristic mega-hit *Avatar*. In a less apocalyptic but equally potent way Hollywood mythologizes contemporary body and beauty conventions in the narratives and characters that construct romantic comedies, superwomen action films, and the popular movie genres colloquially known as "chick flix" and "teenpics" aimed at female audiences. These kinds of films reflect collective body anxieties and aspirations which then resonate to each viewer's personal experiences, memories, and private dreams, creating a constant circulation of meaning and image between screen and spectator.

To better understand how popular movies specifically impact both the body images and eating and exercise behaviors of female spectators, chapter 1 of *Body Shots* examines how the psychological effects identified by media exposure research such as body dissatisfaction and internalization of the thin body ideal interact with established theories about the processes of screen identification and idealization originally posited by film scholars such as Jackie Stacey and Laura Mulvey. Their pioneering psychoanalytic, cultural, and feminist approaches to film analysis can still guide us today in navigating the relationship between the meanings encoded in images of screen bodies and how moviegoers then decode those messages as they construct their own body images.

While Mulvey's theory of cinema spectatorship was premised on the view of Hollywood as a patriarchal system that produced images of the woman's body for the voyeuristic pleasure of a male audience, here I am interested in how theories of cinematic identification help explain the impact of screen bodies on the formation of the *female* moviegoer's body image and consequent eating behavior. In much the same way, the motif of the Lacanian mirror, which figures prominently in psychoanalytic film theories about cinematic idealization, can be re-framed to explain how vulnerable female viewers may get demoralized at the "lack" in their own bodies of movie star slenderness and perfection, seeing in their mirrored reflections a distorted image that engenders body dissatisfaction and shame. Since both processes of screen identification and idealization are centered on the visual power of the movie star image, the chapter also describes the construction of both the all-important screen body as well as of the Hollywood star image, and demonstrates how the themes and structures of star identification are played out in the 1997 film *L.A. Confidential.*

Chapter 2 goes on to trace the heightened influence of the movie star's body in today's celebrity culture where it becomes a kind of "cross-mediated currency" between Hollywood movies and other popular media that propagate the many cultural meanings embedded in her image.[36] The chapter connects the spread of eating-disordered behaviors in recent years to an ever-widening dissemination of media images of celebrity bodies, focusing on how the "body narratives" of such Hollywood celebrities as Lindsay Lohan, Gwyneth Paltrow, and Oprah Winfrey serve as public enactments of the same eating and weight struggles their fans and audiences endure. Celebrity battles with bulimia, post-maternal weight gain, and yo-yo dieting thus become not simply a potent source of popular identification with disordered eating practices but a glamorized validation of the body dissatisfaction, hypervigilance, and self-scrutiny that characterize eating-disordered culture. Finally, this chapter explores how body preoccupation is intensified with the advent of electronic media such as You Tube and social networking sites, as well as digital devices such as "smart" phones and software-laden cameras, which have given rise to a new media environment in which consumers can now construct and circulate their own celebrity images.

The following four chapters of the book then examine how specific popular film genres both reflect and influence different aspects of eating, dieting, and exercise behaviors in female movie viewers. Each chapter includes a close reading of representative films in order to see how their narrative structure, cinematography, soundtracks, and casting construct both implicit and explicit messages not only about contemporary attitudes and beliefs regarding food and weight but notions of femininity and male desire as well. Chapter 3 considers how the "woman warrior" of action blockbusters embodies those ideologies of fitness and body discipline that are implicated in the compulsive regimens and overcontrol of the body that can presage such disorders as exercise bulimia and "gymorexia." Analysis of the figures of the superwomen assassins of *Kill Bill 1* and *2*, for example, reveals that rather than representing genuine images of female strength and empowerment their hypersexualized and stylized bodies in fact perpetuate the cultural dream of desirability and superslenderness that drives obsessive exercising and fitness regimens in women and girls.

Chapter 4 describes how "makeover movies" such as *Maid in Manhattan*, *Miss Congeniality*, and *The Devil Wears Prada* use the motif of body transformation to visualize socioeconomic narratives of class and mobility as well as traditional constructs of gender. But their intertextual resonance with television "reality shows" of the past decade such as *The Swan*, *Biggest Loser*, and *Extreme Makeover* also serves to circulate the notion of the woman's body as a reclamation project. Working in conjunction with new cosmetic surgery technologies and the promises of "plastic" reconfigurations these mediated makeover images fuel the drive for radical reshaping of the less-than-perfect body. In so doing they also reinforce the chronic body dissatisfaction that is an established risk factor for body image disturbances like body dysmorphic disorder and obsessive body preoccupation.

Chapter 5 considers Hollywood's representations of the outsize woman in the romantic comedy *Shallow Hal*, the animated *Shrek* series, and the horror movie *Misery*. For the most part, popular movies construct the fat female body as either monstrous, ridiculous, or asexual—in other words as a cultural "other." The chapter pays particular attention to narratives about the "consuming" body—women with seemingly insatiable appetites who threaten to destroy men or refuse to contain their abundant flesh within the narrow confines of today's tight and toned body ideal. Finally, it argues that these film narratives play a significant role in the social stigmatization of the outsize woman, which not only drives contemporary obsessive dieting and weight loss practices but also engenders the body shame and social isolation in overweight women that contribute to the development of binge eating and emotional eating disorders.

Focusing on such coming-of-age films as *Mean Girls*, *Clueless*, and *American Pie*, chapter 6 investigates how "teenpics" released in the past decade promote eating-disordered behaviors in the most vulnerable populations. Hollywood images of contemporary girlhood migrate to the lucrative teen and tween consumer beauty market where they contribute to a growing trend toward premature sophistication and sexualization of the body known as KGOY—"Kids Getting Older Younger." Cinematic representations of the girl's body encourage adolescents and even younger girls to display their bodies in ways that signal sexual availability long before they have the emotional or cognitive maturity to comfortably manage sexual relationships. Too often the unintended consequences of such early experiences include the confusion, conflict, and trauma associated with development of eating disorders in puberty.

The book concludes with a brief look at how independent films, especially those made by female directors, such as *Real Women Have Curves* and *Lovely and Amazing*, may provide alternative body narratives of adolescent girls and women that challenge the dominant imagery of Hollywood movies and help develop an "oppositional gaze" for new audiences in a multicultural and globalized media world.

Particular attention is paid throughout the book to the way Hollywood movies circulate the complex and troubled relationship contemporary woman have with food. More than a half-century after the memorable opening scene of *Gone with the Wind* when Mammy tightens Scarlett O'Hara's corset and makes her eat *before* the barbeque (lest she be tempted to indulge an unladylike appetite in front of the gentlemen guests), cinematic heroines are rarely allowed to eat at all—unless they are nourishing their unborn babies like the teen mother-to-be in *Juno* or Marge, the very pregnant food-loving police officer in *Fargo*.[37] Films that focus on the sensuality of food such as *Chocolat*, *Like Water for Chocolate*, and *Volver* are almost exclusively foreign productions—and even they tend to depict women *preparing* rather than actually savoring their delicious creations. (A recent and welcome exception to this phenomenon is the American film *Julie and Julia* [2009], which celebrates not only the culinary expertise of Julia Child but the sheer pleasure of eating permitted both its female protagonists.) More typically, as we will see in romantic comedies like *Miss Congenialty* and *The Mirror Has Two Faces*, Hollywood heroines must learn to renounce food in order to restore their insufficient femininity; while in teen films such as *Jawbreakers* food is depicted as the "gross" enemy which must be avoided at all costs to prevent getting fat—always the fate worse than death. Images of women eating are reserved for films featuring plus-size characters who are constructed as either devouring monsters with destructive appetites for power and possession of men—or pathologically repressed and desperately lonely spinsters.

Throughout *Body Shots* we hear the voices of my patients and students—women and girls across the life cycle who share their reactions to the Hollywood films that have shaped their own body narratives. All too often their personal stories reveal how the drive for slenderness inspired by these films triggered the imposition of severe diet regimens and food abstinence, behaviors found in my own laboratory and clinical research to result in eventual "explosions" of binge eating and bulimic episodes.[38] The book omits other important voices, however—in part because of Hollywood's failure to provide screen images that would facilitate identification with more diverse body representations. Conspicuously absent from popular movies are films focused on the bodies of aging women; with few exceptions, such as the box-office hits by director Nancy Myers, *Something's Gotta Give* (2003) and *It's Complicated* (2009) about the sexual adventures of their midlife heroines, Hollywood either writes older women out of the script entirely or sidelines them to peripheral stock roles as asexual mothers-in-law and over the hill seductresses. And beyond such celebrity "crossover" stars from the music industry as Jennifer Lopez, Queen Latifah, and Beyonce, Hollywood more often than not continues to imagine a world populated by willowy blonde Caucasian women and girls, troubling the possibilities of screen identification for a vast ethnically diverse audience at home and abroad. Moreover, while men are surely not exempt from either eating disorders or the media effects on the construction of their body image,[39] an analysis of Hollywood's images of masculinity is beyond my focus here.[40] As noted earlier, while men are increasingly subject to body disturbances in recent years, the incidence of problematic behaviors and concerns is many times higher in women, and the target audiences of the popular film genres I discuss are equally overrepresented by women. At the same time, I do not intend this gender imbalance as a commentary on women's heightened susceptibility to media manipulation due to an intrinsic passivity or naïveté;[41] to the contrary, I assume a female spectator who has the capacity to actively engage in a challenging response to conventional movie images and body myths. The purpose of the book, then, is to provide girls and women (as well as men!) with the critical distance to both resist and "diagnose" those problematic attitudes and values about body presentation in popular film that contribute to the "eating-disordered culture" of my title.

Several other limitations in the scope of this book should be noted. The films selected for analysis here are limited for the most part to movies produced after the late 1990s in order to more accurately assess their impact on contemporary body culture and the most recent manifestations of eating disorders as they interact with new media and the global transmission of visual images. And while Hollywood may still be considered the most dominant and widely distributed movie producer, other world cinemas (such as India's Bollywood and Asian film industries as well as the establishment of Nollywood in Nigeria and Riverwood in Kenya) are rapidly rising competitors. Nor is *Body Shots* designed to serve as a text either on the psychopathology of eating disorders (it does however provide a glossary of relevant clinical terms) or feminist film theory. Rather, it seeks to bridge the disciplines of psychology, cinema studies, and cultural studies to provide ways to read between the lines of popular movie texts and deconstruct those visual messages and narratives which may affect the moviegoer's relationship to food and her own body image.

This is particularly important because today's movies are filled with double messages that can confuse and seduce the unwary viewer. Hollywood can't resist the impulse to tell us a socially redemptive thing or two. After dazzling with luxurious visions of a teen fantasy world in *Clueless*, for example, the film is careful to chastise its valley girl heroine for her mega materialism and teach her the error of her selfish ways. But while a gentle didactic message may render mainstream movies politically correct, their visual conventions far more potently glamorize the same culture they claim to critique. And it is through the "shooting" of the woman's body—the framing, lighting, camera angle, costuming, and placement of her image on the screen—that Hollywood movies most powerfully confirm and valorize the contemporary female ideal of a perfectly contained and restrained body.

Thus, while *Shallow Hal* preaches that a woman's "inner beauty" surpasses superficial sexiness, its heavy-handed message is undermined by visual fat jokes at the expense of Hal's obese girlfriend Rosemary whose bloated fat-suited body is juxtaposed with his fantasized images of the superslender Gwyneth Paltrow. The heroines of makeover movies are reassured that they are loved "just the way [they] are" but hotel maid Marisa of *Maid in Manhattan* doesn't find her prince until she dresses up in a designer suit while tomboy Gracie Hart can't get the guy until she's transformed into *Miss Congeniality's* beauty queen. Ultimately the moralizing messages fail to provide any meaningful challenge to the established "rules" about femininity and beauty that these films visualize: Women should aspire to be slender and toned. They should control and deny their appetites to avoid deadly flab or fat. Body hatred and shame is a necessary prerequisite for the transformation and reform of the imperfect body.

As a result, viewers are left with a series of contradictory messages embedded in the film narratives. As each chapter here will demonstrate, movie makeovers and cosmetic surgery masquerade as self-confidence and self-esteem; body sexualization and a nose job represent female empowerment; uniformity is announced as self-actualization. These representations account for what Tasker and Negra have characterized as the "hollow quality" typical of postfeminist media: "Although a variety of films and genres of the late 1990s and early 2000s hype empowerment, these texts do not sustain any easy or straightforward relationship to women's experiences and social health."[42] Hollywood's refusal to seriously challenge today's eating-disordered culture makes it all the more crucial that we develop the distance and perspective needed to question the cultural assumptions and mythologies embedded in screen images of the woman's body and to identify the stereotypes, contradictions, prejudices, and agendas—both ideological and commercial—they represent. In contributing to such a deconstruction process, this book aims to provide the moviegoer with the critical tools necessary for healthier and more empowering visions of the body and its diverse beauties.

1

Body Identifications

The Movie Screen and the Mirror

Audience identification with movie stars is far from new. Nor is the power of screen bodies to establish, shape, and propagate mass cultural body ideals. Both can be traced back to the early days of Hollywood following World War I when fan magazines such as *Photoplay* found a ready market in the demographic favoring young Americans as the major moviegoing audience, much like today.[1] This in turn gave rise to the widespread circulation of a body ideal defined by youth and slenderness as well as the marketing of products to achieve it, such as La-Mar Reducing Soap and Weil's "Scientific Reducing Belt," commercial ancestors of today's multibillion dollar weight-loss industry. Throughout the 1930s Hollywood stars such as William Powell warned women to avoid looking "fat and forty" to keep their men from wandering, while Jean Harlow endorsed Woodbury's Facial Cream to rid her face of dreaded wrinkles.[2] In this way the professional imperative for Hollywood's leading ladies to stay slender and youthful was transmitted to female moviegoers via a growing consumer culture which encouraged fan identification with the practices of body vigilance and control: "The rhetorical strategy underlying youth advertising in early fan magazines suggests the panopticon," writes film scholar Heather Addison: "All parts of people's bodies were under scrutiny at all times, by themselves and others."[3]

This conflation of youth, sexual desirability, slenderness, and self-scrutiny located in and radiating out from Hollywood movie culture was to repeat itself throughout the rest of the twentieth century. Movie studios invested the images of their stars with enormous visual power and glamour; these idealized bodies in turn became commodified both for the movie industry as well as the thriving beauty consumer market it fed. Notes film scholar Annette Kuhn: "Women's bodies and selling were identified: representations of women became the commodities that film producers were able to exchange in return for money."[4] Seeking to imitate the "look" of their favorite movie star, female moviegoers would purchase not only tickets to see their latest films but also the self-care products and accessories associated with their image. Film historian Rachel Moseley, for example, has traced how the personal styling and shopping behavior of British working-class women in the 1950s and '60s were inspired by the Hollywood persona of Audrey Hepburn, whose elegant style enacted for them the possibility of social transformation through fashion.[5]

Perhaps the most well-known cultural studies of female screen identification are those of Jackie Stacey, whose work marked the shift from earlier "cine-psychoanalytic" theories of film spectatorship to sociohistorical investigations of movie audience reception. Drawing upon memoirs of British women about their responses to Hollywood stars during World War II and the following decade, Stacey's ethnographic study discovered many examples of what she called "identificatory fantasies," which ranged from religious devotion to a screen "goddess" such as Joan Crawford all the way to total psychological escapism into the high society world of Katherine Hepburn's films.[6] One of the most poignant examples of screen identification Stacey cites is a reminiscence from a filmgoer who would gather with her schoolmates at an open coal field to build mounds of dirt dubbed the "Beverly Hills," each girl fashioning her own "mansion" and pretending to be her favorite movie star.[7]

Particularly relevant in terms of Hollywood's potential to influence eating disordered behavior are the identificatory processes of imitating, copying, and consumption documented by Stacey whereby the female moviegoer *actively* seeks to align her own identity closer to that of an admired star. In this way the "look" of the movie star on the screen embodies an aspiration for the viewer which is then internalized in the form of actual cognitive beliefs and behaviors—thus not merely changing hairstyles or hats or purchasing endorsed beauty products but taking on the attitudes and personality "type" each star represents in their screen persona. In this way, notes Stacey "The self and the ideal combine to produce another feminine identity, closer to the ideal"[8]—a kind of reinvention of the self to incorporate the admired star image. A striking postmodern reference to the merging of both body and identity with the image of Hollywood screen icons appears in David Lynch's *Mulholland Drive* (2001) when a mysterious woman who is suffering from amnesia adopts the first name and personal style of Rita Hayworth. The film visually captures this moment of identification in an extraordinary shot: as the woman gazes at her own face in the mirror the viewer also sees the reflection of a poster on the wall behind her which displays Hayworth performing her famous femme fatale role in *Gilda*, the 1946 film noir.

But these same processes of screen identification operate offscreen as well, where they can have a direct impact upon the eating behavior and body image of the individual moviegoer, just as it did in the case of Courtney, a freckle-faced sophomore in my psychology seminar entitled "Eating Disorders in College Populations." Barely five feet tall, she tried to keep her weight under one hundred pounds to maintain a size zero but still struggled to fit into the clothes that she believed made her look "hot." After her current boyfriend broke up with her during the course of the semester, Courtney told me she sought inspiration from a popular romantic comedy she had recently seen:

> In *The Break Up* Jennifer Aniston is so beautiful and has the most amazing body. She's incredibly thin and looks absolutely adorable in these tank tops and slinky little dresses—not

Figure 1.1. Borrowing an identity in *Mulholland Drive*.

one belly bulge or ounce of flab. When I saw it I had just broken up with my own boyfriend and was trying to think of ways to get him back. I took Jennifer Aniston's idea to make him jealous like she did to Vince Vaughn and thought if I looked as good as her maybe it would work. I started to skip breakfast and lunch and go to the gym twice a day all in my head thinking about how I wanted to look like Jennifer Aniston in that movie and maybe just maybe when my ex saw me he would want me back.

Courtney's endorsement of the belief that slenderness and sexiness are necessary prerequisites for empowerment as an object of male desire indicates that she has already internalized contemporary discourses about the body ideal. Thus, she is primed to identify with the movie's representation of that ideal in the image of Aniston's body—so much so that she seeks to copy it through diet restriction and extra-rigorous workouts. Embedded in Aniston's super-thin body is the film's message: to get your man back you have to look perfect—and be perfectly thin, a construction of gender and power relationships that narrowly defines female agency just as it narrows the body ideal to the size zero Courtney yearns for. It is also important here to bear in mind that the *degree* of internalization—in other words just how fervently viewers believe in the thin ideal as synonymous with self-control, success, and attractiveness—is frequently cited in media exposure research as the key to body image disturbance among girls and women.[9]

In order to better understand the formation of such compelling identifications with the body ideal represented by movie stars it is also helpful to revisit the work of feminist film theorist Laura Mulvey. In her groundbreaking 1975 essay "Visual Pleasure and Narrative Cinema," Mulvey described the "apparatus" of the cinema as a patriarchal construction in which the camera produces an image of the woman's body as a source of voyeuristic pleasure for what she posited to be a male spectator.[10] The image of the woman's body is positioned as a performing spectacle in the foreground of the movie frame, an object of erotic contemplation both for the male characters in the narrative as well for the spectator in the audience. Her body is coded for what Mulvey calls its "to-be-looked-at-ness"[11] by the controlling gaze of the camera, which uses the cinematic devices of framing, lighting, and shadows to "freeze" her image on a flattened spatial plane while in contrast, the male characters move actively within the deeper three-dimensional spaces of the screen.

In a departure from Mulvey's focus, however, here we are concerned with what effect these cinematic conventions might have on the psychological and behavioral responses of the *female* spectator as the camera exaggerates the long slender legs and zooms in on the toned arms and narrow hips of action film warriors and makeover movie heroines, eroticizing and glamorizing bodies that represent the ideals of dietary restraint and control—an effect that became part of the story of one young woman I treated for bulimia. Cindy was twenty-six years old, working as a paralegal in a local law firm and planning to go to law school. The tallest girl in her class throughout elementary and middle school, she had always had a troubled body image, feeling herself "too big and bulky," which soon turned into a perception of herself as overweight. In her affluent suburban high school she felt less feminine than the "tiny" popular girls and didn't date. Desperate to reduce her size and failing to stick to ever harsher diet regimens, she began to experiment with purging and eventually became bulimic. During the course of our therapy work, she recalled a defining moment in the early history of her eating disorder:

> I was just about obsessed with the movie *Cruel Intentions*, in which Reese Witherspoon and Sarah Michelle Gellar were beautiful, sexy, and thin. It seemed the whole focus in the movie was on their fantastic toned arms and legs, and of course completely flat abs, and I just couldn't stop focusing on those bodies. I think it was their sex appeal that I coveted. I wanted to be the girl turning heads and getting guys. And by throwing up almost everything I ate for a little over two years, I became that girl. I can actually say I *was* my female ideal: I had big boobs, a nice flat stomach, and at five feet eight inches I was pretty striking.

After leaving home for a big urban university Cindy began to feel more socially confident and developed a close relationship with a college boyfriend. Eventually her bulimic symptoms remitted, only to reappear after graduation when the relationship ended unexpectedly. She described a long painful period during which she would return to her apartment every night to binge on ice cream and cookies, eating until she could barely walk and finally falling into an exhausted sleep after "purging it all out." More recently however, she has begun to move toward self-acceptance in general and of her "natural" body size in particular. She reports feeling less compelled by the thin ideal and is questioning the conventional values embedded in its screen representation:

> It's funny but I don't feel so driven by gorgeous movie stars anymore. When I was younger I really believed what they were always saying—that only skinny women could be sexy and have a life. I know now that's just not true. When I was making myself throw up and lost a lot of weight maybe I got all the male attention I always had wanted, but I was mostly treated as a sexual object and nothing more. I dumbed myself down and lost my own opinionated personality; I became just a shell of my real self. Now I'm feeling happier with who I am because I know I have more to offer guys and the world than my body. My body is for me, not for them.

Mulvey also applied the theories of French psychoanalyst Jacques Lacan to her understanding of the process of screen idealization of the movie star. Lacan described what is known as the "mirror stage" of ego development during which a baby is first held up before the mirror and encounters an image of his or her self that seems more whole and integrated than s(he) feels inside. Mulvey used this notion to explain the ambivalent relationship the spectator has with the movie star: "Hence . . . the birth of the long love affair/despair between image and self-image which has found such intensity of expression in film and such joyous recognition in the cinema audience."[12] In other words, the movie star is like that ideal image in the baby's mirror—more powerful and larger than life because of its cinematic brilliance but enough *like* the spectator to allow for the pleasurable fantasy of identification. For the contemporary female moviegoer, however, the pleasure is increasingly met with an equal measure of discouragement—and even despair—at the gap between the screen image and her own image in the bathroom mirror where she gazes at her body, anxiously inspecting any offending fleshy bulges and bumps and sagging skin.

Thus, the golden glorious tall and tight female bodies on the screen are the ideal against which women measure their own bodies—and find themselves lacking. Such culturally driven body insecurity takes its most extreme form in the distorted body image of anorexic patients who look in the mirror at their emaciated bodies only to see themselves as grotesquely fat. But for the vast majority of female viewers who are not suffering from the symptoms of clinical eating disorders, the effects of the self-ideal gap can be sufficiently troublesome because they create body dissatisfaction, the risk factor that plays such a key role as we try to connect the dots between the impact of movie screen images on unhealthy eating behaviors. Here for example is the response of Samantha, another student at my university, to the gap she perceives between her own body and that of Angelina Jolie:

> My favorite movie star is Angelina Jolie. She has the most incredible body and even though the gossip magazines say she's anorexic, she always looks so hot—especially after all those babies. Even my boyfriend tells me he's turned on by those fabulous full lips and great boobs; I would die for a body like that. Maybe even if I had to become anorexic for real! When I went to see her in *Mr. and Mrs. Smith* I threw out the popcorn I'd just bought (it had butter on it and everything) and didn't eat a thing all the next day. Later I kept thinking about that movie and started to watch what I ate a lot more and noticed a difference in my food, not letting myself eat anything the tiniest bit fattening. It also changed how I saw my own body because the movie made me feel like I don't live up to what is expected to be a sexy woman. I get so bummed about how I look to myself in the mirror compared to someone like Angelina.

Not only is Samantha's perception about her body negatively affected by this comparison but she then goes on to contemplate the benefits of anorexia, a sobering echo of the media exposure research cited previously that viewers most influenced by slender body images are more likely to endorse disordered eating behavior as a means to a much-desired end. And in fact Samantha's fantasy about anorexia is something I frequently hear from both students and patients struggling with weight issues; as one woman confided to me not long ago: "If only I could become anorexic just until I reach my goal weight—and not die in the process!"

Connected to this self-ideal gap is the increased risk of media exposure in those vulnerable girls and women most affected by the process identified by media scholars as social comparison theory: "It could be argued that social comparisons are at their most problematic when there is a large discrepancy between the person's actual (or perceived) self and his or her ideal self, resulting in efforts being made to attempt to close the gap."[13] And for these individuals who constantly check out each other's bodies—both overtly and covertly—at the gym, the mall, or the office, body comparisons don't stop when the lights go out in the movie theater. Not surprisingly, moviegoers who are more compelled in the course of their everyday lives to compare their bodies to others tend to see in images of their favorite movie stars harsh commentaries and critiques of their own bodily and dietary failures. At times these invidious comparisons are so powerful that they actually intrude upon the viewer's pleasurable immersion into the world of the film. Here for example is how Kristi, a twenty-three-year-old graduate student, described her internal experience while watching a surfing movie she had rented from the video store:

> I first saw that surfing movie *Blue Crush* when I was still in high school, and even though I know it's like junk food I got it out again last night. Each time I see it I still think how great it would be to look like Kate Bosworth and also have her athletic ability. Now I consider myself pretty fit, I go to the gym five times a week and lift weights, but I do not look like Kate in any way, shape or form. Watching her surfing the waves in her bikini makes me look at my own body and wonder how come I don't look like that? And last night I couldn't stop staring at her sculpted arms and thinking about how I've worked so hard on my arms and they're still not toned enough. It just makes me feel *I'm* not good enough either. I thought at least I had finally gotten the flab out of my arms but now I see that compared to her I'm not even close. I got so distracted by all this stuff that it ruined the whole movie!

Over the years many other cinema scholars have challenged Mulvey's original model of film spectatorship and its theorizing of the dominant *male* gaze, particularly in view of the diverse "gazes" and spectatorship positions possible for other sexualities, ethnicities, racial, and cross-cultural identities. Notable among such critics are Mary Ann Doane, Kaja Silverman, and Judith Mayne who have addressed the question of the female gaze in reframing other gendered ways of looking and visual pleasure.[14] Others have sought to understand film spectatorship and the politics of "gazing" not from psychoanalytic or feminist theories but from the perspectives of queer theory, postcolonial studies, or critical race theory.[15]

Of particular interest is the work of bell hooks in theorizing an "oppositional gaze" based on her premise that racial identity, far more than gender, shapes the viewing position of the black woman movie spectator.[16] hooks describes the power and pleasure that can come from both active resistance and refusal to identify with the dominant cultural images on the screen, a position of movie spectatorship that has great relevance both for the project of this book and the possibilities it seeks to provide for viewing Hollywood movies with a more challenging "gaze." Just as women of color or gay, lesbian, and transgendered spectators are free to adopt their own subjective points of view toward the movie frame so too moviegoers whose body size and shape do not fit into today's narrow body ideal can assert their own critical agency—instead of desperately seeking to close the self-ideal gap to identify with Hollywood's "glamazons." We can see how the gradual development of such an "oppositional gaze" became a source of resilience to the damaging effects of body dissatisfaction in at least one moviegoer: Elena is a forty-one-year-old single musician who was suffering from what I call "diet fatigue syndrome." In endless attempts to lose weight and fit into a smaller clothes size she had fallen into a persistent habit of breaking her diets with bouts of an overeating reaction (commonly known as the "what the hell" effect), which only made her gain more weight. Her "ideal" was embodied by the figure of actress Gwyneth Paltrow:

> I've seen every movie she ever made, losing myself in fantasies of being that tall and model-thin and blonde—and always feeling really depressed and fat after each movie. But

I'm finally seeing how ridiculous it is to keep wasting my life pining for something that's not ME! Absolutely every woman in my family is short and kind of stocky, but we're all really strong and not unhealthy at all. When I went back to visit relatives in Italy last summer they looked just like me, with thick dark hair and great eyes—and they're really beautiful! Now when I watch those romantic comedies I turn my bullshit meter on—and I can see how they're just selling the same old myths that there's only one kind of beautiful.

  Despite the development of alternative cultural and political models for cinema spectatorship, however, Hollywood productions continue to serve as powerful inspirations for women and girls who yearn to become objects of sexual desire and "visual pleasure" in order to acquire the power, money, or eternal devotion that perfect bodies would seem to ensure in their narratives. To further illuminate how the internalization of the values embedded in these Hollywood narratives has only intensified since the height of the big studios and the star system, we turn to the figure of Veronica Lake, one of the most influential Hollywood screen goddesses of the postwar era. A witty reference to her star power in shaping the body ideal of the period (and possibly Hollywood's sly recognition of its own cultural clout) occurs in Billy Wilder's 1942 comedy *The Major and the Minor.* Disguised as a schoolgirl for most of the film, its adult heroine (Ginger Rogers) is escorted by a group of admiring military cadets to a dance with the girls at neighboring Miss Shackleford's School. Upon entering the ballroom she is told by her escorts that there is an "epidemic" at the girls' school: "They all think they're Veronica Lake!" The camera then cuts to a medium shot of four young women each of whom has copied the star's signature long blonde hairstyle with its deep wave falling over one eye—the key to Lake's seductive screen image. The ensuing long shot then reveals an entire chorus line of girls sitting with the identical look, and then concludes the visual joke in a final shot of the dour headmistress Miss Shackleford herself, sporting the very same hairstyle in a grotesque caricature of the movie star's temptress persona.

  A more contemporary reference to Veronica Lake appears in the Oscar-winning film *L.A. Confidential* (1997) where the process of movie star imitation and embodiment takes on complex resonance as a cinematic expression of the various systems of identification with

Figure 1.2. A bevy of Veronica Lakes wait to dance in *The Major and the Minor*.

Hollywood movie culture that have intensified in the intervening decades. Consciously evoking the *noir* films of the '40s and '50s, the film replicates a world inhabited by the genre's stock figures of corrupt cops and city officials, mobsters and drug dealers, set within the classic *mise en scène* of nightclubs, Beverly Hills mansions, back alleys, and seedy bars. Central to the film's motif of Hollywood images, both "real" and illusory, is the exchange of body identities that takes place in the call girl ring known as "Fleur-de-Lis," where customers hire prostitutes disguised as the most glamorous movie stars of the period—Ava Gardner, Jane Russell, Marilyn Monroe, Rita Hayworth, and once again, Veronica Lake. The women take on their particular star's persona with the help of sophisticated makeup, costume, and plastic surgery. The film's ambiguity of identities—acted, imitated, masqueraded—is heightened by its incorporation into the narrative of such "real" historical figures as crime bosses of the period such as Mickey Cohen and his bodyguard Johnny Stompanato, who in turn was famous for his liaison with actress Lana Turner. In one of the film's lighter moments, the lead detective (Guy Pearce) confronts Stompanato and a woman sitting with him who he takes for a Lana Turner look-alike call girl. When the woman reacts with anger the detective tells her to shut up: "Being cut to look like Lana Turner doesn't mean you *are* Lana Turner"—only to learn to his chagrin that this time the woman was indeed the "real" actress and not a simulation.

While *L.A. Confidential* is far from a "message" film, both the limitations and dangers of overidentification with embodying movie star images is implicit in the relationship between its two main characters, Lynn Bracken (Kim Basinger) and Bud White (Russell Crowe), a romance that ultimately shifts the tone and structure of *L.A. Confidential* from neo-*noir* to love story. As the cool blonde Veronica Lake–styled call girl (the film's screenplay describes her as "looking more like Veronica Lake than Veronica Lake"), Lynn is ultimately drawn to White not because he is the iconic tough guy hero (he may be a macho "Bud" but he's also "White," a reference less to his racial identity than to his rough chivalry toward downtrodden damsels in distress) but more precisely because he sees past her fake image into her own original self-concept and identity: "You're the first man in five years who didn't tell me I look like Veronica Lake inside of a minute," she confides. After they make love, he assures her: "All they [her customers] get is Veronica Lake. I get Lynn Bracken." It is not accidental that the couple are shown having a traditional date at the movies watching *Roman Holiday,*

Figure 1.3. LAPD detectives mistake the "real" Lana Turner for a call girl in *L.A. Confidential*.

the 1953 film starring the virginal and wholesome ingénue Audrey Hepburn; fittingly for this date Lynn has forsaken her Veronica Lake hairstyle for a 1950s-style pony tail and pristine white blouse.

Before the recuperation of her identity Lynn appears in a scene that serves as a self-reflexive statement about the powerful psychological and visual process of screen image identification. Dressed in a slinky evening gown in her Veronica Lake persona she is seen having sex with an "older gentleman" client while a home movie screen behind their figures plays a scene from *This Gun for Hire*, the 1942 *film noir* starring Veronica Lake as a cabaret singer and Alan Ladd as a hard-boiled hired killer. Lynn's client is also dressed in a Hollywood costume of sorts: in addition to his undershorts he wears a tank top undershirt and hat styled like Ladd's and imitates the actor's tough guy stance while pretending to hold an imaginary gun in his hands. The flickering light from the movie screen plays over the figures of the call girl and her customer as they kiss.[17]

But most evocative of the connection between idealized screen images and contemporary body disturbances is the depiction of the film's call girl ring masquerade. The movie star guises of the Fleur-de-Lis

Figure 1.4. Call girl masquerading as Veronica Lake foregrounded against screen image of the "real" Veronica Lake in *This Gun for Hire* (1942).

prostitutes are designed to embody "whatever you desire." The call girls submit to plastic surgery and other cosmetic manipulations in order to accommodate the fantasies of their clients, reminding us of today's beauty culture consumers who employ far more sophisticated technologies to shape, transform, tone, and sculpt their bodies in the image of celebrities and movie stars—even if it threatens their physical and mental health. This drive to literally *embody* the celebrity found particularly striking expression in the makeover show *I Want A Famous Face*, which ran on MTV from 2004 to 2005. In "post-op" interviews during which subjects shared their aspirations and goals for their surgeries "Mike" and "Matt," both age twenty, reportedly chose the Brad Pitt surgical face template "so deep down inside [they could] feel and look like him."[18] Celebrity gossip television shows report other surgical makeover procedures such as the "Brazilian Butt Lift" to imitate Jennifer Lopez's rear end (cost: $11,000) or (for a mere $1,000) fans can purchase snap-on teeth simulating Jessica Simpson's smile in order to make a "fashion statement."[19] Thus, far beyond the possibilities imagined in earlier theories of audience identification, the technological tools of body transformation now enable movie fans to merge corporeal identities with their favorite stars—to literally become their "body doubles."

In order to better understand the powerful influence that images of movie star bodies can exert on such contemporary beauty practices we also need to take a look at how these images are constructed in the first place. Scholars in the field of star studies such as Yvonne Tasker have noted the centrality of the body in the establishment of this all-important image: "The star's body, worked out/on transformed or preserved by surgery . . . is only ever experienced by an audience as an image."[20] The work of Richard Dyer, who is interested in how the visual "signs" and meanings embedded in the star image represent ideologies of the American Dream—particularly the "fabulousness of Hollywood"[21]—documents how the most powerful star images represent contemporary ideologies of body mastery, fitness, and control, ideologies that are then communicated to modern media consumers and inform their own body practices.

A star's image initially takes on these meanings from her professional identity in specific films—an association dating all the way back to the birth of the film industry when the Thomas Edison movie company first began to credit their performers by name. Screen actors soon became linked to the "type" they were cast in their movie roles—just as today we typically think of Kirsten Dunst as the girl next door or Helen Mirren as the dignified aristocrat. Their constructed identity as Hollywood stars, however, goes beyond specific film roles: "Movie stars are not just actors—in some sense they always play 'themselves.'"[22] Their image is thus further constructed by the way their bodies are "read" and given meaning in the public media space *outside* their movies, primarily in gossip and "backstories" about their personal lives, loves, and scandals. A user-friendly way to think about these relationships is provided by celebrity culture theorist Peter Marshall: "Storyworld" refers to the narrative of the star's film, "Realworld" is the star's personal life and legends, while "Audienceworld" points to how the film viewer, armed with this information, interprets the star's image on the screen.[23]

Once constructed through a fusion of these three "worlds" as well as media interviews and product endorsements, the star image must be scrupulously maintained, guarded, and continually embellished so that even a performer's most casual public appearance walking the dog or toting a baby is carefully designed to preserve it. This task is carried out by a large network of industry workers—agents, publicists, events managers, lawyers, plus an entourage of personal trainers, hair stylists, and makeup artists, who develop and share in the maintenance of the star's image. Team members collaborate with popular media to circulate the established image via tabloid fan magazines, official interviews and public appearances, charity causes, and of course, the *paparazzi* who are not on the payroll but whose "candid" shots reinforce the star persona. The final production becomes the star's "brand," which extends beyond her consumer product lines to represent a specific personal style, value system, and targeted fan subculture.[24] Emerging from this commodification of fame is a form of property law known as the "right of publicity," through which both celebrities and their descendants can claim ownership of their brand and their image.[25] In the following chapter we shall examine how these processes are recruited to create a celebrity culture that has rendered the star's image inseparable from the public and private performance of her body. It is the circulation of these images throughout popular media that helps create the social context from which body disturbances and eating disorders emerge. Thus, they mediate the paradoxical effect noted by one cultural critic: "Celebrity images are a reflection of our idealized selves sold back to us. Yet they actually constrain rather than expand our horizon and experiences."[26]

2

Celebrity Bodies

One afternoon in the winter of 2007 I walked into the lobby of the Boston Museum of Fine Arts to meet my undergraduate psychology class for a field trip. We had planned to tour the museum's high fashion exhibit as part of our study of media and contemporary body ideals. I spotted my students huddled around a cell phone, their voices animated and faces registering shock. Was this a national emergency? I wondered. Another international terrorism alert? Breathlessly, the students reported a different kind of crisis: the body of media star Anna Nicole Smith had just been discovered, and news of her death was buzzing over airwaves and the Internet with gathering speed.[1] Over the following days and weeks "legal" and entertainment television shows and Web sites, network call-in programs, and blogs relentlessly hypothesized about the celebrity's sudden demise (was it suicide? foul play? a drug overdose?) seeking clues in the highly publicized battles over the paternity of Smith's five-month-old baby girl, a recent Supreme Court judgment allowing her to inherit the $400 million estate of her elderly oil magnate husband, and the equally mysterious death of her adult son of a suspected overdose.

Why the focus and the fascination? As a popular media icon Anna Nicole Smith's personal story contained three key elements that typically construct the celebrity narrative. First, there was the "discovery" myth: the former Vickie Lynn Hogan had been working as a topless dancer in Houston when Hugh Hefner, seeing in her full-breasted figure an iteration of Marilyn Monroe, chose her for his March 1992 *Playboy* magazine cover, which catapulted her to fame as Anna Nicole Smith. As *Playboy*'s "Playmate of the Year" her image was used to brand Guess jeans, thus circulating her body still more widely throughout public spaces via magazine and billboard ads. Another celebrity narrative component, the "rags to riches" motif, was played out in Smith's controversial May-December marriage to the eighty-nine-year-old oil baron. She invited public access to her newly acquired rich and famous life through the medium of the *Anna Nicole Show*, which in 2002 was one of the first reality television productions organized around the new star's glamorous and wealthy L.A. lifestyle. As such the show served as a reification of the phenomenon of celebrity: you can *get* famous by creating a life dedicated to simply *becoming* famous. The final component of the celebrity narrative, "the fall," was in Smith's case depicted as a descent into risky self-destructive behaviors, suffering personal tragedy, and finally dying young and mysteriously in yet another evocation of Marilyn Monroe. Equally predictable was the ambivalent public response to this narrative, which interpreted Anna Nicole's story either as punishment for her overreaching and "loose living" or as victimization by the media and her handlers. One of her many attorneys gave voice to the latter sentiment in the press: "Poor Anna Nicole. She's been the underdog. She's been besieged . . . nobody should have to endure what she's endured."[2]

But most relevant here is the fact that the site of this celebrity narrative is the *body* of its protagonist. Following the initial circulation of the sexualized image constructed by *Playboy*'s focus on her breasts and voluptuous figure, the drama of Smith's ensuing struggle with weight loss and gain became the subject of much media commentary and not infrequent ridicule. In the year leading up to her death she had become the spokesperson for the diet supplement Trim-Spa, claiming it had helped her lose seventy pounds. A subsequent class-action suit brought against this product led to speculation that Smith's death was in fact caused by the interaction of diet pills with alcohol and drugs as well as her extreme weight fluctuations. And while media obsession with this particular body soon subsided it was quickly replaced with similar "crises" engendered by Britney Spears's pregnancies, Lindsay Lohan's suspected bulimia, Queen Latifah's weight loss, and countless other star body dramas. Public fascination with these events reflects the complex relationship between celebrities, their bodies, and the popular media that circulate their images as part of a cyclical process in which popular media stars both mirror and model the same self-improvement struggles their fans and audiences endure in hot pursuit of the very ideal the stars embody! Oprah Winfrey's weight loss saga, Carnie Wilson's online gastric bypass surgery, Renee Zellweger's "heroic" thirty-pound weight gain for her role in *Bridget Jones Diary*, and the ever-growing legion of young stars confessing (or more often denying) brushes with anorexia and bulimia—each story represents the eating and weight control practices and size and shape obsessions of the audience who "consumes" their films, music, and product lines.

Recent decades have seen a dramatic increase in the power of contemporary star images to influence the body control practices and dieting behaviors of media consumers, primarily because of the historical, economic, and technological developments in celebrity culture that affect both star image making and the fan's relationship to the star. Key among these has been the demise of the Hollywood studio system and its legendary control of publicity. In the past monolithic companies such as MGM and Paramount had rigorously preserved and protected the images of their contracted stables of star properties by tightly limiting access to both their personal lives and physical exposure of their bodies. Other than fan magazines, which for the most part observed a reverential tone aimed at perpetuating star worship, there was little chance for the star's image to be contaminated or subverted. Noting the conspicuous absence of the broad reach of television in the heyday of the studio system, Molly Haskell wryly observes that "there were no celebrity interviews, no talk shows that would expose their 'humanity,' their scandals, their boringness."[3]

Today we have far more access and therefore a somewhat more ambivalent relationship to our celebrities, who are no longer limited to remote and gorgeous iconic stars of the silver screen but crossover performers from the entertainment, fashion, and sports industries as well. We may still want to idealize them but we also want to know that, as a regular column in *US Weekly* reports, "Stars Are Just Like Us," perhaps seeking in what Dyer calls their very "ordinariness" a sense of intimacy.[4] We can feel their pain, forgive their frailties, critique their excesses even while we may continue to worship them.

What, when, and how we get to know about the bodies of our celebrities has further transformed our relationship to them. Their images are streamed from ever smaller and more ubiquitous media screens on laptops and portable DVD players and smart phones, exposing their bodies to round the clock public scrutiny. Expansion of celebrity marketing and branding also guarantees that these images are no longer restricted to screen-based media; celebrity bodies adorn designer product lines and magazine endorsements, dolls and toys, school lunchboxes and T-shirts, videogames, and most far-reaching of all, pop-ups in the endless stream of Internet traffic. In an ever increasingly visual world there is far more opportunity for "leakage" of information about celebrity bodies, particularly their battles with weight, eating disorders, cosmetic surgery, or postpartum recovery. In short, the bodies of the stars have become the property of the public domain, no longer under the watchful parental eye of the big studio publicity department.

Public scrutiny of the celebrity body in fact would appear to be the primary editorial mission of the tabloid press and cable and network television productions such as *E!*, *Vh1*, and *ShowBiz Tonite*. In its regular feature "Body News" *People* magazine offers running commentary on Hollywood stars' weight cycles, dress sizes, and workout routines accompanied by photo spreads in which their bodies are dissected into parts rendered up for critique. Breasts are a particular object of scrutiny, with bold headlines demanding to know "Did Madonna get a Boob Job?" or wondering "Where did their boobs go?," the question posed in a recent article featuring before and after shots of stars such as Anne Hathaway.[5] Tyra Banks, host of the television reality show *America's Next Top Model*, was vilified for allegedly gaining twenty pounds in an unflattering bathing suit shot captioned "Tyra Porkchop." These body indictments in the court of public opinion follow a predictable pattern: suspicion, accusation, "expert" testimony offered by Hollywood plastic surgeons or hairdressers, typically followed by defense or denial of any transgressions by the star's publicists.

The deconstruction of the celebrity body is also a key ritual in the "Red Carpet" show televised at the annual Academy Awards. As each star arrives on the carpet a camera zooms in on legs, hips, breasts, or arms, disembodying the image on one half of a split screen while the other half zooms out to show the star dutifully modeling her designer gown for waiting interviewers. During 2008's Oscar ceremonies the *E!* channel's Web site provided computer graphic software to outline "trouble spots" on each star who had walked down the Red Carpet, including a correction of actress Helen Mirren's waistline, which was judged to be too big. The Oscar postmortem body critique continues for several weeks during which period the entertainment media render opinions of "best" and "worst" bodies, dresses, and hairstyles of the stars, while Internet sites such as "The Skinny Website" or the "Fashion Police" join the conversation with postings ruminating, for example, about whether a star's thighs look suspiciously larger: "I wonder how far she will let this go?" Equally prevalent are tabloid press contests in which fans are invited to vote on "best" and "worst" celebrity bodies. The net effect of this popular media discourse serves not only to reinforce the self-consciousness about bodily appearance so pervasive among many women and girls but also the body rivalry and competition which is such a powerful driver of food and weight preoccupation throughout contemporary culture.

Yet another major change affecting circulation of the star's body image may seem obvious: far more body can now be visible. Social historian Joan Jacobs Brumberg has attributed the increase of eating disorders and body obsessions throughout the twentieth century both to the relaxation of dress codes as well as to the extraordinary range of technologies available to remove any imperfections in previously hidden body parts now freely displayed. "Life in the world of the bikini," she writes, "is obviously different from life in the world of the corset."[6] With increased body exposure comes increased social anxiety about real or imagined flaws now visible for public evaluation. These sociocultural shifts are reflected in contemporary Hollywood film and celebrity culture. Of course, it was imperative during Hollywood's "golden age" of classic cinema that the screen images of the stars' bodies be as idealized and gorgeous as possible. As one Hollywood legend would have it, Louis B. Mayer commanded his camera crews that no matter what befell his heroines—floods, fire, any disaster—"She's gotta look beautiful!"[7] All the cinematic arts—lighting, camera angle, soft focus, the close-up shot, makeup, and costume—were orchestrated precisely to achieve that effect. But while Carole Lombard studied cinematography to learn how to hide a scar on her cheek and Claudette Colbert could only be filmed from her "good" side, the censorship restrictions imposed by the Production Code beginning in 1934 permitted limited exposure of the star's body. Even Marilyn Monroe's highly sexualized image had to be clothed, no matter how diaphanous and low-cut the evening gown she so unforgettably wore in *Some Like it Hot* (1960).

No longer subject to any such restraints, contemporary Hollywood media also has at its disposal a far more high-tech toolbox with which to perfect the fully exposed celebrity body. Today the constructed image is not only sculpted simply by lights and makeup but by digital editing and computer software that "morph" and eliminate any unwanted lumps and bumps that might compromise the illusion of complete perfection.

The high-stakes pressure to maintain this illusion extends to offscreen body exposure displays as well, as evidenced by a 2008 retrospective of *Vanity Fair* photographs of contemporary film stars featuring nude portraits of Demi Moore, Kim Basinger, Julianne Moore, Scarlett Johansson, Keira Knightley, and subsequently and (more controversially) the then fifteen-year-old Miley Cyrus, teen star of the Hannah Montana television and film series.

If "Screenworld" roles force a star to depart too radically from her image of bodily perfection it must quickly be restored. Two Hollywood stars who have been critically acclaimed and honored for their willingness to take on decidedly unglamorous roles are Charlize Theron and Hilary Swank. To play death row murderer Aileen Wuornos in *Monster* (2003) Theron not only gained considerable weight but appeared throughout the film with swollen face and pitted skin; nor was her brutalized appearance ever improved in the film, which rejected the conventional Hollywood transformation narrative. Instead, the recuperation of her image took place in "Realworld"'s public space of media body displays. Theron's subsequent interviews were careful to note both her early career as a *Playboy* cover model and her extraordinary beauty. In worshipful tones, one interviewer describes her skintight pants, stiletto heels, ankle tattoo, and platinum hair as she makes her entrance: "Her legs are endless and she glides into a room. . . ."[8]

For her role based on transsexual murder victim Teena Brandon in *Boys Don't Cry* (1999) Hillary Swank bound her breasts, cut off her hair, and dressed in jeans and a cowboy hat. Appearing that year at the Oscars to accept her Best Acting award Swank recuperated her movie star glamour in an ultra-feminine gown and accessories, an image then reiterated in a *People* magazine spread entitled "From Grit to Glam."[9] Any lingering doubt about her femininity generated by a subsequent performance as the champion boxer in *Million Dollar Baby (2004)* was erased by a breathtaking photo of Swank in *Vanity Fair* magazine in which she leaps across a Malibu beach, lean and incredibly muscular but with a bikini revealing prominent curves of breasts and hips.

Renee Zellweger's willingness to play the buxom heroine of *Bridget Jones' Diary (*2001) was valorized in popular media as a courageous feat. Much was made of the thirty pounds the actress gained for taking on the role of a character who berates herself for having a "bottom about the size of Brazil." In a series of postproduction revelations Zellweger herself marvels at her ordeal, ruefully noting that co-star Hugh Grant must have needed a chiropractor after lifting her during a sex scene. Echoing the body shame I hear so often from overweight women, she confesses: "I didn't look at my naked body in the shower, that's for sure!"[10] In both her subsequent role as the sexy Roxie Hart in *Chicago* (2002) as well as in public appearances Zellweger's body recuperated a highly toned and slender image, so much so that it soon became the object of much tabloid concern that she was now "dangerously thin": in a photo display of the actress weighing 108 pounds, *In Touch* magazine announced "Renee is skin and bones," thus officially dissociating her body image from the plump Bridget Jones.

Not long ago, while speaking at a local hospital at a public health forum on weight and eating problems, I asked the women in the audience for their reactions to these kinds of celebrity body stories in gossip magazines and television entertainment shows. One woman was more offended than moved by the popular media discourse about Zellweger's sacrifice for her art. She spoke to both her frustration at the star's representation of a body ideal beyond the grasp of so many "ordinary" fans as well as the impact it had on her own body image: "Bridget Jones isn't fat—she's just normal. If that's supposed to be fat, then I must be an elephant!" Most audience members had followed the ongoing drama of Oprah's weight losses and gains over the years. While some were inspired by her struggle, others expressed the demoralizing effect it exerted on their own personal weight battles each time Oprah begins to look as if, in the words of one observer, "she's been doing some serious snacking on the side." Said another Oprah fan: "If she can't keep it off with all that money for personal trainers and chefs and God knows what else then there's no hope for me!"

When the conversation turned to famous makeovers a similar demoralization born of social comparison with celebrities was expressed: "If such a perfect star like Cameron Diaz is having plastic surgery, it just makes me feel I'll never even come close to that look. I've got so much more to fix!" bemoaned one participant. As for the constant "true confession" media reports of celebrity eating disorders, audience responses reflected a not uncommon ambivalence. One woman who had been overweight since childhood announced "I think it's disgusting how skinny Nicole Ritchie got." Then she paused and admitted: "But I'd give anything to look like her!"

One person in the audience, a tall slender woman in her thirties who spoke with enormous energy about how much she hated her "cellulite," reflected an equally ambivalent kind of fan relationship with actress Kristen Bell:

> I couldn't get over how fantastic she looked in "Forgetting Sarah Marshall." She spent the whole movie in a bikini looking completely luscious. I was dying of envy. But then I saw this picture of her in *People* "outing" her—you know, about how she's gained weight—and sure enough when I looked close I could swear she had cellulite exactly where I do! It's funny—in a way I was really sorry to see it because it kind of knocked her off the pedestal for me, but at the same time I was kind of glad. Either way, though, when I'm at the gym my own thighs look fatter than ever to me. Since I can't afford to do any surgery right now I'm just going to double my workout time to see if I can tone them up.

In much the same way, as celebrities respond to the relentless public scrutiny of their bodies with revelations of their own insecurity and dissatisfaction, their body narratives go on to inspire their fans to monitor their own bodies with equal vigilance and anxiety. In his inside-Hollywood guide *The Science of Sexy*, celebrity fashion designer Bradley Bayou reveals the body insecurity of "very famous movie actresses" who plead for a dress design to hide their "huge" hips even though they are a "perfect size four."[11] While such celebrity confessions may once again be designed to portray the star's "ordinariness," the actual psychological process being described is disturbingly close to the perceptual body image distortion symptomatic of anorexia, where it is not unusual for a skeletally thin patient to see in her reflection a bloated and obese body. In fact celebrity narratives glamorize pathological practices such as obsessive self-scrutiny as an expected part of the beauty regimen necessary to "sell yourself and your image,"[12] thus normalizing the chronic body dissatisfaction that is endemic to most girls and women as well as a growing number of boys and young men. And body dissatisfaction, as we must continue to bear in mind throughout this book, is a major risk factor in the development of eating disorders.

While celebrity diet and fitness routines are offered up to fans as instructive beauty tips and secrets, in fact a closer study of such features in the tabloid press reveals practices and beliefs about food and weight that are listed as clinical symptoms on the Eating Attitudes

Test, a standard diagnostic scale for the assessment of eating disorders.[13] These include excessive dietary restriction, renunciation of calorie-dense foods, and only allowing "safe" low-calorie choices. Thus, Beyonce and Jennifer Aniston report denying themselves their favorites—fried chicken and any kind of meat, respectively—while Kate Hudson restricts her dinner to raw salads and Jennifer Lopez must satisfy her snack cravings with air-popped popcorn. The trainers charged with controlling the bodies and appetites of Halle Berry and Cameron Diaz share the tips they use to prevent their stars from "bingeing" on the bread basket. Again, eating disorder research has shown that it is precisely this kind of enforced avoidance of proscribed "fattening" foods that often leads to their excessive consumption in the food binges characteristic of bulimia and binge eating disorder.[14]

Other cognitive beliefs and attitudes considered diagnostically symptomatic of eating disorders include seeing food as a dangerous enemy and feeling guilty after violating a dietary restriction. Published excerpts from her food diary in a Hollywood tabloid magazine reveals that actress Kristin Chenoweth is tormented by remorse after satisfying her craving for a doughnut and tries to repent with a Diet Coke; she then worries about being "bloated" but rationalizes, "at least it wasn't the real thing."[15] "Cheating," another behavioral consequence of the strict dietary restriction that leads to compulsive eating disorders, is reported by both Uma Thurman and Gwyneth Paltrow who confess to a "weakness" for M&Ms and fried fish and chips. Typically, these revelations are juxtaposed with photos of the sinning but still super-slender star in a bathing suit; she is almost never depicted actually *eating* these forbidden delicacies. Food abstinence, renunciation, and deprivation are normalized as practical tips to achieve the ideal body; Paltrow, for example, shares her regimen of periodic raw organic fasts to attain her own personal goal of a "Victoria's Secret butt."[16] Extreme exercise, another symptom of eating disorders, is recommended by celebrities and their trainers who attribute militant workout regimens as the trade secret for getting one of "Hollywood's Hottest Bikini Bodies." Reality shows such as "Celebrity Boot Camp" which first aired on the Fox television network during 2002, feature Hollywood celebrities who have "the strength of heart" to sacrifice their luxurious lifestyles for weeks of tough body discipline. Crucially, all these body practices, many of which border on the pathological, are idealized both as "healthy' and more importantly, as mandatory to achieve the "look" of a Hollywood celebrity.

The clinical manifestation of this mediated body discourse became all too apparent to me not long ago as I sat in my office across from a young woman seeking evaluation for anorexia. She had ridden her bicycle more than fifteen miles to the appointment, and at five feet seven inches was still dissatisfied with her weight of 109 pounds. As I looked at her gaunt face with its sunken cheekbones I was struck anew with the recognition that just a few decades ago her medical condition would have been immediately obvious. Today, however, there was very little difference between her superthin form and the images of celebrity bodies that have become the standard fare of our popular media consumption.

Specific celebrity narratives also serve as powerful enactments for their fans of bodily changes and challenges throughout the woman's life cycle. Perhaps no media star represents this better than Oprah Winfrey. Over the years not only has she wielded enormous influence via her ever-expanding media empire, which in addition to her world-famous television talk show includes book clubs, magazines, film productions, satellite radio programs and a retail store, but Oprah's ongoing weight loss battle has remained a compelling drama for her devoted fan base, a large percentage of which are over the age of fifty.[17] They have heard deeply personal revelations of her struggles with compulsive eating, including her vivid confession of devouring stale bread and syrup while in the throes of a desperate binge. While Oprah's public attempts to conquer this life-long problem in an endless succession of interventions ranging from liquid fasts to psychological and spiritual counseling may enact for midlife women their own frustration at decades of "yo-yo" dieting, many of the images embedded in her body narrative also represent a self-excoriating rejection of fat as an unacceptable part of her identity. One of the most memorable moments in Oprah TVland occurred in 1988, when after four months on the OptiFast liquid diet regimen she triumphantly wheeled out on stage a wagon laden with animal fat to symbolize the sixty-seven pounds she had lost. While performing this very public disavowal of her former "fat" self Oprah modeled a pair of size 10 Calvin Klein jeans she had saved for the occasion to the enthusiastic applause of her audience. Soon thereafter, however, a chagrined Oprah confessed to her fans that she no longer could fit into the jeans; like so many crash dieters who suffer from the "diet rebound effect," she had immediately begun to work her way back up the scale.

Figure 2.1. Oprah's triumph over fat (Courtesy Paul Natkin).

Other celebrities, such as Queen Latifah, Kirstie Alley, and "Fergie" (Sarah Ferguson) both narrativize and commodify their struggle with obesity and compulsive overeating while serving as spokespeople for commercial weight loss programs such as Jenny Craig or Weight Watchers; their newly slender images are then immediately displayed in the tabloid press. Still others, depicted as desperate and on the tipping edge of morbid obesity, undergo bariatric surgery in an equally public setting; in 1999 entertainer Carnie Wilson invited her fans to witness her gastric bypass procedure on the Internet. (Most recently, she has capitalized on that notoriety in a television reality series, *Carnie Wilson Unstapled*.) Her very public surgery only underscored the changes in popular media culture that have replaced tightly controlled access to Hollywood movie stars with the capacity to circulate images of a celebrity's digestive organs around the world.

Younger audiences are invited to identify with the glamorized narratives of pregnancy that are constructed in the popular media as guarantees of domestic bliss. Celebrity pregnancies are featured each week in *People, Star,* and *Us* magazines, typically displaying a star couple either radiantly expectant or proudly displaying their newborns. The site of celebrity fertility and domesticity is the pregnant belly of the expectant mother—known in tabloid jargon as the "baby bump"—an image that made its first and most memorable appearance in the now-iconic photograph of actress Demi Moore's nude and very pregnant body on the cover of *Vanity Fair* in 1991 and which frequently reappears on the covers of contemporary fan magazines and in Web sites.

Such images have also become crucial elements in the project of commodification of the pregnant body in a multibillion dollar industry promoting designer maternity clothes modeled by fashion celebrities. The clothes are designed to emphasize rather than hide the bulging belly, a part of the anatomy currently considered to be what social historian Clare Hanson dubs "a fashion accessory, like a sort of handbag."[18] The marketing of "pregnancy chic" significantly includes services that signal self-care and maintenance of both sexuality and visibility such as maternity spa services like "Yummy Tummy" belly facials, luxury apparel including Victoria Secret thong underwear and other prenatal indulgences prescribed in guidebooks for the "The Hot Mom to Be." Still more fundamental to this consumer pregnancy narrative is the recuperation of the prepartum body, that is, getting "in shape" as quickly as possible after giving birth. Postpartum cosmetic surgeries known as "Mummy tucks" including liposuction, breast and belly lifts were first publicized by celebrity mothers and subsequently marketed to the general public as part of the trend for postpartum makeover practices.[19]

The drama of the postpartum reclamation project produces images each week in entertainment media of how celebrity mothers work to retrieve "Amazing 'After-Baby' Bodies." Fans are also invited to witness the challenges confronting the star in maintaining her glamorous image: new mother Gywneth Paltrow, for example, tells *People* that after shedding twenty pounds of pregnancy weight her "biggest challenge" at the Oscar award gala was "expressing milk while getting my hair blown out."[20] The postpartum project typically involves replacing the baby bump with even more desirable "flat abs"; following the much-publicized birth of her first child, Madonna's body was displayed as toned and tight after weeks of strenuous fitness regimens. *Star* magazine exulted: "Angie's [Angelina Jolie] got her waist back—11 days after baby!" noting "if she doesn't see her old shape return soon enough, she's investigating plastic surgery options, including a tummy tuck and breast-lift." More recently, Jolie attributed her speedy reclamation of her "old shape" to the calorie "burn" of breast feeding, modeling it as another diet tip for nursing mothers.[21]

Importantly, these celebrity postpartum narratives stand in sharp contrast to weight loss recommendations from obstetricians who advise a far more gradual return to prepartum weight of between four and nine months.[22] Not surprisingly, the expectations established by the circulation of celebrity body images may serve to promote feelings of inadequacy and shame, which can drive unhealthy weight control and dieting behaviors in new mothers. Here for example is how such cultural expectations impacted thirty-one-year-old Marnie, a stay-at-home mother of two toddlers. A former high school beauty pageant queen who had worked diligently throughout her twenties to maintain her slim shape through rigorous exercise and strict calorie control, she reported in therapy that since the birth of her children she was struggling with the loss of her toned prepartum body:

> I feel like such a wreck—I have all these stretch marks from the babies and now with me staying home and not working there's no way I can afford a tummy tuck like the celebrity moms in *People*. And my boobs—forget it! I feel so guilty but when I'm nursing the baby all I can think about is how old and saggy they look compared to the stars' after they had babies. Remember how Madonna was back at the gym practically right after she gave birth looking like a million dollars. Who has time to go to the gym? I'm so afraid of not losing all my baby weight these days I'm mostly just letting myself drink diet shakes.

Just as celebrity maternity narratives speak to a major moment in female development, so too the dramas of self-destructive body practices of younger celebrities such as cutting, substance abuse, and self-starvation enact the stormy conflicts of identity, sexual experience, and insecurity that characterize the developmental crises of adolescence. In fact, one of the most common understandings of the emergence of eating disorders and self-harming behaviors in adolescence is that these body disturbances are an attempt to gain a sense of control during the often confusing transition to adulthood. The list of young celebrity eating disorder victims is long, with once again entertainment media primarily emphasizing the shock value of photos documenting Mary-Kate

Olson's "ultra-bony bod" and Nicole Ritchie's "scarily pin-thin" image, or engaging in a public scolding of Lindsay Lohan's denial of her bulimia. In its complicity with the circulation of "ultra-boniness" as a body ideal, however, popular media are seemingly blind to the irony of such commentary. And in fact, many young readers are "inspired" by the super-thin celebrities suffering from eating disorders just as they are by "pro-anorexia" Web sites such as "Thinspiration" which encourage active and would-be anorexics in their drive for impossible slenderness. Prominently featured on these sites—along with "Thin Commandments" such as "Thou shall not eat without feeling guilty" and "Thou shall count calories and restrict intake accordingly"—are images of movie stars and entertainment celebrities who are seen as role models for the commandment: "Being thin and not eating are true signs of will power and success."[24]

Without doubt, the relationship between Hollywood celebrity culture and contemporary body disturbances has been dramatically affected by the emergence of new mechanisms of image production and distribution: flashing television screens in airports, subway stations, and apartment elevators; electronic moving billboards on city streets; outsize high-definition screens looming over bars; tiny cell phone screens and mini-laptops, not to mention instant access to any media image past and present via YouTube—the rise is exponential, a quantitative shift so great that it now exerts a qualitative effect in its sheer omnipresence and inescapability. But far more complex in its implications is the recent shift from star-centered media to interactive user-based systems, which free media consumers from their fixed positions as mere spectators to become protagonists of their own video or musical productions. Media scholars recognize that today's information world—fed by user-generated content circulated by programs such as Twitter, YouTube, or Internet blogs—has radically transformed the traditional definition of the "audience."[25] In this new environment in which "each audience member has become a producer of their content,"[26] media consumers now have the mechanisms both to construct, morph, and monitor their own images and then circulate them to an ever-wider audience via the global reach of the Internet, only increasing the intensity of an already visually driven culture. As another media critic has observed: "The web is a place of performance and staging of the self."[27] It is now a predictable feature of contemporary nightlife, for example, that at any given table in a club or restaurant, the incessant flash of cell phones and digital cameras are recording the "show "of the moment performed not by a professional entertainer up on a stage but by the diners seated around the table. Each camera flash is followed by shrieks and laughter at how "good" or "horrible" the subjects appear in the shot, with particular evaluation of whether or not they look "fat." Well beyond the capacity of Polaroid cameras and home movies to capture our images in real time, today's webcams and smart phones can ensure instant personal celebrity.[28]

Such consumer technologies not only have provided a mechanism for popular culture audiences to construct their personal home-grown "reality shows" but they are also actively recruited to interact with media-produced shows as well. ABC's promotional ad for their reality show lineup urges viewers to "Get In The Picture!" while "on the ground" citizen reporters are encouraged to submit their cell phone images of major events and disasters for display on network and cable television and the Internet. When a Dunkin' Donuts store clerk was held up by a robber not long ago he decided to assault the intruder largely because he didn't want to be caught on the surveillance camera looking like a "wimp." He hoped that through the Internet the image of his bravery could soon travel from the store camera to a far larger audience: "There are only a few videos like that on YouTube right now, so mine's going to be the best."[29] The post-9/11 security camera technology developed for surveillance in public spaces such as airports, stores, and office buildings has expanded into private and commercial space as well, including a recent innovation to introduce small cameras into billboards, which allow advertisers to profile potential customers. The notion of constantly being "on camera" allows us to feel that we are no longer the audience but the main act; not surprisingly, we internalize a sense of self-scrutiny and body consciousness in response.

A related media phenomenon is the rise of a new variant of reality television in which the "average viewer" can actively participate in the previously exclusive world of stars. The boundary between screen celebrities, models, and rap stars and their fans dissolves on such formats as *Dancing with the Stars*, *America's Next Top Model*, and the wildly popular *American Idol*, shows that encourage aspiring contestants to compete for their own chance at stardom through contact with "real" stars, in many instances soon becoming "divas" and celebrities themselves. As a result contemporary media audiences, far more than previous generations of fans, want to look like celebrities primarily because they want to become famous themselves. Copying the "look" of their favorite star, then, is more aspirational than devotional. "Sha," a nineteen-year-old subject on the "makeover" show *I Want A Famous Face* talked about her goal for her surgery: She underwent chin liposuction, lip implants, micrografts to her hairline, and breast implants in order to look like Pamela Anderson and become a *Playboy* model. She sees Anderson as an ideal because she "knows how to take advantage of every opportunity that comes with being beautiful and turn it into a great career." And Crystal, a twenty-four-year-old office worker, received both breast augmentation and a nose job in order to gain the confidence she thinks she needs to become a stripper and impersonate Britney Spears.[30]

A growing trend in the pursuit of celebrity for children and adolescents transmits body scrutiny and preoccupation to the next generation. Training programs such as "Idol Camp" in Northfield, Massachusetts, with a tuition of $300 per day, prepare teens for their competitions on reality shows while pre-teen girls are now hooked on television shows such as *iCarly* (which features a "'tween" with the most popular personal Web site) or *Hannah Montana*, a "regular teen" schoolgirl who moonlights as a rock and roll star at night. According to a recent study, more than one-third of American teens, aided by their parents' encouragement, are confident they will be stars: as one thirteen-year-old American Idol aspirant noted: "I think it would be really cool to be a famous singer. . . . Every teenager wants to be famous."[31]

The development of the software Web 2.0, which enables social networking sites such as Facebook and Twitter, is yet another contributor to today's heightened body vigilance and self-scrutiny. As one of my students shared in a burst of candor during a class discussion about the sites: "If I weren't on Facebook I would eat whatever I wanted and stop starving myself." In this regard it is worth noting that the origin myth of Facebook identifies its initial format as a Harvard University site called "Hot-or-Not" in which users were invited to choose between juxtaposed photos of female students—underscoring the potential the concept had from its onset to perpetuate a kind of cultural "looksism."[32] Social network members can build a Web site that constructs an image and persona based on their looks, hobbies, friends, and accomplishments in order to attract interest from a "fan base" of fellow members. Discovery myths about Facebook stardom abound, such as that of the woman whose sexually provocative site gained sufficient notoriety that she graduated from cyberspace celebrity to appearances on an MTV reality dating show. In a related trend on college campuses, student-produced publications are appealing to undergraduate fantasies of modeling and body celebrity by publishing students in various degrees of undress in glamorous and provocative poses.

At the same time that the Internet has increased access to pornography it has also enabled passive viewers to become performers. The results are new forms of "Amature" pornography in which nonprofessionals perform in pornography films or appear online in their own porn displays and body calendars in hopes of transitioning to modeling and acting jobs in the "Adult Industry." This in turn has led to the proliferation both of products to beautify previously hidden body parts as well as cosmetic surgical procedures designed to emulate porn star bodies. One such procedure developed for this consumer market is known as elective genitoplasty, which promises to correct asymmetry and bodily imperfections in pubic areas and genitalia for both public display and private sexual encounters. Thus, both new media and aesthetic surgery technologies not only allow contemporary media consumers to enact their private fantasies but also to become the stars, scriptwriters, and directors of their own performances, enabled by digital editing equipment to perfect their images and circulate them around the world.

It is precisely this quest for the perfect image, and with it the relentless pursuit of impossible slenderness, that drives the food and weight control regimens and obsessive body preoccupation that mark eating disordered behavior. The star image as constructed by celebrity culture is the enactment of this quest: it is represented as a perfected body that must be constantly controlled, improved and toned. Identity and character strengths such as courage, perseverance, and discipline are externalized as bodily fitness, dietary control, and restraint, creating a new kind of corporeal political correctness. In the following chapter we will examine how specific Hollywood films simultaneously establish and reflect such cultural ideologies of body mastery.

3

Body Mastery and the Ideology of Fitness

The women warriors of Hollywood action movies tell us that body mastery is far less about female strength, agility, and athletic skill and far more about looking good, being sexually desirable, and displaying a body that is above all "in shape." This cinematic narrative finds its analogue in the modern fitness movement. While exercise has long been promoted by the medical community for physical health and flexibility, today's fitness culture with its rhetoric of discipline and self-control is driven by powerful social pressure to lose weight, contain saggy and baggy flesh, and "whip" the body into the contour that conforms to the contemporary ideal. In fact, the very notion of being "in shape," originally a reference to cardiovascular capacity and endurance, is more likely to signal a tight and toned appearance, privileging the outwardly "shapely" body rather than an internally sound specimen of metabolic health. In the process, fitness culture conflates healthy exercise and nutrition with obsessive and near-pathological practices that can lead exercisers to become more frantic than fit.

Women in particular learn it is crucial to look attractive during the performance of their body in action. External features of fitness initially marketed to men such as "six-pack abs" as well as toned arms and legs, developed bicep and back muscles, are frequently displayed as female fashion accessories. The bodysuit worn by action movie superwomen has inspired designer gymwear made of form-fitting materials like Lycra and Spandex that are dual purpose: they both reveal the toned body at the same time that the fabric contains and smoothes unsightly bulges and bumps. These garments are modeled on the "unitard," a one- piece suit created for early comic book superheroes of both sexes such as Superman and Wonder Woman which influenced the costumes designed for *Kill Bill's* women warriors and other Hollywood action heroines. The unitard has been described by writer Michael Chabon as a representation of the human body as "unfettered, perfect and free." Significantly, he also notes that "like the being who wears it, the superhero costume is, by definition, an impossible object. It cannot exist."[1] Yet the impossibly perfect superwoman body has become a powerful aspiration toward which women and girls are encouraged to strive. In an episode of *What Not to Wear*, a "makeover" reality show, a firefighter from Orange County, California, named Natalie who is fond of wearing "Supergirl" and "Batman" T-shirts is accused by her family and boyfriend of being sloppy, adolescent in her taste, and still worse, "unfeminine." The goal of the show's fashion experts is to upgrade her wardrobe to make her sexier and more "confident" by shedding her work boots and jeans. The contestant obediently vows to reduce the size of her broad shoulders and big arms to "get in touch with [my] feminine side." Significantly, her "bigness" and muscularity is read as problematic, an obstacle to contemporary notions of sexual attractiveness that define the feminine body as slender rather than powerfully built and strong.

It is just this message that was internalized by Linda, a twenty-three-year-old teacher who has suffered periodically from bulimia, after repeated exposure to a Hollywood film she first saw as a teen ager:

> The movie *Bring It On* came out when I was in eighth grade. It centered around a group of cheerleaders. They all had really thin sculpted bodies. The entire movie they wore either really small tight tank tops or sports bras and tiny shorts. I have been a hockey player my entire life and because of weight training I have always been bulked out especially in the legs. This movie made me very insecure about my body. I felt like I looked too boyish; although I appeared strong it wasn't a "girly" type of strong. This was the first time I ever felt dissatisfied with my body. Since then I have gone through stages in my life where I binge and purge to try to get smaller. Though I can't blame it solely on *Bring It On*, I can definitely say that movie acted as a trigger.

Because women are thus inspired to reform and shape their bodies to conform to conservative constructs of femininity, their exercise regimens are often aimed at becoming more externally attractive than physiologically fit. Fad exercise trends imported from professional sports or other traditions such as "cardio-boxing" and "power yoga" are marketed as weight-loss aids and conditioners for body toning and slenderizing. Typically, they are spinoff products endorsed by celebrities such as Jane Fonda, whose home exercise videos were among the first to exhort fans to reshape the "problem" areas of their bodies through rigorous workout routines. A revealing ethnographic study of aerobic exercisers found that instructors identified the goal of each step not in terms of improving stamina but rather to obtain a sleeker appearance, while muscle building was promoted to burn calories and "carbs" and tighten flabby body parts rather than build strength.[2] A more troubling manifestation of this kind of cosmeticization of fitness is the rise of steroid abuse in young women and girls where the object is not to raise their batting average but to turn hated fat into calorie-burning muscle. A recent study found more than 5 percent of teenage girls admitting to using anabolic steroids for appearance improvement, with the most rapidly growing incidence occurring among seventh-grade girls.[3] Said one recovered abuser: "It's this whole Hollywood thing. Everyone is so affected by movie stars."[4] And while middle school girls may thus confuse physical strength with physical attractiveness to their peril, their little sisters are being encouraged to lose their baby fat earlier than ever: toy manufacturers have begun marketing step gliders and treadmills to pre-schoolers and their anxious parents. Promoting products such as Fitness Fun's My Treadmill and Glide-a-Stride, which are designed for children ages three through six, a spokesperson for the Toy Industry Association says that if the toys "help kids slim down and parents feel good about buying [them] everybody wins."[5] But it might not be such a win-win given the potential of such products to encourage body vigilance and self-scrutiny in the youngest of consumers.

Emphasis on displaying a toned and sculpted body also explains why women who perceive themselves to be "out of shape" often feel exposed and embarrassed in public exercise settings—and consequently avoid them. Just as unshapely bodies are absent on the screen, so too they may be underrepresented in health clubs and gyms, particularly those that are co-ed. This was the dilemma faced by thirty-seven-year-old Tracey, a pediatric nurse who had spent much of her childhood and adolescence being teased at school, sometimes brutally, for being overweight. She recalled the humiliation of being picked last for team games and being taunted during gym class, and the indignity of being sent away each summer by her parents to a special diet camp to lose weight and become more "athletic," experiences that continued to inhibit her physical activity:

> I'm way too out of shape to show up at the gym with all those teeny girls decked out in their spandex tights and tank tops. I swear they put on make-up just to work out because they want the guys to hit on them! And of course I feel worse when I see myself in the mirror with all that flab under my arms when I lift weights. So I'd much rather go out after dark and get my exercise walking around the neighborhood and just hope the boys don't start yelling "Fatso" at me like when I was in first grade.

For Tracey as for so many others the word *fitness* has come to mean whether a person is "fit" to display their body in a social setting and whether they "fit" into today's body ideal. And bodies that fail to "fit" or conform to that ideal must be *re*formed. Contemporary prescriptions for such body reformation through fitness regimens, as well as the notion of physical exercise as punishment for bodily excess, have several striking correspondences to the theories advanced in the treatise of French philosopher Michel Foucault known as *Discipline and Punish: The Birth of the Prison* (1975). In his investigation of Western penal systems Foucault documents how the human body has been subject to forms of surveillance and control through institutions like schools and the military which enforce regimens of uniformity and discipline to create what he calls "docile bodies." What is most important to emphasize about these docile bodies is that they have *internalized* the dictates and standards of the enforcers who establish them. In other words such bodies are neither rebellious nor defiant but rather all too willing to control and monitor themselves in alliance with society's expectations. The analogy here to today's fitness movement is all too clear: in a culture that promotes constant self-scrutiny and body vigilance, self-disciplining practices such as dieting and workout regimens demonstrate our willingness to control our own excessive flesh and appetites by keeping our desires in check through careful "watching" of our weight and food intake.

In contemporary fitness culture, exercise is presented as a necessary penance for indulgence; the aerobics instructor exhorts her "ladies" to sweat and pant to burn off last night's pizza orgy before it gets "stuck" on their hips. This kind of caloric calibration is further institutionalized in the gym by aerobic exercise machines, which feature devices to monitor the number of calories expended in the workout. Women's magazines feature "Splurge and Redemption" workout products such as the "Dessert Wizard," which calculates "the exact number of minutes you've got to work out to burn off those Gummi Bears or brownies."[6] The same anxious calculation informs the weight control practices of college students who atone for the sin of eating a candy bar during study break by running up ten flights of stairs in their dormitories. Not surprisingly, clinical research studies have found that female aerobic exercisers who work out to compensate for overeating have significantly higher rates of eating disorder diagnoses.[7] A particularly striking investigation of more than two hundred college students recently identified a new type of disorder called "exercise dependence" in which subjects reported feelings of stress, depression, guilt, and difficulties concentrating if they failed to meet their exercise goals. They also expressed the need to increase the intensity of their workouts to satisfy their exercise "cravings," symptoms all too reminiscent of the tolerance and dependence effects of addictive behavior. These students also tested higher for stringent dieting and food preoccupation as well as bulimic behaviors; once again they acknowledged that weight control was their primary motivation for exercise.[8]

Fitness and fatness anxiety are thus conflated while the specific fear of becoming fat by eating high-fat foods gets channeled into obsessive exercising. Worry about weight gain drives several new eating disorders that have emerged in recent years. In addition to exercise dependence, more colloquially known as "gymorexia," clinicians have also identified such conditions as "obligatory running" and "anorexia athletica." Preoccupied by what they have eaten or the number on the scale, individuals suffering from these disorders report feelings of overwhelming guilt and stress unless they complete their daily workout routines, a ritual that can send them to the gym several times a day for hours at a time. The compulsion reaches fullest pathological expression in the eating disorder known as "exercise bulimia" where individuals use excessive exercise instead of purging to prevent dreaded weight gain. This is the disorder that brought forty-two-year-old Lisa to me for treatment. A highly competent biochemical engineer, she grew up in a family that demanded peak performance from Lisa and her two brothers, both of whom had become physicians. Their father, a well-known neuroscientist who still played competitive tennis, was a "big guy" and Lisa bemoaned the fact that she took after his body type. Lisa was "incredibly close" with her mother, a successful magazine editor, whom she described as "a really petite size 2 who always ate healthy." She recalls her humiliation when another member of her aerobics class congratulated her for getting out there even though she was "such a big girl." Much of Lisa's day is structured around rigid exercise rituals which she enforces even when she is sick, including a week in the winter when she had the flu and was running a fever of 102:

> Before I let myself have my muffin in the morning I have to run for thirty minutes. Then in the afternoon I swim thirty laps in the pool which allows me to eat a half a sandwich. Otherwise I'll just skip lunch. And if I have to go out for dinner, I'll work out for another hour to burn off the calories I'll have to eat at the restaurant.

Eating disorders among trained athletes and dancers are well documented, often generating publicity and concern when a young gymnast or ballet performer dies from anorexia. Clinical studies of female ballet dancers show disturbingly high rates of eating disorders, particularly among dancers who struggle to maintain a weight lower than their natural body structure supports.[9] But the popular media imagery surrounding the heroism and success of these body masters is so compelling that it can encourage rather than discourage the relentless pursuit of body performance and perfection. Nicholas Hytner's film *Center Stage* (2000) follows a group of aspiring dancers in New York City as they compete for professional careers at the fictitious "American Ballet Academy." The rising star of the class is the driven and immensely competitive Maureen, a dancer who struggles with bulimia. She manages to confront her problem by the film's end and drops out of the race to the top. But if the film intended her story to serve as a warning about the perils of obsessive performance and ambition, it was overshadowed by its visual fascination with the grace and beauty of the dancers' bodies, their fierce commitment to winning and the sheer excitement and drama surrounding their dreams of success and romance against a backdrop of the bright city lights of the New York skyline. As in so many Hollywood movies the "message" backfires and the film becomes instead a virtual training film for eating disorders, as it did for Ariana, a student who had transferred to my university after dropping out of a dance institute. She had received what she called a "fat letter" during the previous semester warning that unless she lost some weight she might not be a successful candidate in advancing her career. After much soul searching she decided not to return to the institute, realizing the price she was being asked to pay was too high:

> When I was growing up I was a tomboy but when I got older I wanted to be more lady-like, like my big sister who took ballet. I noticed my body type was different from the other ballerinas in my class who were taller and leaner while I was more athletically built. I wanted to look more like them, and I got my inspiration from a movie called *Center Stage*. The best girl on the dance team Maureen had an eating disorder and in my mind I correlated that with being the skinniest and the best. Judging from her body, her perfectionism and her skill, she would definitely have become the lead ballerina in a professional company. At the end of the movie Maureen drops out and goes to a regular college where she is popular and successful. Even outside of the ballet world people accept her because of her looks; the men in the movie liked the skinnier girls better and made fun of the fatter ones For a long time after I saw the movie I counted calories, put myself on a pretty strict diet and exercised . . . a lot! I worked so hard at becoming a perfect little ballerina that I lost myself somewhere along the way.

Much as *Center Stage* exerted paradoxical effects on this young dancer, the two-part martial arts saga *Kill Bill* (2002 and 2004) falls short of its intended message. Despite director Quentin Tarantino's assertion that he wanted his heroines to be "empowering women" rather than "eye-candy for guys,"[10] the films do not live up to this intention, constructing instead superwomen images that perpetuate the ideologies of body control and self-denial embedded in contemporary fitness culture. "Chapter Nine" of *Volume 2*, for example, opens with a shot of a sleek black convertible careening through a surreal desert landscape. At the wheel is Elle Driver (Daryl Hannah) her long blond tresses blowing in the wind. She screeches to a stop in front of the battered trailer of the man she will soon destroy in a particularly gruesome way for revenge and possession of a prized samurai sword—but for the moment the camera seems to be more interested in what she is wearing. It zooms in on her impeccably tailored black suit, matching boots and superslender legs as she steps out of the car; the bright red bag she is holding as she strides up the stairs might be just a fashion accessory but for the fact that it contains a deadly snake whose venom will leave her victim writhing in pain. While Elle sits coolly puffing on a cigarette waiting for him to die, the camera continues its appreciation of her body, lingering on her full mouth and glistening red lipstick, alluring neckline, and her signature eye patch which is perfectly coordinated with her outfit.

Elle Driver in turn will soon be savagely destroyed by her sworn rival Beatrix Kiddo (Uma Thurman) who is bent on avenging the wedding day massacre four years earlier in which Elle and the film's eponymous Bill (David Carradine) shot her and her unborn baby. But as the saga sets about unraveling this Byzantine plot of revenge for the martial arts fan, it has much more to say about how Hollywood

Figure 3.1. Fashionable assassin Elle Driver waits for her victim to die in *Kill Bill 2*.

action movies depict their women warriors. To begin with, *Kill Bill* codes its superwomen bodies as fashion models, most obviously with the casting of Hanna and Thurman. Not only are both long and leggy stars over six feet tall but they also have had previous careers as models and frequently appear in fashion magazine photo spreads and advertisements for luxury goods, such as a diamond wrist watch ad featuring the image of Uma Thurman staring out provocatively from the back cover of *Vanity Fair* magazine.[12] Another cinematic resonance is Thurman's earlier role as a beautiful but impossibly dumb high fashion model in *The Truth About Cats and Dogs* (1996), a romantic comedy in which she happens to suffer from a serious eating disorder, blithely confessing: "I don't eat anything so I can look good on the outside, but inside I'm nothing." The fashion in-jokes grow broader still with the construction of the character of "Elle Driver"; while her name is a nod to both the fashion magazine *Elle* and supermodel Elle Macpherson, her color-coordinated eyewear is a visual reference to the now iconic patch sported by the debonair Hathaway shirt man who ushered in the advertising age decades ago. At many instances in both *Kill Bill* films we might as well be in Paris or New York watching Beatrix and Elle on the fashion runway. They are filmed striding, fashionista style, with hips forward, eyes straight ahead, and shoulders swaying to the beat of a pulsing soundtrack which announces their entrance into the frame. These deadly assassins may be on their way to destroy their next enemy but the camera is busy tracking their "killer" designer outfits.[12] *Kill Bill Volume 1* culminates in a ten-minute crescendo of violence as Beatrix singlehandedly vanquishes a rival Japanese gang in a show-stopping battle featuring spurting blood, severed heads and limbs, James Bond torture weapons, and flailing swords clanging in the best martial arts movie tradition. But the long sequence is choreographed more like a Madonna music video, with Beatrix surrounded by a circle of men dressed in identical black suits wielding their swords in perfect unison while the camerawork rivets our attention on Beatrix's willowy body clad in a chic yellow and black bodysuit. The camera swoops up to an extreme high angle affording an aerial view of cleavage and crotch, then does a 360° turn around her entire body as she kicks, leaps, and somersaults through the air, finally dropping down for a slow pan of her seemingly endless legs. The oblique camera angles further elongate her body at the same time as the quick edgy editing evokes the rhythm of a fashion photography "shoot."

Figure 3.2. Beatrix Kiddo battles her enemies in Tokyo.

Thurman describes her Beatrix Kiddo character as "a lean mean killing machine,"[13] and it is indeed her lean body as much as her ferocity that is the feature act. In fact both films are all about style. Together they form a self-conscious homage to a wide array of popular movie genres—particularly kung fu, Hong Kong gangster, and Japanese martial arts sagas, as well as spaghetti westerns and James Bond action adventures; while the soundtrack references still others in a virtual medley of country and western music, blues and rock and roll to the score of Sergio Leone's *A Fistful of Dollars*. The *mise en scène* is a dazzling display of visual style with geometric patterns, saturated colors, and flashy sets used to create what one film critic described as a series of "lacquered glitz-interiors."[14] The virtuosity of the cinematography, with its sudden shifts in camera angles and fast-paced shots zooming in and out of the frame combines with these effects to draw attention to the surface rather than depth of the screen, emphasizing once again the mannered "look" of the fashion world.

Kill Bill constructs its supermodel/superwomen as objects of sexual desire who ultimately embody traditional images of femininity. True, Beatrix and her sister assassins perform feats of kicking, leaping, punching, and sword fighting with the ferocious aggression usually coded for masculinity. Especially impressive is the long sequence in *Kill Bill 2* in which Beatrix is sent to China to train with a harsh master who subjects her body to punishing discipline; later, when Bill's brother buries her alive she uses all her strength and ingenuity against seemingly insurmountable odds to escape from her coffin. In both these sequences she appears muddied and bloodied and decidedly un-glamorous, but not for long. In fact, both films more frequently lose themselves in the erotic possibilities of superwomen bodies as the camera stalks them with its own voyeuristic gaze, using tight focus shots in the classic "view from behind" as Elle and Beatrix stride through airports and sit astride roaring motorcycles in form-fitting pants and leather jackets.

If these images seem familiar, we should not be surprised: Beatrix and the other members of Bill's gang are descendants of the original 1940s comic book figure Wonder Woman, which succeeded in feeding the sexual fantasies of an entire generation of adolescent readers. The figure resurfaced in 1970s television shows such as *Wonder Woman, Charlie's Angels,* and *The Avengers* as a response to new "liberated" images of feminine power.[15] While films in recent decades certainly have given us memorable female action heroines such as Ripley in *Alien,* Sarah Connor in *Terminator II*, and of course, both Thelma *and* Louise, Hollywood for the most part continues to hypersexualize their superwomen, as if to reassure the young male spectators who comprise the vast majority of their viewing audience that their fantasies of big-breasted dominatrixes in leather and high boots can remain intact and unchallenged. These same figures emerge alive and well in such recent superwomen movie iterations as *Lara Croft: Tomb Raider* (2001), featuring Angelina Jolie decked out in a body suit emphasizing her breasts and sculpted shoulders and armed to the hilt with knives and bombs strategically strapped to her exposed thighs and crotch, thereby giving the camera maximum eroticizing "photo opportunities" in its many action shots. As one film analysis points out: "There is hardly a shot that does not zoom in on her bosom or take its departure from between her legs."[16] Jolie may wield the biggest gun, as she does in a subsequent role as Fox, a superwoman assassin in the action adventure *Wanted* (2008), but her sleek dominatrix body remains the stuff of adolescent sexual fantasy. And while these action "dolls" and gun-toting "hotties" may be the product of studio producers appealing to male cultural fantasies, the message to female viewers is still more potent:

the way to embody such fantasies and thus be desired by men is to look like the action heroines the films construct. Here for example is how Carly, a college junior returning from spring break, described her own such reading of the *Kill Bill* saga:

> During the break my girlfriends and I sat around watching movies and I couldn't get over how erotic *Kill Bill* seemed. Somehow it made me feel really self-conscious despite being really drawn in and fascinated by the actresses' incredible bodies. One of my friends was talking about how Uma Thurman spent six hours a day training for the Beatrix Kiddo role with coaches and all kinds of kung-fu masters. So after seeing the movie I really was inspired to work out more and got so gung-ho I actually ended up pulling my hamstring from overdoing the running and calisthenics. I often have this feeling of inferiority when watching sexy movie stars but it's even worse with martial arts movies like this one. I want to be lithe and long like Uma Thurman and Darryl Hanna were but my body seems to be built more like an NFL lineman and less like an acrobatic fashion model.

While Hollywood's fashionable women warriors may wield phallic guns and swords, roar about on motorcycles and in race cars, and master computer technology and foreign languages, they typically work for a more powerful man, thus attenuating any notion of true independence and "female empowerment." The three avenging superwomen in the movie version of *Charlie's Angels* (2000) are dedicated employees of "Charlie" (Bill Murray) their crime-fighting boss, while Bill is the unchallenged ruler of his harem of trained assassins known as the "Deadly Viper Assassination Squad"; the acronym the name implies holds some irony in that the assassins are not "divas" but in fact obedient trainees who vie for Bill's affection and approval. They are also his sexual workers, paid to use their seductive bodies as well as their lethality to advance his power. An arch allusion to prostitution is contained in Beatrix's voiceover narrative: "I was quite the professional [who] worked in an exclusive industry."

True, the men in both *Kill Bill* films are for the most part grotesque sexist caricatures (they refer to Beatrix as "the cutest little blond pussy you ever saw," who is "too smart for a blonde") whose sadism and misogyny provide justification for equally brutal retaliation—such as Beatrix's particularly savage revenge upon the male nurse and his buddies who raped her during her long coma. But the films also perpetuate the iconography of rape and sexual abuse of women in less overt but more troubling ways. The construction of several scenes in fact evokes the glamorization of violence against women used in contemporary fashion ads of models in bondage, in cages, or lying unconscious while displaying designer cosmetics and accessories.[17] After Bill's brother Budd wounds Beatrix with a stun gun, for example, the camera focuses on the decorative red pattern of the blood that spreads across her white blouse while in another scene the camera looks down on Beatrix's body dressed in a stylish two-piece outfit designed to match the décor of the bathroom floor on which she lies prostrate; the extreme high angle of the shot references her form both as a stylized fashion image as well as a sexually vulnerable and exposed female body.

Another sexist trope is evoked by the films' action scenes where for the most part women fight and men watch. During the fierce duels in which Beatrix takes on each of her enemies, the insistent sexualization of female bodies reduces their battles to a "cat fight." In fact when Beatrix and Elle engage in mortal combat Beatrix literally claws Elle's eye out; one cannot help but wonder if the image of Beatrix slowly and sadistically crushing the fallen eyeball underneath her foot is less an over-the-top grotesquerie and more an unconscious expression of the films' lack of insight into their own sadism and cinematic misogyny. And the films may be equally blind to how their narrative structure undercuts any genuine empowerment of the women warrior. Read as a developmental history of the heroine, Beatrix's personal narrative ultimately contains all stages of traditional femininity, each of which is represented by the different sobriquets she adopts. As Beatrix Kiddo, bonded to mentor and father figure Bill, she is a "Daddy's girl" who gazes up at him adoringly as he initiates her into the lore of martial arts. Later she becomes Beatrix aka the Bride who yearns to retire from the contract killing business and settle down in El Paso with a nice guy and raise a family. And she is also Beatrix aka Black Mamba Snake as both worker and mistress in an incestuous relationship with Bill who appears as a perverse and jealous "Dad" at her wedding aiming to shoot her and the baby he apparently sired.

Ultimately, however, it is the identified role of Beatrix aka Mommy that drives the films' narrative structure, for it is the prospect of maternity that both ends her contract killing career and later motivates her "rampage" to avenge the attempted murder of her unborn child. In fact, Beatrix's maternal instincts prove to be sufficiently strong to instantly transform this "natural born killer" into the tender and protective mom we see in the final sequence of the film. The scene in which Beatrix discovers that she is pregnant takes on a special resonance because of the consistent coding of her body throughout the films as a high fashion supermodel. She is filmed standing in her scanty underthings before a long bathroom mirror, inspecting her perfectly flat belly with a worried frown while the camera once again circles and pans up and down her tall and lean form; the image suggests the fear of losing both her model's figure to pregnancy and childbirth as well as her career as a professional killer.

Just at that point in the narrative a rival female assassin arrives at the door to kill Beatrix but, in one of the film's funniest moments, retreats when she reads the positive pregnancy test strip; in an apparent impulse of womanly solidarity the assassin wishes her well through the hole she has just blown through the door with her huge phallic gun. While the films' gamey tone easily can sustain this kind of parody, Beatrix's choice of motherhood over allegiance to Bill in the narrative

Figure 3.3. Beatrix checks for signs of pregnancy.

structure is less ambivalent; rather, it clearly suggests her recuperation of traditional feminine identity after a lifetime of masculinized aggression. In fact, her essential womanhood is confirmed by Bill himself; just before dying from her lethal five-point palm exploding heart assault he pays her the ultimate tribute: "You're a terrific person. You're my favorite person. But every once in a while you can be a real cunt." Beatrix smiles at him with great affection and gratitude, as if he has indeed validated her feminine nature; with this blessing she is finally free to take up her maternal role and conclude her journey.

Not all Hollywood action heroines turn out to be either training models for fashion statement bodies or self-flagellating perfectionists of body discipline. Clint Eastwood's Oscar-winning *Million Dollar Baby*, the sentimental favorite recipient of four Academy Awards in 2004 (the film was billed as a "tale of heart, hope and family"), presents a heroine who stands in sharp contrast to the women warriors of *Kill Bill* and *Lara Croft*. Unlike Tarantino's mind-bending nonlinear structure, *Million Dollar Baby* follows a simple archetypal narrative of triumph over adversity, followed by loss and transcendence. Its three main characters are equally recognizable: Frankie Dunn, the aging world-weary boxing trainer of the "Hit-Pit" gym who is estranged from his own daughter (Eastwood), "Scrap," the beat-up old fighter who now serves as his gym janitor and loyal companion (Morgan Freeman), and Maggie (Hillary Swank), the lost and abused daughter of a "trailer trash" family who enters their lives in search of a chance in the ring. The bonds that grow among these three down-and-out figures as they become first a training team, then a reconstituted family, and ultimately witnesses to tragedy and mortality, lie at the emotional core of the film; but the "action" is centered around the prizefighting women in the boxing ring. The depiction of these powerful bodies, as well as the entire cinematic style of the film, provides a very different message about body mastery than that of the superhero sagas of Beatrix and Lara Croft.

Set in a seedy Philadelphia gym and the sterile corridors of hospitals and rundown dressing rooms, the film's *mise en scène* stands in sharp contrast to the dazzling surfaces of *Kill Bill*'s designer world. Instead, *Million Dollar Baby* is rendered in an elegiac tone, delivered by Scrap's velvety sad voiceover narrative of a tale that is as faded into the past as the dim shadows and dull brown and green filtered light of the film's texture; in nighttime shots the dark spaces give way to silhouetted forms of Maggie's bulky sweat-shirted body diligently pounding away at a punching bag, a far cry from the jazzy patterns of *Kill Bill's* graphic design motifs.

A simple plaintive piano and guitar soundtrack reinforces the somber mood, inviting retrospection instead of the high energy pop music of *Kill Bill's* soundtrack. No trendy designer bodysuits and high fashion accessories for Maggie, who wears baggy sweats and boxy shorts, clunky boxing gloves and sneakers, not a stitch of makeup, and pulls her straggly hair up in a practical braid. Unlike Elle Driver's eye patch, Maggie's mouth guard is anything but a fashion statement. While there are a few scenes in which Maggie is filmed in the soft focus closeup shots suffused with a golden light that cinematically code her as an object of desire for Frankie (the film only hints at a romantic connection between the two characters), for the most part Maggie's body is filmed in middle and long shots as she ducks, jabs, and throws punches in the ring or with sparring partners at the gym; when her body *is* made visible the camera emphasizes the highly developed muscles of back and shoulders in action, pummeling opponents who are equally muscular. These are sturdy athletic bodies and the fights between the women boxers are filmed in the classic tradition of boxing movies as a battle between two professional athletes, with none of the stylized violence or voyeuristic pleasures of Bill's decorative Divas. The gritty realism of the women's fight world is supported by Eastwood's inclusion of "real-life" boxing star Lucia Rijker who behind the scenes served as Hillary Swank's trainer for her role and in the narrative is the reigning champion who deals Maggie her mortal blow. In fact, the only sexualized female images in the entire film are the faceless "babes" in high heels and bikinis who parade across the ring between rounds to hold up the scorecard.

But the film's interest in the woman's action body goes beyond exterior muscularity and agility to the *insides* of bodies as they are bruised, battered, and ultimately broken. Maggie's face is swollen, her nose bloodied, and after her head cracks against a metal pipe in the ring at the final championship fight, her body becomes the site of tracheotomy and naso-gastric tubes, bed sores, respirators, and gangrene infection. While Beatrix's body certainly takes on its share of assaultive injuries, as a superwoman action heroine she magically bounces back, gorgeous and sexy in black leather and designer sunglasses, trendy new hairdo, off to her next adventure. Paradoxically, in its insistence on showing the *limitations* of the human body *Million Dollar Baby* succeeds in depicting the female action heroine as genuinely tough and courageous, thereby

Figure 3.4. Maggie in the ring as her trainer watches from the ropes in *Million Dollar Baby*.

Figure 3.5. Maggie takes a blow to the face.

offering its viewers a more progressive model of female body mastery than most Hollywood films.

Its positive impact, however, is attenuated in two ways. First, we might wonder about the fact that the heroine is killed off before having a chance to realize what was fast becoming a triumphant career as a world champion boxer. Instead, Maggie becomes the victim of a tragic accident who must plead with Frankie to perform the mercy killing that allows her to die with dignity. (It is tempting at that moment to imagine that it is not Frankie her trainer but Eastwood the director who is scripting Maggie out of his film.) A second question arises from the depiction of Maggie's rapacious "trailer trash" family who descend upon the paralyzed and dying patient at her hospital bedside to grab her estate. They represent the world from which Maggie seeks to escape, and the film renders her people all the more hateful and repugnant because they are fat and unhealthy: "My brother's in prison, my sister cheats on Welfare . . . my father's dead, my Mama weighs 312 pounds. I could [just] go home and buy a used trailer and a deep fryolator and some Oreos." Maggie's aspirations are in turn represented by her determination to transform her own body into a lean fighting force, whereas both fat and eating fat are identified with decadence and failure. This equation reaches full expression in the character of Maggie's mother, who is not only a slovenly ingrate but monstrous and unnatural in her rejection of her daughter's success and predatory consumption of her dying child's money. This mother from hell cruelly reminds the paralyzed Maggie that she lost her last fight, then sticks a pen in her mouth to sign over her assets. Mustering her failing strength the daughter resists, and in a final act of assertion of good over evil banishes her mother's "fat lazy Hillbilly ass" from the room.

The equation of the out of shape body with "fat lazy" parasitism is deeply embedded in the ideology of fitness, which reads the "in shape" body as an external manifestation of such inner virtues as commitment and determination. In other words, to look good is to *be* good. "Working out" is also inextricably linked to the American work ethic itself, reflecting shared social and economic values such as productivity, ambition, and upward mobility. Body discipline is not only a national project but a form of self-actualization as well; to become "your best self," one has only to meet the exercise challenge, or as the Nike sportsgear ad urges, "Just do it!" Devotion to body work is even connected to spiritual perfection, articulated explicitly by faith-based fitness programs such as "Weigh Down" which promote body "gospels" like "More of Jesus, Less of Me." It is no wonder, then, that the social and psychological need to reform and reshape the imperfect body has given rise to the group of films that follows, all of which capture a deep cultural yearning for body transformation.

4

Body Transformation

Ugly Ducklings, Swans, and Movie Makeovers

I feel the ugly part of me is gone. I'm a whole new person.

—cosmetic surgery contestant,
Extreme Makeover television show

The longing to transcend the limits of individual identity and escape the boundaries of our bodies—just like the "free and unfettered" superhero—has always been with us, from the classic myth of Pygmalion to countless fairy tales such as the Ugly Duckling and the Frog Prince. The magical shift from poor to rich, old to young, weak to powerful played out in these archetypal stories taps into deep psychological desires which reappear in Hollywood movies, the fairy tales of our time. Contemporary cinema fantasies of sudden success, wealth, and social power are typically embedded in narratives of physical transformation in which the body becomes the catalyst for realizing the collective social dream. The visions of body transformation conjured by the Hollywood romantic comedies known as "chick flicks" are so compelling that they can inspire particularly susceptible moviegoers to reshape their own bodies at any cost—emotional, physical, or economic. While the ideology of fitness promotes the toned body as a state of ethical and spiritual superiority, the transformed body on the movie screen envisions the promise of social mobility, femininity, glamour, and romance. These cinematic visions are then propagated through popular culture via television reality makeover shows, which take up the project of reshaping the unshapely body, harnessing new technologies that can re-engineer and reconstruct it, all the while signaling to women that dreams of everlasting happiness may be as near as their local cosmetic surgeon. In sum, Hollywood movies and television makeover shows both produce and normalize the body obsession, chronic dissatisfaction, and body shame that contribute to the development of serious eating disorders and body image disturbances. They also hold out the promise of escape for women such as Myra, a dietician in her mid-thirties who has never felt comfortable in her own skin:

> Growing up I always felt I was too big for a girl. I sat in the last row because I was usually the tallest kid in the class. I needed the biggest shoe size they sold and my mother had to take me to the Big Girls section of the department store when we went shopping. If that wasn't bad enough I got breasts and my period when I was still only nine, so then the boys would chase after me in the hall and try to feel me up. I never liked my breasts after that and got so self-conscious I would wear my father's shirts to cover them up. For a graduation present I got breast reduction surgery but later I kept staring at myself in the mirror and my breasts still looked weird to me, kind of lopsided. Even though my boyfriend tells me it's all in my head I'm too ashamed to let him look at me with the lights on. I want to get picked to go on one of those TV makeover shows so I can just start all over and finally feel beautiful—or at least normal.

If films of body transformation provide the vision that inspires women to remake their bodies, the cosmetic and "aesthetic medicine" industry sells them the equipment. Central to the marketing of beauty culture are television makeover shows, which reach even bigger audiences than the cinema. These shows and the products and processes they promote thrive on the ever-widening spread of body dissatisfaction and disordered eating behaviors across socioeconomic, ethnic, and racial divides—democratizing and globalizing what has become a universal aspiration for body correction and perfection. As one commentator notes: "Through sanitized, pain-free 60-minute capsules showcasing the transformation of ordinary folks, reality TV has sold people on the notion that the Cinderella story is a purchasable, everyday experience that everyone deserves."[1]

In reality shows such as *The Swan, Extreme Makeover,* and *From Flab to Fab* which have flourished on television over the past decade, self-hating contestants present their bodies as a public reconstruction project to be "nipped and tucked," surgically sculpted and reduced by teams of "experts." After they are transformed, contestants confront their now unrecognizable images in the mirror, squealing with delight through tears of gratitude and disbelief. These shows enact the body hatred many women are conditioned to accept as an appropriately self-critical stance toward improving one's appearance but which in fact contributes to a culture of humiliation aimed at bodies that fail to fit the conventional beauty ideal.[2] It is not accidental then that the format of makeover shows takes on a sado-masochistic dynamic: a contestant is first accused of a fashion "crime," admits her guilt, gratefully submits to her rehabilitation and later disavows her former flawed self to the enthusiastic applause of an audience that witnesses and validates the transformation. "Turned in" by their friends and families, these penitent contestants admit to "letting themselves go" during dietary transgressions of eating coconut cream pie and steak. They are encouraged to publicly display the "flab"—sagging breasts, bulging hips, fleshy bellies—they have failed to contain, desperately pleading for a chance at rehabilitation; this is provided by a squad of "fashion police," knife-wielding surgeons and intimidating body coaches who warn contestants they will soon endure "brutal" manipulations requiring discipline and considerable pain in order to achieve their "life-changing" transformation. The sadism masquerades as salvation; the abuse is for the ultimate good of the ugly duckling. On one show, for example, a self-appointed fashion maven recoils in horror at a contestant who dresses in sweatpants, banishing her to a mirror dressed in a garbage bag to cure her of her terrible taste;[3] on another program "victims" are recruited by roving producers who kidnap them from the streets to correct an egregious appearance, weight gain, and other fashion infractions.[4]

Insufficiently feminine contestants whose partners complain about their lackluster sex lives are turned in for gender reconstruction. A woman motorcyclist who considers herself "one of the guys" is converted into a "real" girl by a "Glam Squad" who dye her hair blonde and perform breast uplift and liposuction, subsequently revealing their handiwork in a followup sequence displaying the woman on her motorbike in tight jeans, low-cut tank top, spike heels, and heavy makeup, delighted that she is now a "sexy" biker.[5] On yet another show cosmetic surgeons roll out their reconstruction project to create a youthful sexy look for Rachel (who was, in fact, a construction worker!), which includes sculpting a more defined waistline, curves, and breast augmentation for a new "killer body" and a "more alluring tantalizing face."[6] The promise of sexual allure to rekindle the flagging interest of boyfriends and husbands is linked in turn to becoming a "confident" beautiful woman; one sexually frustrated husband hopes that after a complete makeover his wife will "feel better about herself and we can be more intimate."

The extraordinary popularity of television makeover shows is connected to two major developments in beauty culture. The first is the relatively recent notion of the body as a project, something to be worked upon and radically re-engineered. In her study of girls' body culture, historian Joan Brumberg notes that in the past century external mechanisms of shaping the fashionable body such as corsets and girdles have been replaced by internal manipulations like liposuction and breast silicone implants which can sculpt and contain the flesh in increasingly invasive and dramatic ways.[7] Technological advances in organ transplants, genetic bioengineering, and artificial joint replacements prime us to think of the body as a plastic machine, subject to endless manipulations of reconstruction and repair. This expectation in turn drives the multibillion dollar market for cosmetic surgery, aptly described by feminist scholar Susan Bordo as "an industry and an ideology fueled by fantasies of rearranging, transforming, and correcting, an ideology of limitless improvement and change."[8]

The second development is an increase in media dissemination of body commodification, a process through which advertising and consumer culture embed high-status values such as youth, health, and affluence—not to mention the moral qualities of discipline and fortitude that underlie the ideology of fitness—within the image of the strong and shapely body. In today's consumer beauty culture the perfected body has thus become both social and economic currency: "[T]he closer the actual body approximates to the idealized images . . . the higher its exchange value."[9] This socioeconomic incentive and the notion of the plastic replaceable body both exert a powerful cultural pressure to *work* on the body, to constantly improve its less than perfect parts. The imperfect body is a problem that needs to be fixed—and today the consumer can choose from an endless array of products and procedures to fix it. Just as domestic consumer marketing played to the fears of the 1950s homemaker with the prospect of that shameful "ring around the collar" or embarrassing "housetosis" it preys today upon the body insecurities and anxieties of her presumably liberated granddaughters. In our contemporary looksist culture the woman's problem is not her housekeeping skills but the size and shape of her body and its deficiencies: teeth that are not white enough, a belly that is not flat enough, breasts that are not big enough—or maybe too big. In such a culture a chronic state of body dissatisfaction is neither abnormal nor maladaptive; it is simply a requisite part of a woman's beauty practice, so much so that for a twenty-eight-year-old waitress named Lori I recently interviewed, mounting credit card debt and economic uncertainty could not weaken her determination to fund her cosmetic surgeries:

> I'm always working on looking better. I used to be so flat chested no boys would ever look at me. Then I got implants and for a while I felt sexy, a little more confident. I even had a rich boyfriend at the time who said if I lost five pounds by Christmas he'd buy me a nose job! But what really bothers me more is my butt—it's too flat. I'm thinking of getting an uplift so I can look more like J.Lo or someone really hot. Right now though I'm saving up for a silicone fix for my lips, which are way too thin. I figure it's the best money I could ever spend.

While body shame and insecurity may be socially sanctioned in media beauty culture, in the mental health community it is an all too reliable predictor of trouble down the road. A recent study of more than a thousand schoolgirls between the ages of thirteen and fifteen found that the more discontented the girls were about their size and shape, the lower their self-esteem and the higher their stress and rates of depression. Most worrisome of all, the more likely it was that just one year later they were severely restricting their diets and engaging in bulimic practices.[10] In another study girls at a private school in the Northeast were followed over an eight-year period from seventh grade through young adulthood and again the statistical findings were sobering: the girls who had the highest and most recurrent rates of body dissatisfaction on psychological tests were twice as likely to have developed serious eating problems by the time they were adults.[11] Equally telling was a study of undergraduate women who were tested with figure rating scales and weight-based self-esteem measures assessing how much anxiety they felt about their thighs, ears, hips, feet, and just about every other body part—and how concerned or depressed they were about their weight. Again, the greater the students' concern about their size and shape the greater the chance that their eating behavior resembled those of individuals with diagnosed anorexia and bulimia.[12]

Gnawing worries about one's body shape and size can continue well past adolescence, often becoming a cognitive habit of self-talk that I call "bad body thinking." It only gets worse when a voice *outside* the self articulates one's worst fears, even if spoken in jest. Brenda is a bright, well-educated mother of three in her forties with a wry sense of humor and clear insight gained over the course of her psychotherapy into the origins of her body obsession. She describes her family, originally from Athens, as a veritable "Greek chorus" constantly critiquing her figure and her food choices throughout her life, while always pointing out it was "for your own good." Whenever she eats a "fattening" food she is convinced that it almost immediately turns up as the "squishy" cellulite on her thighs, which everyone will notice. One of her worst moments took place at the beginning of the summer when her ten-year-old son, all too aware of her sensitivity, squeezed her thighs and "as a joke" told her she was getting fat:

> Ever since then I've tried to avoid the beach because I feel everyone is staring at my cellulite thighs, not to mention my flabby belly. I hate those girls with the flat abs, not a drop of fat on those tight bikini bodies. When I take the kids to swim I wrap myself up in a big beach towel so no one will see my body. Even though I'm sweltering I won't get up to go into the water because then everyone will see me jiggle from behind.

As with so many body practices in a looks-obsessed culture, the line between the "normal" and the pathological is often just a matter of degree. When body self-consciousness becomes so extreme that it forces individuals to literally hide from view or constantly camouflage a perceived defect, spend so many hours at the mirror examining a fatal flaw that it impairs their ability to function, or become so preoccupied with an imagined or exaggerated problem that they even appear delusional, they may be diagnosed with the psychiatric condition known as Body Dysmorphic Disorder (BDD). And while research points to biochemical factors that might predispose a person to both BDD and related disorders such as obsessive compulsive and anxiety disorders, it is also worth noting that BDD has increased in prevalence since its official emergence in 1987 and is highest in the United States and other affluent societies that place a high value on appearance. In fact, many of the telltale symptoms used to diagnose the disorder are just more frequent and extreme versions of how the vast majority of "normal" women think and feel about their own bodies. These include "dissatisfaction with a perceived physical defect, seeking reassurance about appearance from others, self-consciousness about one's appearance in public situations and comparing one's appearance to that of others."[13] It comes as no surprise then to discover that a significant percentage of frequent flyers to the cosmetic surgeon's office suffer from this body disturbance. Buried in the statistics about the explosion in the aesthetic medicine market, a $12 billion-plus industry boasting 500 percent increases in recent years for procedures such as liposuction, breast augmentation and reduction, and tummy tucks[14] is the less publicized data from cosmetic surgeons and dermatologists' offices showing that as many as 15 percent of their patients suffered from Body Dysmorphic Disorder.[15]

> Never in my wildest dreams did I imagine a simple Indiana girl like me could be here in Hollywood becoming as beautiful as a movie star! I feel just like Cinderella at the ball!! (Surgery contestant, *Extreme Makeover* television show)

If television reality shows and the cosmetic surgery industry provide women with the tools for body transformation, Hollywood movies give them the inspiration. In the compelling fantasies of "makeover movies" the possibilities and rewards of body transformation are visualized either in terms of social success or the restoration of inadequate femininity. The fairy tale that has forever entranced with its dream of upward mobility of course is Cinderella—the first and greatest "social climber" of them all. Long after late-twentieth-century female moviegoers outgrew the animated Disney version of the story they could revisit its pleasures in such popular films as *Pretty Woman (1990)* and *Working Girl*

(1988) where the body transformations represent a kind of "cross-class dressing."[16] The notion of restyling the body to literally and figuratively "re-dress" its lowbrow excesses can be traced farther back in cinema history to Hitchcock's *Vertigo* (1958) where the obsessed detective (James Stewart) seeks to recreate his lost ideal love by "dressing *up*" a working class girl (Kim Novak) into her sophisticated body double. So it would be easy enough to dismiss *Maid in Manhattan* (David Wang, 2002) and *The Devil Wears Prada* (David Frankel, 2005) as mere remakes of an old fairy tale. But their power to affect the eating behavior and body images of contemporary moviegoers is potentiated today by trends in celebrity body culture, aesthetic technology, and popular media, which have converged to create a climate in which Hollywood movie visions of body reformation resonate with ever more impact on their targeted female audiences.

Two Cinderella motifs shared by *Maid in Manhattan* and *The Devil Wears Prada* are their heroines' servitude to demanding "stepmothers" and their spectacular arrival at a ball where their magic makeover enchants a modern-day Prince Charming and an awestruck crowd of admirers. This climactic moment most vividly conveys the transformation of cultural and class identity via body beautification; no longer drab and dowdy, the resplendent Cinderella wins social acceptance *and* the man's heart all at once. Moreover, while both films seek to update the regressive aspects of the fairy tale with several heavy-handed messages about their heroine's independence from the prince's patriarchal authority, in the end each manages to reinforce the old equation of conventional beauty with social aspiration: in order for a woman to realize her dreams she has to have the right "look"—and whatever it takes to get it.

Both films are set in New York City and use its urban geography to establish zones of economic class and ethnic identity that define the social mobility of each Cinderella as she travels between them. *Maid in Manhattan* immediately places its heroine Marisa Ventura (Jennifer Lopez) as a hardworking Hispanic single mom with its opening shots of the Statue of Liberty and a singularly sanitized "barrio" marked largely by a quick glimpse of bananas and tropical fruit shot against the soundtrack of Simon & Garfunkel singing "Me and Julio down by the schoolyard." Making her way from this Bronx neighborhood to a domestic job downtown at a posh Manhattan hotel, Marisa grabs a proletarian breakfast of a takeout doughnut and coffee as she rushes to the subway. No time to indulge in dressing or self-care—all efforts are bent on advancing herself and the education of her young son Tyler. To illustrate her embrace of the American dream Marisa is shown pulling out a copy of *The Drama of the Gifted Child* on the bus, while her own professional aspirations are signaled by a lingering close-up of her face as she listens intently to the promotion opportunity announced at work, confirming her belief that in this country "anything is possible." But while this Cinderella may dream of self-improvement through education and job promotion, until she undergoes the magical transformation of a grooming upgrade she must, like all Cinderellas who came before her, serve more powerful and affluent masters. She endures the mistreatment of patronizing and arrogant hotel guests who order her to fetch panty hose, unpack their suitcases, and press and iron their clothes—all the while remaining as optimistic as her Disney counterpart who sings of the day when her prince will come. And indeed he does, in the person of wealthy politician and playboy Chris Marshall (Ralph Fiennes) who arrives at the hotel with his "court," a noisy entourage of publicists, press agents, and campaign managers. Dressed in her maid's uniform Marisa remains invisible to him, so much so that in one of the film's several sly sexual jokes (including the title pun) he uses the toilet while she is cleaning his bathroom. It is not until she undergoes a radical wardrobe change that she can be socially "seen" by Marshall. This initial transformation takes place when a fellow maid convinces Marisa to try on the $5,000 "Dolce" designer suit hanging in the closet of a rich but ditzy occupant of the hotel's Park Suite (Natasha Richardson); without skipping a beat Marisa effortlessly takes on the guest's identity along with the suit. Immediately smitten upon seeing Marisa just after she has slipped into the suit (which happens to be her size, as befits a fairy tale) Matthews seems remarkably oblivious to Marisa's "real" identity and New York street accent during the ensuing series of sitcom situations during which she and her working comrades conspire to maintain her disguise. Her new outfit would appear to give her the "class" and confidence to be totally at ease in her new identity, even proffering savvy political advice to Matthews about how to reach the working-class voter in his senatorial campaign. Here the film suggests that by restyling her look a woman gains not only easy access into worlds of power and money but also boundless self-confidence and new competencies—the very same promise made by the cosmetic surgery and beauty industries.

A still more regressive message is embedded in the film in the form of another sexual joke. During a stroll through Central Park with the now lovestruck Chris Matthews, Marissa gets up from a park bench with a magazine stuck to the bottom of the stolen white suit that she is still wearing. The magazine in fact features a cover story about Matthews, who gallantly removes his printed image from her pants as he casts an admiring gaze at her buttocks. While the moment takes on a special resonance because "J.Lo"'s body is most frequently noted for its curvy anatomy—an association reinforced by the camera's frequent rear view shots of her tight-fitting pants—within the structure of the film it is even more meaningful as a symbol of the "branding" of her body as belonging to the high-powered Matthews.[17]

Both the sequence and the image underscore the important role celebrity media play throughout the film. Soon featured as Matthew's mysterious new companion in the tabloid press, Marisa can now partake of the fame attendant upon her new social identity, which is constructed cinematically with shots of *paparazzi* photos and headlines depicting the course of the couple's glamorous romance. Similarly, the film's "happily ever after" coda is narrated through a series of montage shots of magazine and tabloid covers sequentially announcing Matthew's election, the publication of Marisa's book on "Maid Management" (*sic!*)

Figure 4.1. Hotel maid Marisa and her new admirer in Central Park in *Maid in Manhattan*.

and the success of their marriage one year later. The media images announce that they are now the leading couple of New York—the prince and princess of the realm. They also visually confirm that Marisa achieved her fame and fortune through body transformation, despite the film's sporadic attempts to mark her as worthy of social success because of such middle-class American values as hard work, persistence, and professional aspiration. In fact, any suggestion of the importance of these values is overshadowed by the notion of magical (i.e., instantaneous) transformation rather than the gradual and often laborious process of educational and professional advancement for the immigrant worker; nor does the film attempt to examine the relevant issues of generational assimilation and preservation of Marisa's ethnic identity.[18]

As in all Cinderella stories the peak moment of body transformation is the requisite grand ball, which is orchestrated in *Maid in Manhattan* by Marisa's fairy godfather and mentor Lionel, the hotel butler (Bob Hoskins) and a complicit chorus of the entire housekeeping staff who dance about in glee to the strains of "I'm Coming Out," a filmic moment reminiscent of the mice in Disney's movie as they help pick out Cinderella's gown, shoes, and jewelry—which in this version includes

Figure 4.2. Preparing for the ball.

the secret loan of a priceless Harry Winston diamond necklace from the hotel boutique.

No longer a proletarian subway rider, Marisa is sent off in a limousine coach as her friend reminds her that she is living a dream for all her comrades: "Tonight the maid is a lie, and this is who you really are." The magical makeover allows Marisa's social dream to become embodied in a new identity not just for the pleasure of her workmates but for the screen audience as well. Her "arrival" at the ball realizes the collective fantasies of a benign world in which one can effortlessly rise from housemaid to senator's wife through a fashion upgrade that transforms social, economic, and ethnic identity. Significantly, when Marisa tells Matthews that like all Cinderellas she can only be with him for this one night, he replies: "Then you should have worn a different dress," thereby making explicit what the film has suggested from the outset: how the woman looks and what she is wearing is the prerequisite for the Prince's love and all the fame and fortune that goes with it.

The Devil Wears Prada, another urban Cinderella fantasy, transforms the "ordinary" Andy (Anne Hathaway), a recent college graduate from the Midwest, into a "glamazon." As in *Maid in Manhattan* the film

Figure 4.3. The transformation completed

immediately locates its heroine geographically and socially in a downscale neighborhood in its opening shots of Andy rushing from a cramped rental apartment on the Lower East side and grabbing a bagel en route to her job interview uptown at *Runway* fashion magazine. The cruel stepmother Andy is hired to serve is the magazine's resident high priestess of fashion, aptly named Miranda Priestley (Meryl Streep). Hypercritical and demanding, the imperious Miranda literally dumps her Prada bags and fur coats on Andy as she strides past her desk, barking out orders to fetch everything from coffee to unpublished editions of Harry Potter for her bratty twin daughters. Andy also finds herself at the beck and call of a wicked stepsister, a more senior assistant named Emily who demeans and overworks the new hire. In this ultra fashionable world where all her office mates wear elegant black outfits and designer high heels Andy is subject to constant ridicule about her lack of style; the other women in the office giggle at her rumpled schoolgirl "polyblend" sweaters and skirts in all the wrong colors and consider her "fat" at size six—which she is told is the new size fourteen.[19]

If Miranda Priestly is Andy's harsh stepmother, her "fairy godmother" is Nigel (Stanley Tucci) a snide but heart-of-gold design assistant who takes pity on the clueless Cinderella, even giving her the "glass slipper" equivalent of a pair of designer heels to replace her sensible clunky walking shoes. Instead of a magic wand he taps her on the forehead with a pen, scolding her to "Wake up sweetheart!" to the crucial importance of fashion. He wraps Andy in Chanel designer samples and whisks her off to the "beauty department," all the while dispensing grooming wisdom to the wide-eyed novice who is now desperate to be "reformed" from her fashion crimes. Even before she is presented at the ball, however, the miraculous transformation of this Cinderella is witnessed first by her stepsisters (the catty Emily and another office mate played by supermodel Giselle Bundchen) who gaze in disbelief at the new Andy and then by the formidable Miranda herself, who sizes up her chic hip-length boots and accessorized ensemble with grudging approval. These reaction shots in which women gaze at women, checking each other out, capture the competitiveness that often drives the body preoccupations and practices of girls and women. But like so many Hollywood genre films *The Devil Wears Prada* makes little attempt to critique or investigate the significance of this kind of female body rivalry, using it instead as a comedic device to heighten the viewer's pleasure at the dramatic impact of Andy's transformation.

In fact, the sequence that follows Andy's makeover would seem to be filmed precisely for the visual pleasure of a female audience who know all too well how to read and decode the meaning of the fashionable body. Just as the camera in *Kill Bill* displayed its women warriors as runway models battling each other in stagey set pieces, so too this film interrupts its narrative with a slick montage of images of Andy on the streets of Manhattan crossing an intersection, running to catch a cab, and emerging from a boutique; in each shot she is modeling a different designer ensemble, hairstyle, hat, and accessories to the soundtrack of "Vogue," Madonna's anthem to fashion and the "ladies with attitude" who can "strike a pose." The cinematic ambiguity here makes us wonder if we are still in the movie narrative or suddenly looking at a glossy fashion spread in the pages of *Runway* magazine. It also reflects the film's generally confused stance toward the world of fashion versus the more socially responsible values Andy represents before her seduction into Miranda's glamorous world. On the one hand the power brokers of the *Runway* domain are portrayed as ruthless and cutthroat; even Miranda Priestley's hegemony is threatened by younger competitors biting at her heels. There are also sporadic attempts to lampoon the fashion industry's obsessive dieting and weight phobia: when Andy points out to Emily that she looks very thin her rival beams with pleasure, confiding that it's the result of her new diet rule, which is basically "don't eat anything . . . I'm one stomach flu away from my goal weight." And when Miranda selects Andy as her assistant for a Paris fashion show Emily wails: "You don't deserve it. You eat carbs!"

Once again, however, the film refuses to explore the complexities behind cultural obsessions with fashionable slenderness and youth. As one critic notes, it chooses instead to "wink[s] knowingly while kicking sand in our eye."[20] In a heavy-handed attempt to privilege Andy's small-town girl natural style over the artificial fashion world she is about to enter, the film opens with a parallel editing sequence of shots contrasting Andy's decidedly unglamorous dressing routine—brushing her teeth, throwing on practical underwear and plain serviceable clothes, barely running a comb through her hair as she runs out the door—with shots of the long-stemmed attenuated torsos of exotic models as they slither into leopard panties and lacy black bras, step into stiletto heels and boots, carefully select earrings and perfume, and artfully make up brows and lips in the mirror. The sequence culminates in a shot of manicured hands counting out a "breakfast" of seven almonds juxtaposed with a final shot of Andy taking a healthy bite of a bagel liberally smeared with cream cheese. And in case we have missed the point, the film just as sharply contrasts the hostile relationships between *Runway's* sleek but vicious fashionistas with Andy's circle of downtown buddies, a supportive and loyal bunch of struggling young artists and writers who love Andy just the way she is. As Andy crosses over to the dark side of money and influence she abandons this loyal community, which includes both her understanding dad and salt-of-the-earth boyfriend, an aspiring chef who makes her grilled cheese sandwiches.

The problem is that despite how hard it initially tries the film can't sustain its critique of that dark side of Andy's world. Before long it seems to fall under the spell of its own fairy tale enchantment: as Andy enters the dazzling spaces of New York's high fashion industry any intended message about its superficiality and venality gets lost in the film's own cinematic attraction to surface beauty and glamour. Famous designer names—Hermes, Prada, Bill Blass—are dropped at every opportunity while guest appearances by "real" fashion moguls and models, such as Valentino and Heidi Klum, and New York's "A-list" people are featured in scenes of the townhouse and gallery parties and receptions Andy gets to attend as Miranda's new protégé. Fashion, it turns out, is not simply a backdrop but the film's central character and focus. Projected through Andy's wide-eyed point of view the camera luxuriates in the lush fabrics and colors of designer clothes, the sparkle of jewelry and rich leather belts and bags and the sleek interior designs of the *Runway* office suites. The visual seduction culminates once again in the archetypal ball scene at which the now transformed Cinderella completes her social arrival. Just like Marisa Ventura, Andy drives through the bright city lights in a black limousine to arrive at the red carpeted stairway of the Metropolitan Museum; her ascent is shot in slow motion as press cameras flash and onlookers murmur at this new beauty resplendent in her black evening gown It is on these steps that Andy soon encounters Prince Charming, this time in the form of a successful writer with connections who soon sweeps her off her feet in Paris during a magical night of romance and lovemaking.

One might say that much like its heroine the film tries to have its cake and eat it, offering up an obligatory critique of the very world in which it so clearly delights. Like *Maid in Manhattan* it nominally promotes socially redemptive values such as economic advancement and the American work ethic; just as Marisa aspires to a managerial job and education for her son so too does Andy finally reject the frivolous *Runway* world for an entry-level job as an investigative reporter in a gritty newsroom. In a symbolic act of liberation she tosses her office cell phone into a Paris fountain, gives up the Prince Charming and the designer labels and heads for home and her old boyfriend. Their reunion appropriately takes place in a humble downtown coffee shop that serves "comfort food" where he not only forgives her but—in a vision of domestic bliss to come—promises to still fix his grilled cheese sandwiches. In the end, again like the film itself, Andy manages to have it both ways; she gets the chance to have been a "glamazon" in the world of fashion and wealth but doesn't lose the security of a domestic future. She even gets Miranda's approval and a good recommendation for her new job.

Above all, Andy's magical makeover turns her from an awkward girl to a sexual and sophisticated woman, a progression documented in the later section of the film by camera shots displaying her body in sexy black underwear revealing cleavage and curves and close-ups of increasingly fuller red lips and alluring eyes; no longer apologetic and clumsy, she now knows how to flirt. Recognizing that "his work is done," her fashion trainer Nigel toasts Andy's crowning achievement: never again will she have to wear a shameful size six. And while she has toned down the makeup and the fashion-plate look by the end of the film, its final shot of Andy dressed in high heel boots and tight pants emphasizes her slender and stylish figure as she strides confidently through the streets of Manhattan. Her body transformation complete, we are assured our glamorized heroine is headed for a happily-ever-after life with her own prince charming.

Curious about the potential impact of this very successful makeover movie on viewers concerned about their own body size and shape, I asked members of one of my group treatment programs for women with eating and weight problems about their response to the film. Paula, a thirty-four-year-old radiology technician who considers herself a diet "failure," spoke up first:

> I'm embarrassed to admit the effect the movie had on me. Of course all the time I was watching it I kept saying how really superficial and obvious it all was and you knew of course Andy had to see the light in the end—but when I got home from the theater all I remembered was those

incredibly thin and gorgeous models at *Runway* and how amazing Andy looked when Nigel dressed her up. By then she had gotten down to a size four—and here I am at size fourteen. I got so depressed I went through every box of cookies I had in the house. The next morning I vowed I wouldn't buy myself anything new to wear until I lost ten pounds on my next diet.

Not all group members shared her reaction, however. Representing a more "oppositional gaze" at the film was the response from Brenda, a physical therapist in her late thirties who described herself as a lifelong diet "yo-yo-er" who cycled up and down the scale and bought new outfits for each size she passed along the way—ruefully relegating the clothes that no longer fit to the back recesses of her closet. She felt manipulated and patronized by the film's double message and ultimately rejected its transformation narrative. In fact, Andy's grateful submission to the body makeover only made her angry:

> There's this scene in the movie when that guy Nigel tells Anne Hathaway she's basically a fat slob at size six. I got furious—especially because Andy herself didn't! Instead of telling him where to go she gets humiliated and crushed and works her butt off until she's as unbelievably skinny as all those supermodels parading around the office. I'm so sick of feeling like I have to apologize like she did for not fitting into teeny size zeros, or only finding cheap polyester in larger sizes, like I have to wear sack cloth and ashes to atone for being bigger. I'm starting to go into stores and remind myself that I'm the customer—and I ask what do you have that fits ME instead of feeling how I don't "fit in!"

Not only can makeover magic transform Cinderella's social and economic status but it can restore her femininity as well, turning her from tomboy into temptress—or at the very least into a "girly girl." This becomes the central project of *Miss Congenialty* (Donald Petrie, 2000), starring Sondra Bullock as FBI agent Gracie Hart who despite her name is constructed as a woman with a total lack of any feminine "grace." A case of arrested development, she has never outgrown the tomboy childhood depicted in the film's introductory flashback of a seven-year-old Gracie in glasses and blue jeans fighting schoolyard bullies. The film then cuts to a shot of the now-adult Gracie still in jeans and braids, disheveled hair, and untweezed bushy eyebrows practicing karate chops. She tries hard to be "one of the guys" in her predictably sexist detective unit; indeed, while her male co-workers confirm her lack of feminine appeal by telling her she "looks like hell" they still send her out to fetch coffee and refuse to promote her up the agency ladder. Gracie is yet another workplace Cinderella, this time a victim of institutional misogyny and gender discrimination. Nonetheless, the film minimizes any sympathy for her plight by working hard to establish Gracie's unattractive traits: she snorts, picks her ear, and defends against any identification with "airhead bimbos," proudly asserting "I don't even own a hairbrush." Her seemingly incorrigible masculine identification is described as a phallic preference: "[Y]ou're an incomplete person. In place of . . . a relationship you have sarcasm and a gun," fumes the fashion stylist assigned to transform her.

Significantly Gracie's questionable femininity is signaled by her eating behavior. She attacks her food with gusto, digging into extra-rare steaks as big as a cow and polishing off hefty containers of Ben & Jerry's ice cream.

Figure 4.4. Agent Gracie Hart has one more for the road in *Miss Congeniality*.

The coding of the woman's masculinity by endowing her with a hearty appetite is hardly new in Hollywood movies. In *The Mirror Has Two Faces* (1998) another romantic comedy about gender "gentrification," women's studies professor Rose (Barbra Streisand) is a feisty feminist who uses four-letter words in her lectures, follows wrestling on TV, and eschews makeup and fashion. She is first seen cheering at a basketball game biting into a huge coconut snowflake; at home she dunks bread into gravy, to the horror of her diet-conscious mother, and at restaurants asks the waiter for extra salad dressing. But when she determines to become sexually attractive to men Rose colors her hair blonde, gets contact lenses, works out at the gym and restricts her diet to nothing but salads—this time without the dressing. This kind of food-for-sex exchange is a familiar cultural constraint: the woman must renounce the pleasure of eating in order to access the pleasure of sexual desire. As we will see in movie depictions of the overweight overeater, the obverse is also true according to Hollywood-style psychoanalysis, which inevitably diagnoses the big woman desperately stuffing herself with cupcakes as suffering from sexual repression. These cinematic codes of conduct are not lost on female moviegoers such as Marnie, a divorced mother of two teenagers who has recently been trying to find a new partner:

> I would sooner starve than chow out in front of a guy—especially when you're first dating. I usually say I'm not hungry and just pick at a little salad or something small so I won't look gross eating. What if God forbid I dribbled spaghetti sauce down my face or got something green stuck in my teeth? I once watched a movie called *The Heartbreak Kid* where the bride was on her honeymoon and she orders this huge messy egg salad sandwich. It gets all over her mouth and it completely turns her husband off. He actually *leaves* her in Miami right during the honeymoon for this gorgeous blonde girl who never eats a thing in the whole movie!

Gracie Hart's gender identity restoration takes place when she is assigned to infiltrate a national beauty pageant which is endangered by a bomb threat. The formidable task of transforming the recalcitrant Gracie into a credible Miss New Jersey is reluctantly taken on by yet another gay fairy godfather, "charm consultant" Vic Lemming (Michael Caine).[21] In two days, Gracie's matted hair is untangled, teeth straightened, body hair waxed, skin de-blemished, and nails manicured. Images of the punishing treatments employed to whip Gracie's body into shape may be delivered in comedic style but like all makeover narratives, the film insists she deserves to suffer for her fashion "crimes" and neglect of feminine grooming responsibilities. In return for submitting her body to the reformation process she will ultimately be rewarded with admiring crowds and—most importantly—the appreciative gaze of the man she loves.

The ugly-duckling-to-swan conversion is filmed in the standard format of montage shots; in this case the sequence is depicted as a massive emergency room operation in which Gracie surrenders her body to the skilled hands of a clinical team of white-coated beauty experts. As with *Maid in Manhattan*'s rendition of social transformation, the quick montage pacing of this sequence conveys the prospect of instantaneous change rather than the gradual and decidedly undramatic nature of true bodily modification. As such, Hollywood makeover motifs reinforce the same quick-fix imagery that the cosmetic surgery and diet industries use in their "before" and "after" advertisements. After a crash course in grooming, the transformed Gracie emerges not at the customary gala ball but at an airport where an expectant crowd has gathered for her unveiling; the scene is shot in slow motion against a rhythmic soundtrack as the hangar doors part and Gracie appears in a slinky blue dress, big sunglasses, and even bigger lips. While the hyperbolic presentation of her body transformation sets this moment up for a slapstick follow-up shot of Gracie tripping on her high heels, the scene nonetheless succeeds in establishing the powerful effect her makeover has on the other FBI agents, particularly the handsome Eric (Benjamin Bratt), whose face in a reaction shot registers awakened desire for his previously unappealing colleague.

As a beauty pageant contestant Gracie must learn how to "float" when she walks, close her knees when she sits and her mouth when she chews, and restrict her hearty appetite to a diet of celery stalks. She is reduced to stashing doughnuts in her bra and crotch—another conflation of food and sex—and finally defies the regimented diet deprivation by seducing the other pageant contestants with pizza and beer. Gracie dryly notes that these calorie-phobic beauty queens are "gonna throw it up anyway." As in *The Devil Wears Prada* the film contents itself here with a simplistic caricature of female food and weight obsessions rather than offering any insight into their construction and perpetuation by contemporary beauty culture.

Like Andy's fashion coach Nigel, Vic takes proud ownership of his makeover magic: "I've taken a woman without a smidgen of estrogen and turned her into a lady." But incomplete Gracie must still "complete" her gender recuperation through initiation into two crucial feminine rites of passage—sisterhood and a mature sexual relationship. Both experiences are now open to her because of the successful bodily transformation from frump to beauty queen. Her initial contempt for the other pageant contestants gives way to an appreciation of their talents and socially responsible interests, which suddenly emerge from underneath their bitchy competitiveness and superficiality. Gracie relinquishes her former male-identified contempt for "girly girls" to join the sisterhood of body and beauty culture; she takes her place in the swim suit lineup, a willing participant in the ritual of feminine body display.

By the end of the film, a mutual admiration between the former tomboy and the other beauty queens culminates with Gracie's selection by her new girlfriends as the pageant's "Miss Congenialty"—evidence

Figure 4.5. Miss New Jersey takes center stage.

of the social inclusion that allows her to bond with her own "kind" at last.[22] Gracie's teary acceptance speech, delivered against a swelling sentimental soundtrack, confirms that she has at last acquired a "feminine" soft side. (The film seems to miss the irony of this speech, in which the chastened Gracie announces that "this has been one of the most rewarding and *liberating* [my italics] experiences of my life"). Her final task in the film's exercise in adjustment therapy is to finally recover from her arrested sexual development by engaging in a romantic relationship, a task that would appear to be under way during the film's concluding embrace between Gracie and Eric—even though she is allowed a vestigial snort or two from her old tomboy behavior. The recuperation of her feminine sexuality is now complete as Gracie tells Eric, "I'm suddenly very aware of my breasts." She also signals that her suitability for a domesticated future is at hand. "You think I'm gorgeous," she teases her new suitor. "You want to love me and marry me!"

Like most makeover movies *Miss Congeniality* again represents Hollywood's attempt to have it both ways—to deliver a socially redemptive "message" while essentially appealing to conventional beliefs and values about body culture and femininity. Thus, while these popular "chick flicks" would have us believe that in the end the heroines are loved for their natural *inner* beauty, they send a far more compelling visual message that in fact it takes *outer* beauty to realize collective and individual dreams of success. This message is all the more potent today because filmic visions of transformation speak to the normative body discontent of so many women and girls. And if makeover movies embody their dreams of perfection then Hollywood's depictions of the fat body is their worst nightmare. In the next chapter we will see how our national horror of "flab" informs the cinematic spectacle of the outsize woman.

5

Body Stigmatization

Fat Suits and Big Mamas

By the start of the fall 2008 television season, *The Biggest Loser* was widely considered one of the most popular reality shows of all time. Launched by NBC in 2004 it now aired in more than ninety countries, spawned diet books and an online "lifestyle club," spun off branded products from scales to protein supplements, and blossomed in franchises and chapters on college campuses and in workplaces. During a long writer's strike in 2007 the show even doubled its airtime since the networks were desperate for nonscripted material. Prospective contestants filled the show's Web site with plaintive appeals pleading for a chance to compete for "life-altering" weight loss transformations backed by generous cash rewards.

Once accepted on *The Biggest Loser* contestants are pitted against each other on teams, voting members off if they fail to lose sufficient weight and—as in other makeover shows—exhorted to complete brutal workouts by svelte and buff fitness trainers. A reality TV version of the journey of the mythic hero, the show banishes team members to live in the "wilderness" on a California ranch where they must stare down the "temptation challenge" of snack machines loaded with chips and candy bars to reach the holy grail of a thin body. Resonating with the *double entendre* implicit in the show's title, not to mention the more explicit irony that acts of courage and endurance should be dedicated to the project of obliterating one's former self, is the visual symbolism of each episode's climax: the moment when a contestant marches up to a giant scale clad only in workout shorts and (for women) a sports bra. Swelling music heightens the suspense while the contestant stands, tense and expectant, as a huge number announcing his or her current body weight flashes across the screen. Although the enormous scale has been acknowledged by show producers to be only a prop (contestants are actually weighed behind the scenes before appearing on the set), the televised image resembles nothing so much as the slave auction block—recontextualized here in a social economy that commodifies the body as an object whose worth is based on the scale number that looms over the contestant's head. Unwittingly, the show's weigh-in ritual succeeds in expressing the dehumanization of obesity in a culture of humiliation that gives institutional permission to blame and shame the fat person.

The social construction of obesity in general and of outsize women in particular builds upon many elements—political, economic, psychological, racial, and ethnic—all of which are quite separate from the biological, genetic, and metabolic markers that determine our body composition and weight. In this chapter we will see how this social representation is shaped by attitudes toward women and power, their appetites for food and sex, as well as by notions of femininity and masculinity, which find cinematic expression in the depiction of the "Big Mamas" of Hollywood films. Most important is how these screen images can impact women viewers in ways that directly affect their relationship to their bodies and to food.

The culture of humiliation enacted in shows such as *The Biggest Loser* is expressed in a sanctioned form of discrimination often referred to as "weightism," which operates from cradle to grave. Studies abound: preschoolers pick the thin rag doll to play with, tossing out the chubbier choice; ten-year-olds describe their overweight peers as "lazy, stupid, ugly, and sloppy," ranking them lower on the social scale than kids on crutches or in wheelchairs or kids with amputated hands or facial disfigurements.[1] Overweight teens are far more likely to contemplate suicide, have high blood pressure, and fall victim to violence and peer teasing, while college students would abort their baby if they knew it was going to be obese and would rather marry a drug addict, shoplifter, or embezzler than someone who is fat.[2] It gets no better in adulthood, according to studies that show that over a lifetime, overweight workers earn hundreds of thousands of dollars less than thinner colleagues.[3] Nor is this anti-fat bias limited to America. During the 2008 Olympics in China, for example, government officials enforced several strict fashion codes for its citizens; high on the list was an ordinance forbidding overweight residents from wearing horizontal stripes on the streets of Beijing.[4]

The public sector has sounded both a medical and military national alarm about the cost and danger of fatness. In fact, a U.S. Surgeon General recently determined obesity to be a greater threat to America than terrorism,[5] joining former president Bill Clinton (himself a self-confessed chubby child and junk food "junkie") in a national "war on obesity" in which we seek to marshal an arsenal of pharmaceutical, commercial, and technological weaponry against this public health enemy. New bills have been proposed and passed in state legislatures across the country mandating public programs to trim down the ever-expanding girth of Americans. The state of Mississippi even introduced a bill to bar obese citizens from being served in a restaurant.[6] In what I call the "great weight paradox," the more we spend on fighting the dreaded scourge of obesity, the fatter we have grown; surveys show soaring rates in the number of Americans who are now considered morbidly obese.[7] And while the dire warnings continue to escalate, other evidence suggests overweight may not always be the death warrant that medical, political, and pharmaceutical communities would suggest. In fact, recent studies conducted by the Centers for Disease Control and the National Cancer Institute show that a subset of overweight Americans live longer than many "normal" weight people. In other words, you can be fat *and* fit: it may not be that number on the scale but cardiovascular and metabolic levels of fitness that ultimately protect bodies from the ravages of high cholesterol and hypertension. The fact that these studies are underrepresented in the medical discourse about weight suggests that the now universal panic about fatness drowns out any competing evidence.[8]

The rush to judgment of the overweight American is fueled by something more than public health concerns. Weightism is inextricably linked to notions of religious piety, discipline of desire, and condemnation of gluttony embedded in Puritan and Victorian ideologies of the past, which resurfaced again in the twentieth century as a reaction to growing consumerism and sexual freedom.[9] Such a "morality of orality" locates the outsize body as the site of failed will power and unrestrained appetite—not to mention laziness, disorganization, and lack of personal hygiene.[10]

Weightism is not gender blind, however. A study at Yale University of close to three thousand adults found that weight discrimination, including name calling and insults from partners at home and colleagues at work, was twice as prevalent against woman than their male counterparts.[11] It is also well documented via marriageability rates, earned income statistics, and self-esteem measures that the overweight woman is the object of persistent stigmatization socially, economically, and psychologically; she is, in short, a victim of "oppression, recession, and depression."[12] A decades-long anti-fat bias in hiring, promotion, and compensation practices accounts in part for the correlation between socioeconomic status and obesity, as well as the prevalence in low-income populations of environmental risk factors for obesity, such as more fast-food restaurants, fewer exercise opportunities, and less access to fresh affordable produce. The outsize woman more than her male counterpart bears the brunt of weightism's most devastating effects: she has overall one-third fewer years of formal education, is 20 percent less likely to marry and 10 percent more likely to live in poverty than thinner women, in what amounts to a spiral of "downward mobility."[13]

The overweight woman faces a painful paradox which underscores this harsh social reality: in a culture that overvalues slenderness and undervalues substantiality she is rendered politically and socially invisible—a "full-figured phantom" who at best achieves only a "negative visibility."[14] Ana, a twenty-nine-year-old technical writer who tends to avoid the dating scene because of her large size, experiences just this sense of social invisibility when she attempts to meet new people:

> I've tried to find someone to be with by joining an online dating service but they usually ask for your weight and a photo and I know when guys see all that they probably don't even bother to read my profile. Lots of them put up requirements like "No BBW" (Big Beautiful Women); they're looking for thin "athletic" types. One jerk even had the nerve to tell me he was sorry for being such a "Shallow Hal" but he couldn't date someone who looked like she was a size eighteen. It's just like what happens when I walk into a singles place; no one even notices I'm there. Guys look right past me, like I'm invisible. It's so weird—the more of me there is, the less I seem to matter.

The socioeconomic and cultural erasure of the overweight woman has been likened to a sanctioned form of eugenics with both racial and ethnic overtones since it so often targets women in the African American, Native American, and Hispanic community. While their fuller figures might represent "internal sites of resistance" to the hegemonic skeletal aesthetic they are more frequently demonized as the culprits who fail to take personal responsibility for their ingestion of greasy fries and doughnuts, threatening our national will and pride as well as depleting our health care coffers.[15] Weightism has in fact been likened to racism—and just as racial profiling can lead to traffic arrests for "driving while black" so too many obese woman fear social punishment for the crime of "eating while fat."

Why is the big woman both feared and ridiculed? Feminist theorists, pointing to the inverse correlation of the rise of the women's movement with the narrowing of the body ideal, have viewed weightism as a collective social response to challenges to traditional gender and power paradigms. Writers such as Susie Orbach, Kim Chernin, and Susan Bordo were among the first to interpret the disempowerment of the large woman and the concomitant idealization of "anorectic chic" as a drive to neutralize patriarchal anxiety about increasing female political and economic power; the fragility and childlike body of the "waif" aesthetic speaks of restraint, abstinence, and passivity, while the big woman represents the threat of assertion, dominance, and the ability to "throw her weight around."[16] For a threatened male establishment the tiny "size zero" colleague at the boardroom table may ease anxiety about female dominance while the big woman represents the threat of demanding equality or—still worse—the power to take up too much psychological and social space at that table. While "liberated" women might have welcomed the new ideal of boyish, slim-hipped bodies as marking an escape from their grandmother's procreative fate, in yet another paradox their obsessive preoccupation with achieving that body shape has only drained them of the psychological and professional energy needed to really achieve full equality in the marketplace. Eve Ensler, author of *The Vagina Monologues*, agrees: "What a way to control us. This skinny thing is genius. If you're hungry you don't have a lot of energy, and it's really hard to think."[17]

From the feminist perspective, then, the outsize woman's body is essentially subversive; by allowing herself to be out of shape, she's out of line—not buying into the collective enterprise of getting smaller and thinner. This understanding of the social construction of the big woman stands in sharp contrast to the traditional psychoanalytic notion that "the fat body is the symptomatic body," manifesting in each pound of excess adipose tissue every possible psychopathology from repressed rage and sexual dysfunction to fear of maturity and unresolved Oedipal conflicts.[18] Thus othered, the fat woman becomes society's "identified patient," literally embodying the displaced fears of a fitness-crazed culture, which in fact is far more pathological in its capacity for self-denial and appetite control.

Weightism exerts two major impacts on the eating behavior and body practices of women. First, fat phobia drives overzealous weight loss control in both normal and underweight girls and women who seek a "quick fix" by subjecting their bodies to the endless array of harmful drugs, surgeries, and crash diets that fuels the multibillion dollar weight loss industry. Second, weight stigmatization has devastating effects on women who *are* in fact overweight—not only on their social, economic, and professional lives, but by making them vulnerable to two serious conditions, known as emotional eating and binge eating disorder. Overweight women often subject themselves to severely restrictive diets that can create so much psychological deprivation that they eventually erupt into uncontrollable impulses to consume huge quantities of the very foods "forbidden" on the diet regimen. As a consequence, many refrain from eating anything except sanctioned "legal" food in public, a constraint that often leads them to binge eat in secret. Margaret, a fifty-two-year-old hospital administrator who came for treatment of a persistent binge eating disorder, describes one such frantic junk food odyssey:

> After two weeks on the protein-sparing fast and weighing in at the weight-loss clinic I just had to bust out and get some *real* food—but I was completely mortified to be seen eating, especially anything fattening. So I drove five miles from my house where no one would recognize me, and went through three separate drive-thrus on the strip. At each one I ordered a double cheeseburger and fries and a coke like maybe just one person would eat so no one would figure out how much I was eating. Then to top it off I went to the doughnut place and got a box of donut holes "for the kids." And all the time I'm thinking if they only knew it was all for me I would die of shame.

Margaret's narrative is not surprising in view of laboratory research confirming that the most frequent and stringent dieters are at higher risk for binge eating and bulimia.[19] Demoralized and ashamed at their failure to conform to a body norm that is often incompatible with either their genetics or their metabolism, many overweight women engage in periods of alternately starving and stuffing food in an endless cycle of "yo-yo dieting," which in the end is disruptive not just to their health but also to their self-esteem. Internalizing body shame and avoiding body exposure, they are less likely to exercise and more likely to retreat from social contact; it is not hard to imagine then why food ultimately becomes a primary source of comfort and a constant and reliable companion in an increasingly isolated world—and why they succumb to emotional eating, habitually using food as an opiate to cope with stress and painful feelings. For Adrian, an accountant in her early thirties who described herself as "forever fat," the roots of what she saw as her food "addiction" went deep into her childhood. An only child in a family that constantly monitored her weight, her body was treated as the "Big Problem." No one stopped to figure out that she was sneaking candy bars under her bed because she felt misunderstood at home and badgered at school. Unable to give voice to her feelings Adrian learned to "just stuff everything down" and soothe her hurt and anger with diet "no-no's." Recently married, she described her rage and helplessness at her mother's control of her body even at her wedding:

> Of course my parents took over my whole wedding just like everything else, and all my aunts said that white made me look too fat—so I ended up in a dark green wedding dress to "slim me down." And then at the wedding buffet after the ceremony my mother kept watching what I was eating. Can you believe it—she actually came over and started muttering that I had piled too much on my plate!

Try as they might to confront weightism head on, mainstream films and television shows have for the most part failed to allow the outsize woman to transcend her stereotypical roles as freak, buffoon, or, at best, just "one of the guys." Very few productions feature large women as central characters and fewer still cast them as romantic leads. This stands in sharp contrast to their male counterparts, establishing a kind of cinematic double standard of fatness: from John Goodman to Seth Rogen (and even to Eddie Murphy's *impersonation* of the obese Sheldon Klump in *The Nutty Professor*), the big guy manages to get the cute girl. This is one reason why the romantic comedy *Shallow Hal* (2001),

Dreamworks' animated series *Shrek* (2003–07), and the television reality show *Fat Actress*, each of which features overweight or obese heroines, are worthy of attention. Like many Hollywood comedies they vacillate between iconoclasm and conservatism, initially challenging the status quo with a provocative premise only to retreat into a reaffirmation of our deepest held prejudices and conditioned assumptions. Each production initially seeks to articulate a political correction of contemporary weightism or suggest the subversive possibilities of "living large," but ultimately negates its message through comedic conventions of ridicule and visual caricature.[20]

Shallow Hal, like much of the Farrelly brothers' work (most famously their 1998 comedy *Something About Mary*) elicits a wide range of responses. At one end of the spectrum some film critics have praised it as a form of socially corrective slapstick which uses grotesque images of deformed bodies to confront us with our own misapprehensions and "shallow" prejudices even while it entertains with gross-out humor and outrageous bad taste. But while Gwyneth Paltrow herself defended the film as a "love letter to people who are overweight"[21] most recipients of that letter were far from amused. In fact, The National Association to Advance Fat Acceptance condemned the film as "an insult" to the majority of Americans, more than two-thirds of whom who are now considered overweight.[22] Typical among this audience was my patient Sheila, a high school teacher in her forties who voiced her offense at the film's premise when we discussed it in our therapy group:

> After I saw the trailer I knew I couldn't bear seeing *Shallow Hal*. I hated the main joke of the film—that the guy only falls for the fat girl because he's deluded into thinking she's skinny. It reminded me of how horrible I used to feel when my mother would say there's got to be something wrong with a man who wants to be with a fat woman—because that "fat woman" is me.

The mixed bag of reactions derives from the tensions in the film between its intended critique of three social injustices—looksism, sexism, and weightism—and the disarming visual spectacle that undermines it. To its credit, there are many subversive possibilities that *Shallow Hal* does in fact realize through its over-the-top caricature of our appearance-driven culture, beginning with its very first scene, in which

Hal's dying father urges his young son never to settle for an "average" woman and to dedicate his life to the pursuit of "hot young tail"; the irreverent moment certainly captures the generational transmission of patriarchal objectification of the woman's body—the sexist law of the father being passed down to the son. The film has no illusions either about the double standard that allows both Hal (Jack Black) and his equally looks-obsessed buddy Mauricio (Jason Alexander) to quibble about their girlfriend's imperfect toes and other minute bodily flaws while unflattering camera shots emphasizing their own squat and distinctly un-hunky bodies tell us these two buddies are no bargain themselves. It continues its critique in a pivotal scene which places Hal face to face in a stuck elevator with self-help guru Tony Robbins. The reaction shot of Robbins's bemusement as he listens to Hal's unregenerate deconstruction of celebrity bodies (which includes comments such as, "Britney Spears has great knockers but she's a tad muscular") reinforces the film's didactic message. The encounter also leads to the intervention that will determine *Shallow Hal*'s narrative structure: Robbins exorcises Hals's hopelessly shallow looksism with a spell that enables him to see people's *inner* goodness manifested as *outer* beauty. This reversal is then played out in the film's characterization of the attractive women Hal meets as mean-spirited and arrogant, while the handicapped and obese become not only physically beautiful in his eyes but also prove to be unfailingly kind and caring.

In fact, *Shallow Hal* delivers its socially redemptive message with such a heavy hand that it succeeds in patronizing both the subject and the audience. Here for example is the critique of one disaffected viewer, another therapy group member named Sonia whose identification as a large woman helped her retain a more skeptical spectator "gaze" at the film's didacticism:

> Because everything is topsy turvy from Hal's magic spell brainwashing, all the deformed people are suddenly beautiful and we're supposed to get the message that they're good on the inside, not selfish and vain like the thin and gorgeous women in the movie. But I was really disgusted at the scene where Rosemary is at a disco dancing with all these other disabled people—that terribly crippled guy Walt who has to walk on all fours and her friends from Peace Corps who have psoriasis and are pretty gross and the burn victims she

helps—it made me feel that being overweight I get lumped together with all of society's misfits.

Most problematically, the visual structures and comic devices of *Shallow Hal* are at cross purposes with its didactic intent. The comedy relies primarily on visualizations of stereotypes organized around the spectacle of the enormous body of Rosemary Shanahan, the woman courted by Hal immediately after his enchantment. The manic energy that drives the comedy arises from sight gag images coding the fat woman's body as giant freak. The central joke of the film is sourced in the problematics of her size; she continually breaks the chairs she sits on, collapses a sports car, and creates a *tsunami* when she dives into a swimming pool. But for forty-three-year-old Marion, another therapy group member, this visual conceit was anything but funny. A sales representative for a large pharmaceutical company who travels frequently, she has become increasingly self-conscious about her size since gaining sixty pounds following two pregnancies and periods of inactivity from an automobile accident injury. She shared with the group her embarrassment during a recent business trip when she was sitting between two "skinny guys" and had to ask the flight attendant for a seatbelt extender. Experiences like that have led her to avoid situations that will call attention to her body:

> I was sitting in the movie theatre with my husband when everyone in the audience cracked up during that scene in *Shallow Hal* when Rosemary breaks the chair in the restaurant. All I could think of was that they were basically laughing at me, because I could barely squeeze into my own seat in the row. I spent the whole rest of the movie panicking I wouldn't be able to get out of it.

Equally caricatured is Rosemary's bottomless food capacity, another fat woman stereotype, as she downs super-sized burgers and chili cheese fries, inhales a gigantic soda she shares with Hal, and hacks off a huge piece of his office "congratulations" cake. (Significantly, she devours the chunk that has his name inscribed in frosting, an image that makes us wonder: will she soon devour him?) In each instance, the comedy is structured around the reversal of cultural expectations of feminine fragility and restrained appetite. The film works hard to masculinize

Rosemary through her hearty appetite and physical strength, which relegates her to the perpetual state of being "always a friend, but never a girlfriend"; here her lament reflects the social reality that just as fat men are derided for their feminine breasts and flabby bodies, so too the body of the big woman is coded for masculinity or asexuality.[23] The series of comic reversals based on such gender constructs culminates in the film's closing image of the enormous Rosemary as a "big mama" picking up little Hal and carrying him off to their honeymoon.

The film's other source of comedy lies in the dissonance between the "real" (i.e., obese) Rosemary and Hal's vision of her as beautiful and slender. The same spell extends to the other deformed bodies that figure prominently in the film, which magically transforms the disabled bodies of spina bifida and burn victims into images of perfect beauty in the eyes of the enchanted Hal. This plot device allows the able-bodied characters in the film (who register shock, derision, and disgust toward Rosemary's body, to Hal's constant bewilderment) to collude with the spectator in the "joke" of that body to which Hal is now blind. The joke may be on Hal, but it is really at Rosemary's expense—as well as that of the overweight viewer.[24] The narrative structure built around this central

Figure 5.1. The bride carries her groom over the threshold in *Shallow Hal*.

joke in turn informs the film's cinematic point of view and casting: the object of desire Hal envisions while under his spell appears throughout the film in the form of the actress Gwyneth Paltrow—supermodel tall and slender, blond, and scantily clad—while quick shots of the "real" Rosemary only appear when we are temporarily outside Hal's subjectivity, entering what his friend Mauricio calls "third-person objective reality." This perspective, we are instructed, is the harsh reality of social conditioning against which the film opposes Tony Robbins's utopic corrective for a new social order, one where "the brain sees what the heart wants it to feel"—namely, people's inner goodness. But rather than constructing a genuinely radical alternative to the conventional looks-based value system, *Shallow Hal* ultimately sustains it by recruiting the cinematic conventions of the romantic comedy genre. The central components of that genre—boy meets girl, the courtship idyll, the misunderstanding and temporary separation, the reunion and concluding marriage—are driven by Hal's pursuit of his lady love who appears not in the form of the obese Rosemary but as a famously slender movie star icon. Because as spectators we are invited to share Hal's cinematic point of view during these moments, we can enjoy the familiar pleasures of screen romance without the destabilizing rupture and readjustment we would be required to make had the film visualized his courtship of the obese form of his lover. When Rosemary is sprawled on the floor after collapsing a steel-frame chair for example, the camera privileges Hal's gaze of the willowy Paltrow's body gracefully and provocatively lying on the ground, rather than the spectacle of the fat lady in a humiliating pratfall.

Only at the film's didactic conclusion, when Hal finally forsakes his shallow values and proposes to the "real" Rosemary does her outsize image occupy the same frame as her lover; for the first time in the film the camera lingers on her whole body, a shot followed by a soft-focus close-up as we see her face in a reaction shot to Hal's rather limp apology for his bad behavior. Until this point the camera primarily relies either on fragmented cuts and long shots when filming Rosemary's obese form or on the view-from-behind, the cinematic shot traditionally used to share the "dirty joke" of the woman's body with the spectator.[25] Significantly, this final scene is the only instance in *Shallow Hal* where Rosemary appearing as an obese woman is embraced by her (comparatively) normal-weight lover—although the film immediately undercuts any subversive possibilities of such coupling with a predictable sight gag of Hal's failed efforts to lift his new bride in his arms.

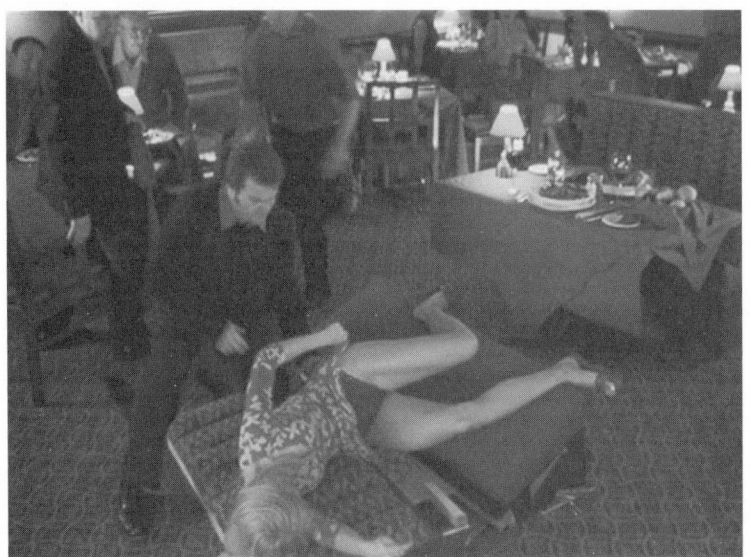

Figure 5.2. Hal rushes to the aid of his date.

Figure 5.3. Together at last in the same frame.

In fact, throughout the film its visual structures persist in negating the possibility of the large woman's sexual desirability. When Hal and Rosemary are presumably about to consummate their love the monstrous nature of her body is signaled by the sudden appearance of a pair of gigantic purple panties, which she tosses to the puzzled Hal. And since cinema can so economically and powerfully embed multiple meanings in one image, the visual joke here gains resonance by its reference to weight loss ads, which typically display the huge pants abandoned by the triumphant dieter who now stands slender and safely distanced from her former fat self. In the shot immediately preceding this joke we see the vision that is making Hal drool with anticipation: a nude rear view shot of a woman's slender body bending over to remove a tiny purple bikini thong which she tosses in his direction. Her foregrounded image is bathed in a soft radiant light while Hal is shot in the far background as he lies in his bed gazing with longing at this vision in a composition replicating the visual conventions of a sexual fantasy.

But these two shots, both of which were featured prominently in the film's promotional ads and trailer shots, signify more than just a sexual sight gag. Actress Gwyneth Paltrow as Rosemary, the presumptive owner of these super plus size panties, insisted on having a body double stand in for the nude shot because she has always been dissatisfied with that part of her anatomy: "I hate my butt, I really do!," she revealed to celebrity gossip columns shortly after the film was released.[26] Complicating this back story is the fact that many of the shots of the obese Rosemary are performed by yet another stand-in wearing a fat suit, forcing us to make a dizzying number of adjustments for what is "real" both inside and outside the movie screen. Still more striking is that within the screen narrative Paltrow's character Rosemary derides the mammoth size of her "butt cheeks" to Hal, a reminder of how the body hatred of the filmic fat woman might be closer than we imagined to the "perfect" thin woman's body dissatisfaction.

In fact, the film's manipulation of the different visions offered to Hal, his friends, and the spectator forces us to question both how we look at celebrities and how we are limited by our subjective visions of other people's bodies. It does this through its constant interplay between images of Hal's view of Rosemary as the superslender movie star Paltrow and momentary flashes of the bloated form of the "real" Rosemary. The effect of these point of view camera shifts, which inform the cinematography, structure, and central theme of the entire film, has

Figure 5.4./5.5. The mystery of the giant underpants.

been read by one observer as an important critique of contemporary body culture: "To put it simply, by asking us to gaze fetishistically at the body of an obese woman in the same way that we normally would at the body of any given starlet, *Shallow Hal* makes a comedy of the moral and political implications of the basic visual protocols of contemporary culture. This gaze reminds us, importantly, that Gwyneth Paltrow's famous body is as much at stake in this visual economy as is the body of an obese woman."[27]

But in the end *Shallow Hal* vitiates any such meaningful social critique of weightism through its dependence on the device of the fat suit Paltrow wears to represent the "real" obese Rosemary. The costume allows us to surrender to the fat jokes at her expense because we remain safe in the knowledge that underneath that suit is the "real" Gwyneth Paltrow, as slender and glamorous as ever. The other unfortunate effect of this representation is that when Rosemary speaks of her body insecurity and shame as an obese woman or articulates her struggles with dieting and weight loss, she is merely *impersonating* the body and subjectivity of the stigmatized fat woman rather than allowing for any empathic connection to her dilemma. This failure to provide a truly radical challenge to weightism lead Rachel, a thirty-six-year-old artist overweight since her teens, to challenge the film's project:

> Why not cast an actress who really is overweight, maybe someone like Camryn Manheim? It just made me feel worse to see Gwyneth Paltrow dressed up in that phony suit and special effects makeup like some Latex mask you'd rent for Halloween or a King Kong gorilla costume. By casting a superskinny movie star it just reminded me that there's no way Hal would ever have fallen in love with Rosemary if she really was as big as I am. I still believe if a guy ever really had the chance to get to know me, to get past what I look like at first glance, he could grow to like me—but how can I ever hope to get someone to want to be with me long enough to find that out? By the end it felt like that movie was all a cruel joke on women like me. They never make movies about what it's *really* like to be a fat woman in a thin world.

Still more importantly, the fat suit serves as a signifier of the bodily transformation from "before" to "after" so crucial in the collective social enterprise to "disappear" the fat woman. It is precisely this promise that drives not only diet infomercials but also television makeover shows such as *The Biggest Loser* or *From Flab to Fab*. So too in Shallow Hal the fat suit encasing the slender body of Paltrow facilitates the image of the thin body which can magically emerge from its shell of fat, literally obliterating the formerly obese woman—a clear reference to her social invisibility and nonpersonhood. Thus, the fat suit serves to reinforce the cultural fantasy of the thin person imprisoned within the fat body, waiting for the magic diet or pill which will allow the excessive flesh to disappear and the *true* self to manifest, a fantasy expressed to me recently by a patient who said: "Sometimes I feel like my fat is like an abcess—I wish I could just pop it and then the real me would come out."

Despite the film's homiletic message about reversing inner and outer beauty, the central image of the fat suit suggests that while the fat Rosemary may possess a "thin" (i.e., competent and generous) nature as evidenced by her community service and Peace Corps volunteerism, its corporeal manifestation remains the image of the thin-bodied Paltrow, thus in the end reinforcing rather than subverting the traditional moral and aesthetic notion that inner goodness is represented by outer beauty. The film's more potent unconscious message is that the potentially worthy self must be disconnected from the alien fat body, a separation transacted throughout the film in its cinematography and editing via camera shots that "disembody" Rosemary, focusing on one huge leg or thigh, super-sized arm, or lumbering back. The camera cuts and fragments her body in an evocation of such surgeries as liposuction, gastric bypass, and other bariatric procedures that slice, suck, and drain the noxious adipose tissue from its owner's body. Flashing shots of Rosemary's "excessive" flesh spilling over the margins of furniture and cars or reaching over into Hal's plate to devour his clams casino at the restaurant threaten the maintenance of the idealized, slender Rosemary, an image generated by a patriarchal establishment represented here by the self-help "guru" and his acolyte Hal. When Rosemary arrives at Hal's door after he is longer protected by his optical illusion, he frantically enacts a range of sitcom avoidance strategies, finally smearing his eyes with Vaseline to blur the bulky form of the woman he must now recognize as his girlfriend. The violence of his struggle to keep her out of his domain as well as his sight is perhaps a measure of how much the big woman threatens to transgress the boundaries of an established order of feminine bodies—bodies that must stay contained and restrained within the bounds of that order through strict weight control and denial of appetite.

The computer-animated series *Shrek*, launched by Dreamworks in 2001, might appear even better suited than *Shallow Hal* to the devices of enchantment. Set in the realm of "Far, Far Away" where kings turn into frogs, donkeys sing rap music, and evil princes vie for the throne, the central trope of *Shrek 1* and its sequel *Shrek 2* is the magic spell cast by a corrupt fairy godmother on Princess Fiona which renders her slender and beautiful by day but a little "fatso" by night. The real Fiona, in fact, is an ogre—albeit a very good-natured one. Ogres are known to devour little children, and like many fairy tales from Hansel and Gretel to Red Riding Hood, such a fearful prospect immediately connects Fiona's chubby body to dangerous undisciplined appetites. Her desperate rush to hide before her transformation at sunset also serves as an apt metaphor for the shame of the fat woman who dreads the exposure of her body in public.

The extraordinary box office success of the *Shrek* franchise[28] is attributed in part to the fact that the films rely on a sophisticated cynical reframing and deflation of classic fairytale characters aimed at adult audiences who buy the movie spinoff products their kids demand. Bemoaning the series' pop-culture spoofing of Hollywood and Walt Disney—including the appearance of a cross-dressing princess with a garter belt—a film critic reviewing *Shrek the Third* mused: "Maybe seven isn't too early for irony. S*hrek* is postmodernism for towheads, pastiche for the potty-trained."[29] But in fact the entire *Shrek* series provides a particularly trenchant reflection of American weight preoccupation. Like *Shallow Hal* the films work hard to drive home the message that beauty is in the eyes of the beholder as they trace the journey of self-acceptance and true "seeing" that Shrek and Fiona must take to achieve everlasting love and happiness. Repeating the same easy-to-read sermon as *Shallow Hal*, the *Shrek* films are careful to endow the outwardly alluring characters with arrogance at best and utter malevolence at worst—represented here by an astonishingly evil Fairy Godmother who schemes to promote her son (Prince Charming) to the throne while operating an underworld pharmacopeia of beauty-enhancing potions with the iron fist of a Mafia drug lord. She rules over a fairy tale equivalent of the cosmetic and diet industry, luring her victims with promises of riches and sexual success; her business card says "Happiness," while the magic potion she markets as "Lust" might as well be Viagra. Similarly, the slender "daytime" Princess Fiona (Cameron Diaz) rescued from her tower by the ogre-hero Shrek is imperious and self-absorbed, but when transformed back to her true chubby self proves to be spunky and strong with a striking resemblance to the famous Muppet Miss Piggy, dispatching her enemies with deft karate kicks and flips—much as Rosemary's size is used for comic gender reversal expectations of strength and fragility.[30]

In *Shrek the Third*, when Fiona, along with Snow White, Rapunzel, and Sleeping Beauty, is imprisoned by villains, her feisty activism is contrasted to the passivity of these traditional fairy tale princesses, archly portrayed in the film as entitled and bitchy Beverly Hills glamour girls; in unison they announce that like all princesses, they are "waiting to be rescued" until the fearless Fiona rallies them into a band of pro-active power girls to free Shrek from the clutches of his enemies.

Princess Fiona in her natural big body manifestation is no-nonsense and down to earth—a perfect partner, in fact, for the mud-loving Shrek. And this is precisely where the films' subtext undermines not only its message of unconditional love for the inner beauty that lies beneath the "spell" of artifice but also of the self-acceptance the couple presumably learns at the end of their journey. This last hard-earned wisdom is articulated in *Shrek the Third* when Shrek, having overcome both his low self-esteem and doubts about fatherhood, delivers the films' message to his young protégé Artie (Justin Timberlake): "People

Figure 5.6. Fiona defends her man in *Shrek 2*.

used to think I was a monster and for a long time I believed them, but after a while you learn to ignore the names people call you and just trust who you are." While the affirmation speaks to the possibility of outgrowing internalized body hatred and developing self-confidence and self-esteem, the lesson was far from clear for at least one young viewer named Hannah whom I met during a talk at her middle school:

> Although my friends thought all three *Shrek*s were just funny kids' movies, there are lots of scenes where it shows people who are unhappy because of how they look. Shrek is upset that he is "a hideous ugly beast" especially when he falls in love with Fiona, and it seems like she's only really happy when she is beautiful, thin, and the princess that every guy dreams of. When she is in the form of an overweight ogre, she's unhappy with herself and wants to hide. When you feel that you may not be the prettiest or the thinnest person in the world, the message you get from these movies is that if you are born unattractive like Fiona and Shrek you will live a life of unhappiness.

The series' failure to more clearly convey its feel-good message may be found in its subtext about the social realities confronting conventionally "unattractive" bodies. From the opening credits of *Shrek 1* where we first meet the ogre-cum-hero in his natural swamp habitat, bathing in slime, farting and belching, and slurping his food with rotten teeth, to the happily-ever-after closing shot of *Shrek the Third* showing Fiona and Shrek raising a bevy of baby ogres back in their swampy home, by so firmly rooting Shrek and his bride in the domain of the bodily fluids and wastes of the subhuman and scatological, the films avoid the more transgressive possibility of a world where an outsize princess could indeed mate with a dashing prince—or for that matter where the obese Rosemary could be pursued by Hal without the aid of a magic visual spell. Thus, the less optimistic message of the *Shrek* series is that fat, monstrous (read ogre here) freaks of nature can indeed live happily ever after—as long as they stick to their own kind. The mating of Shrek and Fiona allows for the harmonious union of like with like not in terms of social class and power but of body shape; in other words when Fiona is no longer a svelte princess but a fat and frumpy ogre like her lover. The beloved William Steig tale on which the films are based says it best: "Like fire and smoke, these two belonged together . . . /And they lived unhappily ever after, scaring the socks off all who fell afoul of them."[31]

When she is not a clumsy "fat lady" or a good-natured ogre, Hollywood's outsize woman is depicted as a monstrous man-eater. This fearsome figure has been interpreted in psychoanalytic theory as a representative of the omnipotent mother of primitive childhood fantasies who threatens to engulf the infant with her insatiable appetite for food or sex. Instead of being an object of male desire, she is the embodiment of his worst fears of annihilation. Her powers are legendary, even appearing in the 1960s rock song: "Watch out boys, she'll chew you up, she's a Man-Eater!"[32] This threatening female archetype with voracious appetites for both food and sex is culturally inscribed onto the "Big Mama," the fat woman whose flesh represents the non-nurturing maternal, the life-threatening aspect of the unnatural mother who would abandon—even devour—her young to feed her own selfish desires. In an alternative reading of these fearsome man-eaters, feminist theorists see them as a patriarchal warning to women that they should remain within the boundaries of a construction of femininity as passive, with little appetite for either sex or food, a construct signaled by the slender form of the restrained dieter.[33]

But whatever their origins, Hollywood images of large women "pigging out" succeed in rendering the disorders that underlie obesity and eating problems either ludicrous or horrific, further isolating and stigmatizing the women who suffer from these very real and difficult to treat conditions. Women who struggle with a compulsive relationship to food come to think of themselves as "pigs" who are pathologically devoid of will power and discipline when in fact many times their problem can be traced to the socially imposed need to "get down" to a size smaller than their bodies can metabolically maintain. This constraint in turn frequently forces them to break out of the "prison" of severe diet restrictions with uncontrollable bouts of binge eating. Perhaps the most chilling rendering of the pathological nature of the large woman who "pigs out" is found in the film version of Stephen King's thriller *Misery* (1990). Kathy Bates is cast as Annie Wilkes, a psychotic nurse with a criminal history of infanticide who takes in a best-selling author (James Caan) after a car accident and sets out to consume the mind as well as the body of her captive. Sequestering him in her isolated mountain lair, she immobilizes the author by literally tying him down in bed and exploding into rages like an angry demanding mom: "You better start showing me a little appreciation, Mr. Man!"

In psychoanalytic terms Annie is the suffocating infantilizing mother who won't allow separation, first "castrating" her prey by hobbling his legs and then threatening him with an endless arsenal of phallic weapons—hypodermic needles, knives, axes, and rifles—to prove the point. She is also the ego-engulfing mother who seeks to control and co-opt his creativity, forcing him to churn out pulp fiction best-sellers— perhaps a rueful comment by King himself on his own artistic dilemma about "selling out." But the film seems most interested in visualizing the insatiable appetite of the devouring maternal figure as a series of bad puns: nurse Annie trots out her pet pig (the eponymous Misery) watches old Liberace TV shows in bed while "pigging out" on potato chips, and in the mortal struggle of the film's finale is bludgeoned to death by her captive with her very own prized statue of a pig. Thus is sanctioned an extraordinarily brutal assault upon the controlling monstrous mother who must be destroyed to free the hero's creative energies. In the film's "happy" coda, our chastened author goes on to write his first critical success: no longer artistically drained and

Figure 5.7. Death struggle with a pig in *Misery*.

devoured by catering to the lowbrow tastes of his admiring female fans, he triumphantly announces to his publisher that he wrote this new book "for myself."

Are there any media depictions of the outsize woman where she is not "reduced" to either a ridiculous spectacle, an ogre or a homicidal monster? In her work on the popular TV sitcom series *Roseanne,* scholar Kathleen Rowe finds an empowering alternative in the figure of the "unruly woman" whose transgressive body challenges cultural fears and phobias about fatness and female appetites. Unapologetically loud, rude, and ravenous, the outrageous excess of the unruly woman questions mainstream conventions for a provocative purpose: her willingness to offend endows her with the "disruptive power" to effect social change. As Rowe notes: "Concerning her fatness, she resists any efforts to define herself by her weight. Publicly celebrating the pleasures of eating, she argues that women need to take up more space in the world, not less."[34]

At first glance, it might seem that just such an unruly woman resurfaced in the pseudo-reality TV show *Fat Actress,* in which Kirstie Alley's predicament as an overweight actress in Hollywood virtually unemployable at her current girth takes dead aim at weight-obsessed celebrity culture. Her wild and unruly hair, flesh spilling over too-tight clothes, stentorian voice, and bawdy language all promise her subversive possibilities compared to either the passive Rosemary Shanahan (who is submissively grateful for Hal's courtship), the happily domesticated Fiona, or the homicidal Annie Wilkes. Thus, we might read Alley's histrionic performance in the show's initial episode (characteristically entitled "Big Butts") as an attempt to critique the world of celebrity beauty consumerism, particularly in the comedy of her frantic weight loss tortures. In one episode, for example, an anorexic personal trainer—who consumes nothing but water and Kleenex (*sic*) for dinner—instructs the desperate Kirstie to contract an intestinal parasite in a "third world country" to solve her weight problem once and for all. But the power of caricature as critique is soon blunted by the show's construction of Alley's character as endlessly needy, hysterical, and self-hating as she submits to her handlers' exhortations to control her gluttony and her apparently insatiable libido. Again, the comedy works to sanction social aggression toward outsize women which is then internalized and turned against the self, enacted here by Alley's loud moans and *mea culpas* for "letting herself go." Significantly, the series is scripted around the frantic star's landing an offer to become a poster girl for the Jenny

Craig diet company, a deal that in fact did take place in the "Real World" outside the show's story line. Meanwhile, numerous articles in the tabloid press charted Alley's weight loss as part of the promotion of the series throughout its run, while an insert in the DVD edition included an advertisement for her new book, entitled *How to Lose Your Ass and Regain Your Life*. After the demise of the show, a triumphant Alley was featured in *People* magazine displaying a fifty-pound weight loss. Like her excessive body itself, the image of the celebrity "Big Mama" spills over from the screen into public spaces where it is used both to sell products and serve as the focus of endless ridicule and applause, depending on whether her body is shrinking or expanding.

In this sense, the project of the comedic spectacle depicting the excessive woman negotiating physical and social space is to "cut her down to size." Laughter is directed *at*—not *with*—her, serving to justify weightism as it simultaneously establishes spectator identification with the contemporary imperative of slenderness and fitness. Ultimately, these Hollywood images of outsize women serve to perpetuate rather than challenge body preferences and prejudices. In their failure to escape the "weight" of their own stereotypes they end up embodying the cultural nightmare of fatness. Explains Susan Bordo: "As our bodily ideals have become firmer and more contained (we worship not merely slenderness but flablessness), any softness or bulge comes to be seen as unsightly—as disgusting, disorderly "fat," which must be eliminated or "busted."[35] Fear can be the strongest motivator of all, and it is our cultural fear of fatness that drives the body practices and eating behavior of contemporary women and—as we shall see in the next chapter—their daughters as well.

6

Teen Bodies

Valley Girls and Middle School Vamps

Hollywood has imagined the lives of American girls in some of the most beloved and enduring films of all time—*Gone With the Wind*, *Meet Me in St. Louis*, and *The Wizard of Oz*. But it was not until after World War II, when social scientists became interested in adolescence as a key developmental stage, that studio heads saw in "teenagers" an expanding moviegoing market with expendable incomes of their own and began to make films designed specifically for them. An even younger demographic known as "tweens" has since become a still more profitable market; girls between eight and twelve are now the biggest consumers of both Hollywood movies and the spinoff products—TV shows, soundtracks, branded clothes and makeup, lunchboxes and dolls, cell phones and other electronic toys—that make or break a film's bottom line.[1]

Teen movies and the girls they target have much to tell us about a culture that circulates eroticized and glamorized images of the body in shaping conventional constructions of femininity. Teens, tweens, and their little sisters, undefended by critical judgment and experience, are especially vulnerable to such media imagery, and as a result their bodies are inscribed not only with tattoos and belly rings but also with the markings of body insecurity, premature sexualization, and disordered eating behavior that have become an all too "normal" part of contemporary beauty culture. Recent decades have witnessed what would seem to be a growing epidemic of eating disorders in teenage girls. Countless studies have quantified this trend with alarming statistics, such as those reported in 2007 when close to five thousand middle and high school students in urban and suburban Minnesota were given a battery of surveys and diagnostic tests about their eating habits and dieting behavior. While the rates of those subjects meeting the psychiatric criteria for anorexia and bulimia and binge eating disorder were not necessarily higher than those for Americans diagnosed across all age groups, it was worrisome to see how many girls reported such seriously disordered behaviors such as laxative abuse and self-induced vomiting (9.4 percent) and out of control binge eating (11 percent). Still more striking was that more than thirty-six percent of these girls reported that they felt their body size and shape was key to their self-esteem and happiness, while even more (41.5 percent) suffered from disturbances of their body image, which was either distorted (many of them were underweight, for example, but thought of themselves as needing to lose weight) or a source of shame and obsession.[2] Such behaviors and beliefs are part of a contemporary girls' body culture that is powerfully influenced by cinematic images of adolescence constructed in teen movies, the marketing to teens and tweens of products and clothes needed to achieve those images, and most of all by the drive among younger and younger girls to be sexy and sophisticated in a national trend known as KGOY—"Kids Getting Older Younger."

The teen movie genre provides tween and teen girls with both representations of the years between middle school and high school graduation as well as visions of the female adulthood that awaits them. Films such as *Clueless* (1995), *Mean Girls* (2004), *Never Been Kissed* (1999), and *Jawbreakers* (1998) both intentionally and unconsciously capture the experience of adolescence: the self-consciousness and self-absorption, the desperate need for conformity and the merciless exclusion and humiliation of not fitting in—all perils along the bumpy journey each adolescent girl must make as she completes the developmental task of separating from home and creating her own identity. But in Hollywood movies the complex internal psychological changes necessary to truly "come of age" are neatly glossed over. Instead, working within a consumer culture that is all about images, teen movies encourage the notion that identity comes from the outer surface of the body. To the adolescent asking "Who am I?" they offer up a quick and easy answer: "My brands. My clothes. My size. My weight. My sexy shape."

At first glance teen movie heroines might look like reliable role models for the negotiation of the adolescent experience, but it doesn't take long to figure out that they are not your typical teenagers. Blessed with flawless complexions and pearly straight teeth, they are somehow miraculously free from the zits and braces that are the bane of adolescence. They come to school wearing killer outfits straight from the pages of *Teen Vogue* and the trendiest boutiques, pick up their friends in snazzy cars and seem to have no limit on their credit cards. Their designer bedrooms are pink and frilly, impeccably decorated in homes that range from spacious comfortable suburban houses to Beverly Hills mansions. They attend well-appointed high schools peaceably integrated with what has aptly been described as a "Bennetton-esque American diversity" sprinkling of Hispanic, African American, and Asian students and which are remarkably free of any real problems, from graffiti to guns.[3] The sparkling sunny world they move through is enhanced by the films' standard production design featuring vibrant colors, sparkling lighting and stylish sets accompanied by bouncy soundtracks playing "bubble gum" music and pop rock tunes.

Most of all, these teen heroines come in three sizes—thin, thinner, and thinnest. One size does not fit all, however, and the narrow definition of the popular girl's body immediately establishes a disturbing gap between the image on the screen with which viewers are encouraged to identify and their own images in the mirror. And in truth how could the average tween or teen viewer ever bridge that gap when the actresses cast as high schoolers look at least ten years postgraduate and whose boyfriends display the sculpted muscular bodies of professional athletes or male models? Actress Alicia Silverstone, who plays the privileged sixteen-year-old Cher, popularity queen of her Southern California high school, was not only close to twenty when she appeared in *Clueless* but had been a professional fashion model since the age of six.

The format of teen movies is as uniform as the body types they feature. In each film we meet a clique of powerful popular girls revered as flawless royalty who "totally rule." Like Regina George, the Queen Bee of "The Plastics" in *Mean Girls*, the clique leader is a ruthless intimidator attended by fawning adjutants typically depicted as dumb blondes and entitled material girls who speak and gesture in unison and display slavish devotion to the rules of their clique.

The "drama" occurs when an innocent newcomer is initiated into the power circle and soon outshines the clique leader. After a series of betrayals and deceptions all social conflicts are resolved at the inevitable Prom finale; the scheming clique Queen is exposed, wrongs are righted, and harmony is restored in time for graduation. The misguided new girl who has sold out her solid values (like Andy in *The Devil Wears Prada*) for the lure of popularity must learn the error of her ways. Her penance

Figure 6.1. A trio of Barbie dolls in *Never Been Kissed*.

is about as serious as a time out in her room; in *Mean Girls* the heroine Cady (Lindsay Lohan) apologizes to the buddies she has abandoned and even joins the geeky "Mathletes"; while in *Clueless* Cher, in recovery from her shallow shopping ways, heads the school campaign to fight world hunger. While the films insist that their heroines be chastened for their dalliance with superficial clique cruelty, in the end each is allowed to emerge more popular than ever and ready to succeed in the world. Their final reward is the acquisition of a boyfriend. While boys play secondary roles in the films they serve as the prime motivators for the girls' rivalry and drive for acquiring a sexy body; as such they are the "queen makers" who promote the girl not just as their Prom date but as the object of their desire. Thus, Cady "gets" her rival Regina's old boyfriend, while Cher convinces her attractive ex-step brother (who as the film earnestly reassures us, is not biologically related) that she is now worthy of his attention and his love.

But while their narrative arc may neatly close with a feel-good ending, if teen movies intend a corrective message about the cruelty and superficiality of adolescent social rituals it is unfortunately lost on many adolescent moviegoers. During a course on gender and popular film genres, I asked my undergraduate students to reflect on the effect these kind of films had exerted on their own adolescence. A lively conversation ensued, ranging from the films' influence on their body image, dieting, and eating behavior to their impact on early sexual encounters. Nicole, a sophomore English major, talked about her initial response to *Mean Girls* as a younger teen and her concern that any satiric intent could be overridden by its seductive images of glamour:

> The popular kids in the movie all look gorgeous and are rich and even though they try to show how ridiculous these people can be I would say that for kids who don't see the bigger picture it can definitely put your self-esteem in danger. The first time I saw it I cut out breakfast and lunch for the whole term to get as skinny as the Plastics. Those people who don't understand that it is a comedy film can definitely take this movie literally.

Julie, a senior, agreed with her critique but added with a sheepish expression that the film continued to have the power to affect her behavior and her body image:

> Each time I watch *Mean Girls* I feel like no one should look like me because I am not skinny like those popular girls in the movie. I need to go buy lots of expensive clothes like the Plastics wear. I need to dye my hair blonde and have it look just right. It probably sounds weird but I love and hate this movie because I can sort of tell it's actually trying to make fun of the Plastics and their lifestyle—in spite of how bad it makes me feel.

And indeed many young moviegoers do take teen movies "literally," just as my student Nicole had suggested. While their parents or big sisters are quick to pick up on the genre's satiric elements younger viewers are more likely to be beguiled by the glamorous cinematic reconstruction of what is presumably their own high school world. Tina Fey, commenting on her *Mean Girls* screenplay, recognized the dual nature of its reception: "Adults find [the film] funny. They are the ones who are laughing. Young people watch it like a reality television show. It is much too close to their real experiences so they are not exactly guffawing."[4] And even when teenage moviegoers do suspect the satiric intent of *Mean Girls* that does not inoculate them from the psychological effects of its images. While they get the caricature of teen materialism in the "clueless" Cher with her private masseuse and sports car, teen girls are often so overwhelmed by her sheer gorgeousness that they forget they are watching an artfully produced illusion of adolescence. Their visual pleasure at the glamorized body of the high school heroine is aligned with the "male gaze" of the boys in the film's narrative who are depicted looking at her with longing and sexual desire, reminding us of Mulvey's original theory of cinema spectatorship. Both these looks and the moviegoer's gaze are directed at the body of the heroine by camera shots that tightly frame her trendy outfits and perfect shape.

The visual power of these images is so compelling that in the end teen films perpetuate rather than challenge the very superficiality they profess to satirize. More problematically, by their failure to clearly critique the "looksism" of adolescent culture the films provide susceptible teen viewers with tips on controlling body weight and restricting food intake while simultaneously increasing their body insecurity. Trish, another sophomore in the class, recalled how she internalized the enactment of weight obsession in *Mean Girls*:

> Regina easily could be crowned the hottest girl in the school, but when she says she wants to lose three pounds and her best friend talks about her flabby arms, it really disturbed me. If these already beautiful girls need fixing,

Figure 6.2. Cher as the object of the male gaze in *Clueless*.

I figured I must be in terrible shape by comparison. And when Regina gets heavier after she's tricked into eating those extra calorie bars, the message I got was: "Don't ever gain weight because you will lose all your friends and popularity!" Even today when I watch the movie I still feel like I should be ashamed of my body, which weighs much more than Regina ever did.

Another idealized depiction of the teen girl's chronic state of body dissatisfaction is enacted in *Clueless* when Cher, who mostly munches on raw vegetables throughout the film, is horrified by her calorie count for the day. Moaning that she feels "like such a heifer" she frets that she may never reach her personal aspiration "to be five feet ten and one hundred and ten [pounds] like Cindy Crawford." No matter that the film inserts a few sharp jabs at valley girl beauty culture—Cher airily reveals that her mother died after a "routine liposuction" while one of her classmates prominently sports a post-rhinoplasty bandage on her nose. The film's more potent message to young viewers is that even perfectly gorgeous girls such as Cher aren't quite perfect enough and that constant vigilance and "watching" one's weight is still obligatory. This cinematic advice is reinforced by two cultural forces discussed in previous chapters: the first is celebrity culture in which stars glamorize body insecurity and appetite control as part of their own well-publicized body regimens; the second is makeover beauty culture in which body dissatisfaction is validated as a necessary motivator for self-improvement and transformation. In other words, *all* bodies need work, all the time. These two forces manifest in adult culture combine to act upon an adolescent subculture in which the price of physical imperfection is exclusion, stigmatization, and loss of social power.

Teen movies capitalize on body anxiety with scenes that invite audience laughter at comic visualizations of any adolescent's worst humiliation nightmares. Opening with "new girl" Cady's nervous pratfall entrance into a classroom of jeering students, *Mean Girls* later ratchets up the embarrassment with a scene showing a very drunk Cady vomiting unceremoniously all over her boyfriend; while the irreverent *American Pie* features both an episode in which the entire school witnesses a boy's attack of diarrhea as well as a still wider public humiliation via Internet of another classmate's premature ejaculation during his first sexual encounter. Such filmic moments anticipate and evoke the peer gossip and shaming revelations on social networking sites, which too often exert devastating effects on young members.[5] Cyber-harassment of a girl is most explicitly directed at her body: a frequent and particularly toxic accusation by an Internet saboteur is that a girl is either "fat" or a "slut." The language of these attacks suggests the complex connection between cultural notions of female appetites for food and sex and the problematic response to their full expression; the double message here is that attractive girls keep their eating in check—and good girls don't sleep around.

Cinematic images of body humiliation also capture the heightened self-consciousness of adolescence that marks the end of childhood, a time usually free from concern about bodily appearance. The little girl at the beach engaged in the immediacy of her experience doesn't worry about whether she *looks* cute when she's playing in the waves, while her thirteen-year-old-sister is more likely to be preoccupied with whether her belly is flat enough to be seen in a bikini. Teen movies capture body obsession in such scenes as the one in which the Plastics line up before the mirror in Regina's palatial bedroom to exchange "fat talk" comments such as "I hate my calves!" and "my pores are huge!"; but the images of both the girls' super stylish figures and the glitzy interior set are so seductive that ultimately these moments serve not to critique as much as validate what has become today's normative discontent.

The same normalization is achieved in the genre's depiction of the body rivalry between girls. As Cady learns in *Mean Girls*, the "fittest" who survive the Darwinian high school jungle are popular by virtue not only of their "fit" bodies but by their capacity to engage in fierce competition for sexual and social power. The near-lethal nature of these beauty battles is more unambiguously satirized in the mockumentary *Drop Dead Gorgeous*(1999), where (just as in *Miss Congenialty*) the pageant organizer for a Miss Teen beauty pageant commits a series of fiendish murders to literally bury the competition. Again Hollywood uses the hyperbolic for comedic effect rather than to explore just why the expression of female aggression is diverted to beauty wars. Nor do teen movies interrogate why teen age girls' hostility so often takes the form of food sabotage, as it does in *Jawbreakers* when a jealous clique member "accidentally" kills her rival with a gumball, or in *Mean Girls* when Cady feeds Regina weight supplement bars to make her too "fat" to zip up her size five prom dress.

Figure 6.3. Regina struggles with her Prom dress in *Mean Girls*.

Since studio teen films are still churned out by Hollywood's mostly male-dominated corporate studios, the depiction of lethal rivalry among women and girls may represent a vestigial patriarchal resistance to notions of sisterhood and feminist solidarity, a regressive indulgence in a misogynist vision of women battling for male attention much like the cat fighting warriors in *Kill Bill*. But while allowing for this possibility it is equally true that women do in fact report feeling competitive with other women about their size and shape and according to many body image studies hold their bodies to much harsher standards of acceptable body size and shape than their male counterparts.[6]

Hollywood teen movies are even more problematic in their depictions of the dieting practices of food restriction and extreme weight control measures that are symptomatic of eating disorders. References to acute conditions such as anorexia, bulimia, and binge eating disorder are either trivialized, lampooned, or dismissed as just another typical teen girl pastime—like shopping at the mall. In a key scene in *Mean Girls*, the Plastics, whose lunch trays consist of identical cans of Perrier and unopened salads, initiate newcomer Cady into the cafeteria table subcultures, which include "the girls who eat their feelings" and "the girls who don't eat anything" who are caricatured in fleeting shots of obese girls with hamburgers and skeletal girls with empty trays.

A similar orientation in cafeteria etiquette takes place in *Jawbreakers*, where ringleader Courtney points out the "Karen Carpenter table" of presumably anorexic students to new girl Vylette. And in *Drop Dead Gorgeous* the black humor reaches its fullest expression in two scenes featuring the winner of the previous year's beauty pageant who is now in the acute stages of anorexia. In a mock interview for television she is interviewed from her hospital bed hooked up to intravenous feeding tubes, her Miss Teen tiara still perched atop her head. In a barely audible voice she recalls her pre-victory regimen: "I was practicing my talent, finishing my costume, brushing up on my current events, and running eighteen miles a day on about . . . four hundred calories." The night of the Pageant she appears in a ghoulish wig and garish make up, lip synching her theme song while a nurse pushes her about the stage in her wheelchair.

While the black comedy may be designed to amuse, many younger viewers go beyond the "just kidding" joke to borrow ideas for regulating their own eating behaviors. Clinicians and parents are all too aware of the mimetic effects of girls learning from other girls in high school bathrooms or summer camps how to get rid of "fattening" food through

Figure 6.4. Lunchtime at the Plastics' table.

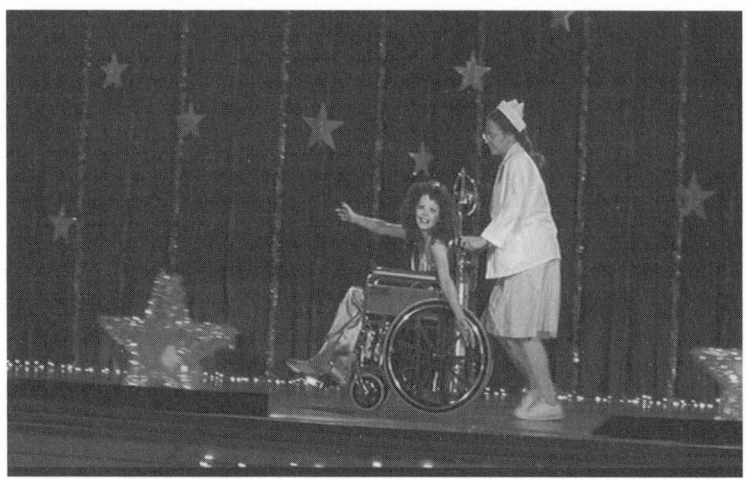

Figure 6.5. The anorexic Miss Teen takes a bow in *Drop Dead Gorgeous*.

self-induced vomiting, much like patients in eating disorder inpatient units report learning from each other the tricks of hiding food and outwitting the staff who monitors their food intake at meals.[7] Thus, it is possible for the more satiric moments of a teen movie to double as a weight loss manual for impressionable viewers, as it did for Allison, a junior history major in my course who had been treated for an eating disorder during high school:

> When I was fourteen I saw *Never Been Kissed* with Drew Barrymore. In this movie the "popular" girls are very pretty and thin. One of the popular characters talks about how she uses laxatives to make herself lose weight. This was the first time I ever heard about someone doing that to make herself thin or drop pounds faster. I was going through puberty and just entering high school back then, and noticed how the pretty girls ruled the school. I knew that vomiting was unhealthy, but I remember thinking that laxatives was a good idea. I mean how bad could they really be for you?

Such diet "tips" embedded in teen movies also reinforce the long-standing connection between food abstinence and femininity, a linkage that has been traced to notions of sexual purity in the Victorian era and still farther back in history to traditions of asceticism and spiritual piety in the fasting girls of medieval Europe who became saints and martyrs.[8] Ever since the screen "debut" of Scarlett O'Hara, Hollywood's young heroines and the moviegoing girls who watch them have been taught to observe the social etiquette of appetite denial. The savvy girls in *Jawbreakers* know this all too well; their clique's code of conduct in the high school cafeteria is simple: "We never never eat at lunch." Often teen viewers take the warning to heart, as Melanie, another student in the class vividly described:

> In *Jawbreakers* the thin pretty girls are teaching a geeky girl to be popular and telling her the "rules" of the cafeteria. They explain that eating in public is a big no-no, especially messy stuff like tuna fish with mayo. They made it sound so disgusting. I'll never forget this quote from the movie: "I mean, food's cool and all. It tastes good and you need it to live, but the mere act of eating involves thoughts of digestion, flatulation, defecation, even, shall we say, complexion defection." This made me so self-conscious that for the longest time after that I would cover my mouth when I was chewing, as if I could prevent people from seeing me eat. I also steered away from eating tuna fish sandwiches in public for about three years even though I love tuna!

Hollywood teen movies not only link slenderness with popularity and food abstinence with femininity but they also dramatize the shift from parental to peer influence in teaching adolescents the "rules" of social survival and success. It is precisely this separation from parental authority and supervision that gets expressed in the food choices and dietary practices that girls begin to exhibit as they seek autonomy through control over their food intake. While many changes in diet are a function of the adolescent's experimentation with different ideologies or political affiliations, it is not unusual for certain practices·such as vegetarianism to grow out of a girl's desire to avoid eating meat because it is "fattening." Less interested in saving the planet than in "feeling light," weight-conscious girls find in strict vegetarian regimens a politically correct stance to mask the fear of getting fat. Like the Queen Bee in *Jawbreakers* who announces "I wouldn't be caught dead eating a greasy pizza," dieting girls associate "grease" or the macronutrient fat with the body fat on their developing hips and rumps. They reject animal-based foods because it makes them feel "gross"; the revulsion toward the food is conflated with their horror at transferring extra fat to their bodies. No surprise then that research on the eating habits of female adolescents reveals compelling correlations between vegetarianism and disordered eating behaviors, with one study of high school girls finding that vegetarians were twice as likely to be frequent dieters, four times as likely to be purgers, and a startling eight times as likely to be laxative abusers.[9]

Driving all these efforts to control body weight and shape is the powerful force of adolescent sexual development. The social equation established in teen movies is no longer merely that popularity equals being thin and pretty; it also requires being sexually desirable. This is the visual message delivered in *Jawbreakers'* opening montage of a girl's scrapbook collage featuring slogans such as "Be Hot" and "Most Wanted," which then cuts to a shot of the reigning girl clique as they stride down the high school corridor displaying big earrings, tight skirts, stiletto heels, and lots of cleavage.

Figure 6.6. Courtney's clique makes their entrance in *Jawbreaker*.

In this and most other teen movies the "Queen Bees" of the school are depicted as seductive and sexually adventurous, eager to demonstrate their sophistication and offer sexual favors to their boyfriends in images more reminiscent of porn movies than high school dating rituals.

While the famously successful *American Pie* could be dismissed as a wet dream fantasy for adolescent boys, for female viewers it vividly demonstrates the power of the girl who is a sexual sophisticate.[10] Jim, the least experienced of a group of four high school buddies determined to lose their virginity before graduation, invites the willowy exchange student Nadia to his bedroom which has been secretly wired by his friends for instant Internet video distribution of his inept attempts at sexual intercourse. Shots of this comic enterprise taking place in Jim's bedroom are juxtaposed not only with shots of his cheering male classmates all over town eagerly watching what is essentially a porn movie on their computers but also by other shots depicting groups of girls gazing at what for them is more of a training film.

The role of "Nadia" is played by a twenty-six-year-old actress (Shannon Elizabeth) whose prior career included stints as a model in both *Playboy* and *Maxim* men's magazines. Her voluptuous body and seductive skills may serves as a compelling role model for the adolescent viewer

Figure 6.7. Courtney seduces her high school boyfriend in her bedroom.

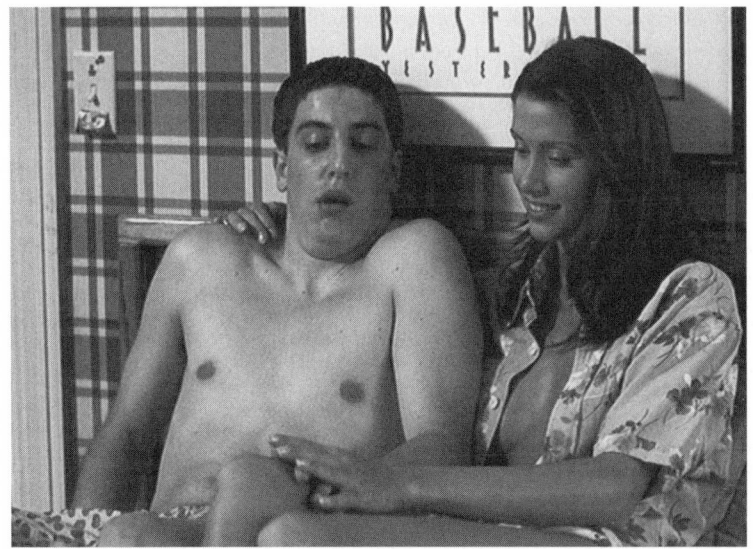

Figure 6.8. Jim and Nadia "live" in his bedroom in *American Pie* . . . .

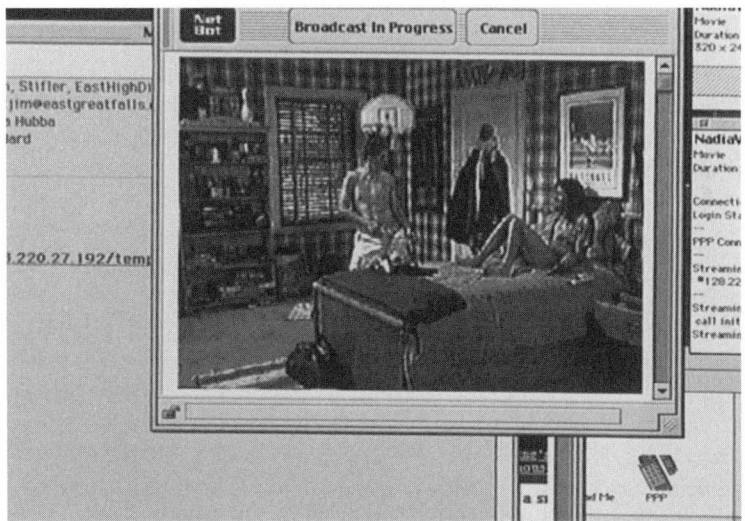

Figure 6.9. . . . and online.

but establishes an expectation far beyond many teens' understanding and capacity. Meghan, a junior in my course, talked about the way in which this particular scene affected her own early sexual encounters:

> When I was a freshman in high school my girlfriends and I would watch that scene in American Pie where Nadia strips and starts masturbating in Jim's room and all the boys watching go wild. We would practice stripping like that but our boobs just weren't that huge and anyway the rest of her was so thin and amazing. Anyhow I figured if I acted like I knew how to do stuff like she did boys would start drooling over me too. Of course when I finally got into a bedroom with this guy at this party I got really scared because I had to pretend I had done everything before and I really didn't know how to do what he wanted, which grossed me out anyway.

Hollywood films about the raging hormones of adolescence tell teen viewers that the route to being in the know—signaling your social savvy and sophistication—is not through academic achievement or autonomous self-expression but through sexing the body with breasts, bellies, and butts revealed for display. And just as Hollywood makeover movies and reality shows promise poise and confidence as the reward for cosmetic transformation, so too do teen movies and television programs, music videos, and fashion magazines link social ease to the display of sexual sophistication.[11] But a far different connection is made by a report issued by the American Psychological Association Task Force on the Sexualization of Girls warning that the heightened sexual objectification of girls in entertainment and commercial media actually results in low self-esteem, depression, as well as higher risk for eating disorders.[12] Media critics have noted the correlation between increased exposure to sexual content on television (where typical teenage viewers get to see more than two thousand sexual acts per year), magazine advertisements, and music videos with early sexual activity.[13] Of still greater concern is that these eroticized media images serve as a form of social coercion, urging ever younger girls to perform sexually not because of their own desire but to please their boyfriends. The proliferation of "sexting" images through which girls circulate photographs of themselves and their friends in provocative poses is but the most recent response to this kind of environment. Citing these trends, educators and parents' consumer watchdog groups worry about the disappearance of childhood innocence into a "pseudo-adulthood"[14] in which "before they even abandon their teddy bears contemporary girls embrace the erotic."[15] Media researchers point out that young consumers lack the cognitive awareness to notice the "stealth marketing" techniques used to promote products embedded in movies and television shows.[16] The same marketing mantra to "grow a consumer" that led to advertisements aimed at the tween demographic has more recently targeted a niche of even younger girls known as "pre-tweens" who are between five and eight years old and are the biggest consumers of such beauty products as glitter, nail polish, and lip gloss. A strategic marketing consultant cynically notes that the growth of this "starter market" is driven by a culture of "insta-celebrity. . . . Our little girls now grow up thinking they need to be ready for their close-up [when] the paparazzi arrive."[17] Just as high school girls regularly get nose jobs and breast surgery for graduation, five-year-olds are celebrating their birthdays with a "primping party" at mall chains like Club Libby Lu and Sweet & Sassy. And if little girls are hanging out at the spa, their toy dolls are keeping up with them. Barbie dolls, once the glamorous staple of girlhood, have been superseded by Bratz fashion dolls which come equipped with such sexy wardrobe accessories as micro-miniskirts studded with rhinestones, "Bad Girl" tight-T-shirts, biker tattoo tank tops, fishnet stockings and enough makeup to equip a cadre of call girls. Given the lure of such a toy, it is no wonder that attempts to offer "healthier choices" such as the "Happy to Be Me doll" designed with more ample waist and hip measurements than either Barbie or Bratz dolls have flopped.

No surprise either that with the ever-earlier sexualization of girl's media images and role models, shows such as "The Baby Borrowers" have recently made their way into the reality television market. In this format teenage couples, inspired in part by celebrity teen pregnancies such as that of Britney Spears's seventeen-year-old sister, get to rehearse for impending parenthood by setting up house and taking care of an infant. (Significantly, one would-be teen mom burst into tears at the indignity of having to spend twenty-four hours dressed in a "pregnancy simulator" fat suit!). The alluring vision of accelerated adulthood also accounts for the commercial success of the teen movie *13 Going on Thirty* (2004), which cast Jennifer Garner as an unpopular school girl who gets her wish to skip over the rest of a painful adolescence by flash forwarding to adulthood where she has become a single professional woman working at a fashion magazine and living a glamorous life in New York City. The trend is another reason why adult "chick flicks" such as *Bridget Jones Diary* and *Legally Blonde* are equally popular with teen audiences eager for glimpses of the adult lifestyle they often await so impatiently.

Increasingly early exposure to adult body and beauty culture is only one part of the larger picture of adolescence, a period when sexuality, eating behavior, and body image interact with biological, social, and economic realities. The biggest biological factor is puberty itself, which often results in girls developing sexual bodies before the other parts of their make up—emotional, cognitive, experiential—have a chance to catch up. The earlier girls reach menarche the greater their risk for developing eating disorders: if girls go through puberty before age eleven (and for Caucasian girls the average age of menarche is trending to age ten), research shows that they are more worried than their prepubescent friends about their body shape and size and more anxious about eating the foods they loved in childhood. Add to this the hormonal and neurochemical changes in adolescence, which often lead to turbulent mood swings and impulsive behaviors, and we get a perfect storm in which chubby girls crash diet and learn to purge, desperate girls get hooked on steroids and diet pills, and diabetic girls stop taking their insulin for fear of gaining weight.[18] For today's pubescent girls, biology is at odds with contemporary body image ideals, troubling their relationship with both food and weight. While boys' hormonal development makes their bodies muscular and tall, naturally aligning them with the "buff" masculine ideal of hunky movie stars and celebrity jocks, it's just the opposite for girls: getting fleshier hips, thighs, abdomens, and buttocks may have been accepted as nature's time-honored way of preparing a girl's body for childbearing in the past but today it can be an infuriating and frustrating detour from the slim hips, narrow waist, straight thighs, and long tapered legs of the feminine body ideal circulated in popular media.

Teen movies and other mainstream media construct social sophistication as not just looking sexy but *acting* ready to "party." As a result the adolescent girl is pressured to become sexually active before gaining the emotional maturity and assertiveness skills she needs to negotiate the welter of confusing feelings about sexual experience and expression. With both her developing body and emotions spinning out of control she may grab onto an illusory sense of control over her body weight and diet. The imposition of overly strict food restrictions, however, may soon lead to explosive bouts of binge eating, while frantic attempts to regain control through purging and overexercising can only push her farther into the vicious cycle of eating disordered behavior. Lindsey, a twenty-five-year-old hair stylist who has been in treatment for bulimia for the past two years, recalled a similar kind of sexual history:

> When I was in middle school I was never popular with the boys until I got my period and my breasts got really huge. It made me kind of embarrassed but at the same time I thought being sexy was cool—guys want you and you get attention, just like in the movies and MTV music videos. So I would do anything with anybody. Later though I started to feel really bad about myself—you know, kind of used, and then the kids in my school started calling me "slut." I felt so messed up inside I began to eat tons of junk food and then throw it up, kind of to get rid of the bad feelings I stuffed down along with the cookies and ice cream.

Just as confusion and ambivalence about being sexually attractive to boys can trigger these kind of bulimic behaviors in some young girls, the reaction to male criticism and rejection of their bodies may lead others to overeating as they seek solace in food from the resulting hurt and anger. Often it can lead to the behavioral disorder of emotional eating, where food is continually used to anaesthetize painful feelings, like a psychological Band-Aid. Teasing by boyfriends, fathers, or brothers about a developing girl's "thunder thighs" or "hippo hips" can send her on a desperate quest to regain their approval of her body, as it did for another patient named Andrea, a financial analyst who describes herself as a chronic emotional overeater. Now in her forties, she traced her eating and weight history to just such an experience in adolescence:

> In junior high school I had a huge crush on this guy Mike. He teased me about getting a big belly so to get rid of it I just stopped eating, pretty much just drank water and some juice. By the end of the week I lost six pounds. I remember my friends staring at my flat belly and saying "You look

sooo skinny!" I was so excited; God, it really was pathetic. But when I called Mike to tell him I was thinner, he still dumped me. He probably was dating other girls the whole time anyway. For weeks after that I would crawl into bed with a box of graham crackers and peanut butter, just trying to comfort myself. It's been that way ever since with me and food and men. When I'm in a relationship with someone I stop bingeing and usually lose weight—then it ends and I'm back to my old love-hate relationship with food.

Complicating the adolescent girl's struggle with emerging sexuality and other developmental challenges is the shift away from reliance on her parents as the primary source of guidance. Movies for and about teen life serve a transitional function during this period by taking on a kind of parental or authorial voice, presenting young viewers with cinematic role models for peer social values and codes of conduct. But more seductive is Hollywood's appeal to teen fantasies of a peer-driven world free from adult intrusion in which parents are either "disappeared" or marginalized as shadowy figures who pay the bills and open their palatial homes and their bars for all-night bashes for their kids and their friends. When parents do appear at all they are either benign onlookers like Cady's parents in *Mean Girls* or hopelessly inept like Jim's father in *American Pie*, who tries to initiate his son into sex by sharing his *Hustler* magazines and embarrassing him with heart to heart talks about masturbation and erections. By far the sharpest satire in *Mean Girls* is saved for the character of Regina's mother, who dresses in the same pink outfits as the Plastics and tries to "bond" with them much to her daughter's utter disdain. "You guys" she gushes, are "my best friends." Announcing that she is a "cool mom" she passes out Happy Hour drinks to the girls and assures them: "There are no rules in this house."

While mothers may be absurd or irrelevant in Hollywood's Girlworld, in reality they play a crucial role in the generational transmission of the very attitudes and practices that can make their daughters either resilient or vulnerable to eating disorders. Both clinical research and anecdotal experience have confirmed time and again the relationship between mothers' weight concerns and dieting behavior and the development of eating and body image disorders in adolescent girls.[19] The figure of Regina's mother, who has "boobs as hard as a rock" from

Figure 6.10. Happy hour with *Mean Girls'* cool mom.

her latest breast surgery and heartily endorses her daughter's grooming obsession, is but a grotesque caricature of the enmeshed relationship in which the boundaries between mother and daughter are confused by the transmission of body preoccupation. Theresa, a fifty-three-year-old management consultant, connects her ongoing diet and weight battles to a complicated food relationship with her mother:

> As far back as I can remember my mother was always on a diet—or more often off it. She'd lock up the cookies in a cabinet but at night I could hear her sneaking downstairs to get them; in the morning they'd be gone. When I was six she put me on a diet too and taught me to count the calories and fat grams of everything in the house. Later we went to Weight Watchers together—I lost track of how many times we stopped and started—and cheated together on the "illegal" food. I guess you could say long after the umbilical cord was cut we were bonded by the scale.

In identifying for her daughter just what is "for her own good" the mother thus transmits both the contemporary body ideal and the imperative of dietary control and restraint—as well as the dominant cultural definition of femininity. Speaking to the enmeshment of mother/daughter psychic boundaries in classic maternal melodramas, film scholar E. Ann Kaplan has written about "the difficulty of separating the Mother's desire from the daughter's needs. Mothers who are closely bonded positively with their daughters often identify their own desires with what is good for the daughter, as that has been defined by patriarchal culture."[20] Thus, the quest of the adolescent girl to define her own needs about her size and shape hits up against her mother's definitions of what is good for her daughter as it is prescribed by conventional cultural ideals. The difficult conflicts that arise as the child struggles to break free from these bonds while holding on to the support and love of her family is the real stuff of adolescence—but not of Hollywood movies. Teen films are not constructed to show the complexity of the "push-pull" separation process between parent and child in adolescence, just as they refuse to explore the other thorny issues of the adolescent girl's journey to adulthood—sexual orientation, anger, and identity confusion or the expressive possibilities beyond the conventional social currency of good looks and popularity. Films that seek to address these powerful realities are found instead in the "independent" cinema, which produces the alternative visions of the female body we will encounter in the next and final chapter.

7

Alternative Visions

By now it is all too clear that with very few exceptions Hollywood movies, especially popular film genres such as teenpics and chic flix targeting the youth and female market, are designed to encourage and promote the values of eating disordered culture. Throughout the book we have identified and examined the cinematic structures with which they create this problematic effect: First, by recruiting film conventions that "shoot" the woman's body as a surface image displayed not just for the male spectator's pleasure but for the female spectator's inspiration; Second, by privileging bodies that are uniformly tall and slender, presumably naturally endowed with taut skin and toned limbs, very flat "abs" and voluptuous breasts; Third, by constructing within the film narrative the flawless body as the object of sexual desire and social power. Notably, these structures produce an aspirational image that is beyond the reach of most female spectators unless they restrain their appetites and commit to the rigorous "work" necessary to reshape their own bodies; makeover movies valorize this body work as a prerequisite for personal empowerment and liberation in a Hollywood version of "feminism lite." And finally, while these films typically tack on dutiful messages about inner beauty and self-acceptance, such sermons are only skin deep—as shallow in fact as the bewitched hero of *Shallow Hal*. Thus, through cinematic devices of enchantment designed to disarm our critical faculties these Hollywood genre movies ultimately both create and sustain the established values of a culture based on externality and body dissatisfaction.

Happily, the outlook for contemporary cinema is not completely dismal. Recent decades have witnessed the emergence of a number of independent films that successfully resist Hollywood's one-size-should-fit-all image of the woman's body. Instead of glossy surfaces and facile feel-good endings, these more socially resonant films interrogate the experience of being born female into a looks-obsessed culture. The screen images they construct thus provide new sources of empathy and identification for adolescent girls and women at the same time that they provoke challenges to the dominant body ideals and values promoted by Hollywood and other popular media. Instead of reassuring us that a good makeover will solve our problems or a great dress will guarantee everlasting happiness, these independent films—some outrageous and transgressive, others thoughtful and more subtly subversive—reject easy explanations and neat resolutions, destabilizing viewers' expectations with ambiguity or disturbing their complacency with harsh images indicting American weight obsessions and narcissism, the realities of living in a large body, or the anguish and confusion of growing into puberty and sexual awareness. Distributed outside the mainstream multiplex and corporate studios these "indie" films typically are first screened at art houses and film festivals and later reappear on the Internet and in DVD format, thereby allowing many of them to "cross over" and reach wider audiences than when they are initially released. Through such outlets films such as *Thirteen* (2003) Catherine Hardwicke's dark evocation of a troubled girl's sexual initiation, and Todd Solondz's *Welcome to the Dollhouse* (1995), an unblinking look at the brutal rejection of its nerdy middle school heroine, have provided access to alternative visions of adolescence far from the sanitized pink and pretty world of Hollywood teen pics, while Solondz's still more transgressive film *Happiness* (1998), with its unforgettable depiction of a desperately lonely obese binge eater has gone on to develop a cult following. The films discussed here are but a small sample of this rich body of work, selected precisely because they counter the conventions of the Hollywood genre films represented in the previous chapters—specifically the makeover movie, coming-of-age teen pic, and romantic comedies about the outsize woman.

Nicole Holofcener's *Lovely and Amazing* (1999) embeds its deadpan critique of cultural narcissism and body insecurity within the domestic tale of an affluent West Coast family of four women.[1] The film's narrative is organized around the liposuction surgery undergone by Jane (Brenda Blethyn), a single midlife mother who has raised Elizabeth (Emily Mortimer), a would-be actress who worries that she is insufficiently sexy, and Michelle (Catherine Keener), an unhappily married stay-at-home mom who bitterly dwells on her former success as high school homecoming queen. Jane has also adopted Annie, a chubby eight-year-old

African American girl who tells people that her biological mother was a "crackhead" and is badgered by her adoptive family to stop eating cookies—even though she protests that they're fat free. Unexpectedly, Jane's surgery goes terribly awry with a postoperative sepsis from which she only narrowly recovers. During her hospitalization, each daughter's life goes through additional upheavals: Elizabeth, an inveterate animal rescuer, is bitten on the face by a stray dog, leaving her with stitches on her lip and her acting career in jeopardy; Michelle is arrested for having a tryst with an underage boy, and Annie runs away from home in search of junk food.

Set in the heart of southern California's entertainment and consumer beauty culture, the characters move on the periphery of a world populated by cynical agents and cutthroat competitors at casting auditions, all of whom scramble to be seen at the right parties with the right people. Here the film's *mise-en-scène* is designed not as a seductive high fashion fantasy like *The Devil Wears Prada* but as a grim reflection of a contemporary social order driven by celebrity images and body preoccupation. The female characters' restless dissatisfaction with their outward appearance is matched by equally unsatisfying relationships in which they continually miss out on the possibility of meaningful connection; instead of making eye contact with each other or their boyfriends and spouses they gaze distractedly at a series of circulating images—the television screen, Elizabeth's promotional spread in a fashion magazine, the prints in the "one stop photo" shop where Michelle finally lands a job—and most insistently at the images in the mirror where they nervously inspect their reflections. Within the female sensibility that permeates this world men either mysteriously disappear like Jane's husband, who abandoned the family years ago, prove unfaithful like Michelle's husband, who has an affair with her best friend, or finally get exasperated by the women's body obsession and move on, like Elizabeth's frustrated boyfriend. Most of all *Lovely and Amazing* is about the loss of self-integration each woman experiences as she seeks to "fix" her appearance, mistaking body image for a true sense of identity. This psychological disconnection is vividly captured by the film's very first image: Elizabeth is posing for a magazine "shoot" wearing a black dress and bright red lipstick. As a camera clicks away, she nervously asks the offscreen fashion photographer whether she is wearing too much makeup. Unconvinced by his reassuring response that she looks "totally hot," she stares down at the see-through dress, which exposes her breasts, shifts with discomfort and murmurs: "I just don't feel like myself," to which the disembodied male voice coolly responds: "Who does?"

The film's commentary on the compulsive body insecurity and self-scrutiny signaled here finds fullest expression in a remarkable scene during which Elizabeth, who has just made love with fellow actor Kevin (Dermot Mulroney) steps out of the bed and stands naked before him. She plaintively asks him—as a "favor"—to assess her entire body: "You're going to tell me everything that's wrong with me." Reluctant at first, the man protests that he "hardly knows her," as if the sexual intimacy they have just shared is far less important than this transaction; in the looks-based world in which they both operate, revealing body flaws is the true intimacy and point of connection. He soon warms to his task, appraising her entire body from her breasts—"perfect from the front but a little droopy from the side"—to her smile—"really sweet but your teeth are a little yellow"—and at the end, marvels at what has been a "refreshing" experience—even better, it would seem, than sex.

While it is easy to read the scene as yet another cinematic enactment of the power of the male gaze to objectify the woman, it is still more expressive of the chronic body anxiety and insecurity that

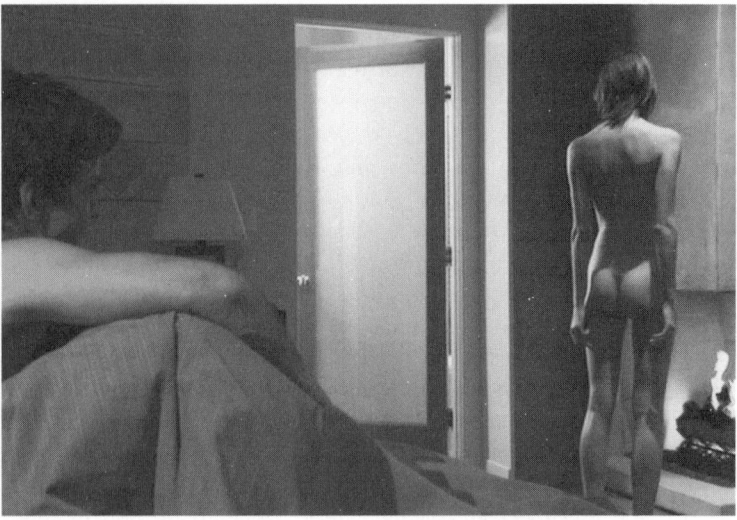

Figure 7.1. Elizabeth stands for her body assessment in *Lovely and Amazing*.

accounts for Elizabeth's willing submission to external sources of validation. In other words, the woman is far less victimized and far more complicit in her body objectification here than feminist film theory would suggest, a potent reflection of how contemporary fitness and beauty norms drive female aspirations and behavior. During the scene's shot-countershot sequence the camera moves from Kevin still in the bed gazing at Elizabeth to her body framed against a soft fireplace light; the viewer sees her image as genuinely "lovely and amazing" but one which Elizabeth herself can only see as deeply flawed and imperfect. Rather than eroticizing the woman's image the film is more interested in emphasizing the dissonance between Elizabeth's actual loveliness and the critique she requests from her new lover. The dissonance serves too as an eloquent reminder of the chronic body image distortion that eating disordered women bring to their own reflections in the mirror as part of a troubled relationship to their size and shape. The final exchange in the scene underscores the emptiness of a life dedicated to body preoccupation: Elizabeth asks, "Is there anything else?" and Kevin answers, "No, that's probably about it." We are left to wonder if indeed there really *is* anything else beyond her body image with which she can define a true self.

With equal toughness, *Lovely and Amazing* exposes the damaging effects of generational transmission of this culture of narcissism in its depiction of Annie, whose identification with her white, economically privileged family is complicated not only by her little girl chubbiness but by her black skin. Echoing the media mantra about body makeovers, mother Jane describes her forthcoming liposuction to the curious Annie as a "procedure to look better and feel better about myself." "It's an improvement," she adds, for her "old and wrinkled and saggy" skin. The mother thus provides a model for the child's fantasy of her own body transformation, which Annie goes on to articulate: "I want to tear my skin off . . . I want it to look the same as yours." Just as her mother is filled with self-loathing by her aging skin and the "yellow puffy lumpy fat" that lies beneath it, so too her daughter yearns to "improve" her appearance by violently shedding her skin and with it her racial identity to look like her adoptive white family. After she gets an opportunity to straighten her hair Annie stares at her round little girl face in the mirror, anxiously appraising her new look as she applies purple eye shadow and glitter in a sad and grotesque caricature of her big sisters who allow her to tag along at a Hollywood cocktail party. At age eight, Annie has learned both the self-hatred and worried self-scrutiny of her adopted culture.

Meanwhile, her mother's reach for body transformation proves to be a nightmare. In sharp contrast to Hollywood makeover mythologies, Jane's romantic fantasies about her attractive cosmetic surgeon and the "reward" of a size eight dress are dashed as she barely escapes with her life in a humiliating and painful experience. In stark contrast to the Cinderellas of *Maid in Manhattan* and other makeover movies, no Prince Charming or magical life transformation awaits her upon her return home. What she does find, however, is that the ordeal has strengthened the bond between the members of her fractured family. The three sisters come out from under their self-absorption to a renewed sense of love and connection as they welcome their mother home from the hospital, while the film gently hints at the possibility that each has discovered within their sisterhood something more meaningful than the quest for a better body.

Like *Lovely and Amazing*, Patricia Cardoso's 2002 film *Real Women Have Curves* made its way into distribution via independent film festivals, but only after a decade-long search for a production company willing to take on an "ethnic" film featuring relatively unknown actors and starring

Figure 7.2. Annie contemplates her image.

a novice whose buxom body would be deemed "fat" by Hollywood's Draconian standards. As one film reviewer noted, "In the casting of the heroine with a new actress (America Ferrara) whose body does not conform to the gruesome anorectic standards of teen stars, Cardoso offers an answer to the demands of the heroine to see her as a subject. 'I am not just a body. I have thoughts. I have a mind.'"[2] In fact, Ferrara was one of the few candidates for the lead role who actually fulfilled the production's casting call for an "overweight" actress; the majority of women who came to audition perceived themselves to be fat but in reality were too slender for the role![3] The film's low-budget/low-tech production values belie its ambitious project: to capture in its powerful and moving coming-of-age narrative not simply an adolescent girl's initiation into womanhood but also her battle to break free from the constraints of the cultural and family traditions that seek to control her sexuality and her weight. It succeeds in presenting a wise understanding of generational conflicts around body regulation as well as the ethnic woman's struggle to rise economically and educationally—all without lapsing into Hollywood's formulaic renditions of making it in America. This complex task is accomplished through a simple story arc: when eighteen-year-old Ana (America Ferrara), a Mexican American high school senior from East Los Angeles, is offered a scholarship to Columbia University her family insists that instead she stay home to work in her older sister's dress factory, lose weight, and set her sights on getting married. The film follows both Ana's internal conflict about leaving her tight-knit community as well as the stormy confrontations with her controlling and possessive mother as she struggles to make the separation that will determine her ability to truly "come into her own."

In sharp contrast to *Maid in Manhattan*, which can't seem to escape fast enough from Marisa Ventura's Bronx barrio to luxuriate in its setting of posh downtown hotels and red carpet galas, here the film's establishing shots linger long and lovingly on the compelling bright colors, Latin rhythms and street dialect of a coherent ethnic community. It renders the faces, storefronts, and factories of East Los Angeles so vividly that the setting itself becomes an important character in the film—not merely for nostalgic reasons (both the film's director and screenplay writer grew up in this particular neighborhood) but to firmly establish Ana in the embrace of a community that nourishes her, thus dramatizing and reifying her aching dilemma as she imagines leaving it behind. The unsettling transition from childhood to adulthood that marks adolescence is mirrored by Ana's journey from her Mexican immigrant neighborhood to the easy affluence of the larger Anglo culture beyond; both these developmental and cultural transitional spaces are visualized by the bridge she traverses by bus from East LA to her high school in Beverly Hills. In contrast, the predictable Hollywood makeover magic of *Maid in Manhattan* dramatizes Marisa's cultural assimilation as an effortless and instantaneous transformation (*not* a transition) from first-generation hotel maid to society gala princess—all without skipping a beat of the waltz. And while Marisa' s social aspirations are achieved by the right ball gown, Ana and her fellow workers spend their days laboring in a sweaty and dusty factory sewing and ironing those gowns, clothes seemingly beyond Ana's reach not only economically but also—as her mother is quick to point out—because she could never fit into them.

The film departs still more radically from the conventions of the Hollywood teen pic genre in which middle and high schoolers occupy a parent-free zone, neatly eliminating from consideration the very real family conflicts that emerge in adolescence. In *Real Women Have Curves* it is precisely this conflict—as Ana and her mother negotiate the tension between her desire for protection and safety and her desire for freedom and self-definition—that lies at the very heart of the film. Ana's midlife mother Carmen (Lupe Ontiveros) is deeply rooted both in her Mexican traditions of Spanish soap operas, religious rituals, and household icons as well as in her conservative convictions about femininity and sexual regulation. Carmen's aspirations for her daughter are inseparable from her own life experience as a woman who has labored in factories and labored to give birth to her children—her proudest accomplishment. She is terrified to face not only Ana's blossoming womanhood but also the loss of her own procreative function; refusing to accept that she has reached menopause Carmen insists instead that she is pregnant—much to the frustration of her sexually more knowing daughter. For Ana this mother is a source of repression seeking to oppose her own energy for freedom and adventure, a containment symbolized throughout the film in images of entrapment—bar-covered windows and grates, caged lovebirds, and the cramped spaces of the family apartment where personal and spatial boundaries and privacy are all too permeable: Ana sits at the kitchen table trying to compose her college application distracted by the TV, music, street noises and the chatter of her relatives flowing around her—just as Carmen violates

Ana's bodily boundaries by poking at her "fat" and intruding on her daughter's exploration of her sexuality.

The mother/daughter battle centers in part around Carmen's attempt to control Ana's virginity and her rage when Ana engages in her first sexual relationship with a high school boyfriend. But she is still more infuriated by Ana's weight. She constantly taunts her for her "enormous" size, calling her "fatty" and intoning dire warnings that she will become an old maid like her older sister Estella, oblivious to the fact that Ana is in reality no more overweight than Carmen herself. Ana suffers repeatedly (as do so many girls with a "weight problem") from the mantra of conditional acceptance that Carmen reiterates: "If you lost weight you could be beautiful!" Carmen insists that Ana obey another equally paradoxical edict regulating the girl's body: to be sexually attractive she must be slender but she must not dare satisfy her own sexual curiosity or desire until she has safely landed a husband. In other words, like generations of women before her Ana must learn to deny her own appetites for both food and sex. The film captures both the comic and all too serious nature of this tortured mother/ daughter bond around food and weight in a particularly memorable scene: Ana and Carmen sit at a café with a plate of flan before them,

Figure 7.3. Ana and her mother battle over dessert in *Real Women Have Curves*.

arguing about weight and marriageability. Carmen forbids Ana to take a bite—and the camera zooms in on the two pairs of eyes locked in a suspenseful showdown. The scene ends with a shot of Ana, in an eloquent gesture of defiance and self-assertion, popping a forkful of the forbidden dessert into her mouth.

But Ana's oppositional stance to her mother's regressive body politics is juxtaposed with displays of her deep affection and tenderness as she seeks to protect Carmen both from her lack of insight and her vulnerability in a culture she is not equipped to understand. The film mirrors Ana's ambivalence toward this difficult parent with scenes establishing Carmen as manipulative and emotionally blunted, oblivious to her envy of her daughter's youth and sensuality, but so incapacitated by her grief at Ana's eventual departure that she retreats to her bed, unable to come to the door to say good-bye.

Two key events in the narrative serve as the catalysts that finally free Ana from her enmeshed relationship with her mother and allow her to set off on her journey across the country to college. The first is the sexual initiation she shares with her equally virginal young boyfriend Jimmy. Unlike the teen pic's hypersexualized fantasies, which cast high schoolers as practiced porn stars, this film presents a far more credible reflection of the hesitancy and awkwardness of a first sexual encounter between two adolescent lovers. And unlike the Hollywood "Queen Bees" who collude with their own sexual objectification in the drive to "get" boys and enhance their social status, Ana displays genuine interest in the sensuality and ownership of her sexual body. When she decides she is ready to "lose" her virginity she insists to Jimmy that they keep the light on because she wants him to see her just as she is; she shares his appreciation of her body because she has the resilience not to internalize her mother's shaming judgment. And unlike Elizabeth's request for a postcoital critique from her lover in *Lovely and Amazing*, here Ana moves to the mirror to gaze at her reflection after she and Jimmy make love—clearly enjoying her own image and her body's newly discovered erotic capacities. With heightened confidence and pleasure in her body, Ana is now ready for the final act of body assertion, which marks the film's defining moment. This takes place at Estella's dress factory, where the summer heat has become so oppressive that Ana takes off her sweat-stained T-shirt, revealing her ample breasts and fleshy hips—much to her mother's horror. Ana's self-possession is infectious, however, and before long her three fellow workers have also stripped to their underwear, laughing and comparing their "cellulite" thighs and stretch marks with a mixture of camaraderie and relief at "letting it all hang out." Ana turns to her mother and announces triumphantly: "This is who we are Mama—real women."

The scene is clearly the film's "teaching moment," allowing Ana to articulate its message about body acceptance and rejection of conventional beauty culture: "How dare anybody tell me what I should look like or what I should be when there's so much more to me than just my weight!" Happily, the scene is rescued from sinking under the cinematic "weight" of its didactic burden by the women's playful humor and an infectious upbeat soundtrack; unlike the redemptive messages artificially appended to Hollywood films, here the political statement grows organically from the narrative and visual structures that have so vividly realized the world in which these "real women" live and work and love. And while the film's final image of a more stylishly dressed Ana walking through the streets of Manhattan (a shot reminiscent of *The Devil Wears Prada*) might seem a capitulation to the Hollywood feel-good ending, Ana's confident stride appears more a function of a credible psychological maturation into adult womanhood than the high fashion makeover that transforms Andy.

Figure 7.4. Letting it all hang out at the dress factory.

The film's ending can also be read as a commentary on the nature of cultural as well as developmental transitions. While Ana's liberation from her mother's repressive traditions might derive from her exposure to more progressive American models of sexual freedom and intellectual equality, she refuses to adopt the weightism and narrowly defined body ideal of her assimilated culture.[4] This oppositional stance carries particular resonance in view of the research data cited earlier documenting the recent rise of body dissatisfaction and compensatory eating disordered behaviors in Hispanic women and girls.[5] In this regard, it is also interesting to note that America Ferrara went on to star in the acclaimed television series *Ugly Betty*, adapted from a Colombian *telenovela* originally aired on Spanish-language Telemundo. Some social critics have seen her character Betty Suarez as emblematic of the marginalized position of her ethnic identity, claiming that she is "a metaphor for US Latinos in general and their standing as 'ugly ducklings' in US society . . . the unacknowledged parenthetical presence that stands for Latinas and Latinos in few positions of power."[6] But many Latina viewers report they are happy to identify with a dark and "average" looking heroine from Queens and were inspired by Betty's refusal to appropriate the high fashion beauty standards of her upscale Manhattan workplace.

It is more difficult to find inspirations for positive identification in cinematic images of the obese woman. While we have noted earlier the subversive power of the figure of the unruly woman in such incarnations as the Muppet Miss Piggy and television's Roseanne, she has remained mostly on the margins when it comes to full-length feature films.[7] She is more likely to be found in the work of standup comedians and performance artists who enact outrageous "over the top" exaggerations of fatness and the diet culture that fears it.[8] Their performances reconfigure the outsize woman as a politically active agent opposing conventional body culture rather than as a passive victim of weightism; in this reframing she is a "revolting" body not because she is an object of disgust but rather a transgressive figure of social revolution who unapologetically indulges her appetites for both food and sexual pleasure.[9]

It is this iconoclastic spirit that informs the utopic vision of director John Waters's 1988 *Hairspray*, a relatively unknown film until it was resurrected first as a Broadway musical and most recently as a big-budget Hollywood movie (*Hairspray*, 2007) featuring well-known stars

John Travolta and Queen Latifah. Set in segregated 1963 Baltimore, the original film uses the racial integration of the "Corny Collins" television teen dance show to upend white establishment reactionary institutions in an antic fantasy of justice and social equality where both weightists and racists get their just deserts. The rebellion is spearheaded by Tracy Turnblad (Ricky Lake) a very short and rotund high school girl who manages to beat out the competition to win both the show's dancing prize as well as the school's heartthrob Link Larkin as she forges an alliance with the kids on the "Negro" side of town to introduce "colored music" to the show. But the film's most unruly "woman" of all is Edna Turnblad, Tracy's obese mother, here played by Divine, the drag artist whose riotously campy performance challenges not only racial and weight prejudices but conventional gender constructions as well. As Angela Stukator notes, the excessive body of the unruly woman such as the one depicted in this film serves to express "a revolutionary cultural politics, one that releases the body from the restrictions of socially sanctioned gendered, racial, and sexual roles."[10]

An interesting effect of the liberating possibilities of the radical vision of Waters's *Hairspray* was documented in one of the very few controlled media exposure studies conducted with film to date. College students were shown two film clips: one depicting the slender actress Olivia Newton-John dancing in the musical *Grease* (1978) and the other showing Ricky Lake in a dance number from *Hairspray.* Although the study subjects were exposed to just a few moments of footage, the results were striking—as well as statistically significant: based on a battery of body image and body satisfaction scales the female students (but not the males) showed considerably more body dissatisfaction after seeing *Grease* than after seeing *Hairspray.*[11]

In its reincarnation as a Hollywood hit musical the original film's radicalism is recast as a predictably politically correct ode to racial harmony set in a fabricated Baltimore world of harmless "homogenized shininess,"[12] created by period sets and fashions, and glossy song and dance numbers. While Tracy Turnblad's spunky character and agile dancing succeed in offering another filmic image of a self-confident overweight young woman, Hollywood's depiction of her mother Edna is more regressive than progressive. This time the role is played by Travolta, who appears stiff and embarrassed to find himself not only in drag but encased in a fat suit. As with *Shallow Hal's* juxtaposition of the bloated fat suit image with that of the superslender Gwyneth

Paltrow here again the prosthetic device invites a cruel contrast with Travolta's early performances as the lithe and leggy dancer in *Grease* and *Saturday Night Fever*. The film's construction of Edna Turnblad is thus more caricature than celebration of the big woman, notwithstanding the insertion of such songs as "Big Blonde and Beautiful" as anthems to her self-confidence and charm. Still more harshly stereotypical are moments in the film where Edna is helplessly seduced by platters of soul food and doughnuts, suggesting once again the monstrous nature of the fat woman's body and her compulsive appetites.

The irresistible food is offered to Edna by Motormouth Maybelle, the leader of Baltimore's black community, played here by a stately Queen Latifah who tries to instill body confidence in the socially isolated Edna. Another iteration of the unruly woman has in fact been the "big black mama," whom Latifah represented in earlier roles as the intimidating prison matron Mama Morton in *Chicago* (2002) and as a downtrodden saleswoman transformed into a daring world adventurer and gourmet chef in *Last Holiday* (2006). While Latifah's offscreen image would appear to be equally provocative, an image cultivated by popular media emphasizing her "voluptuous" figure and powerful presence as a "spunky, ballsy, buxom lady," it is undercut by her prominent endorsements of the diet industry, which she credits for her much-publicized weight loss. Other representations of the big black woman that have appeared in mass marketed comedies such as *Diary of a Mad Black Woman* (2005) and the *Big Momma's House* series (2000; 2006) draw upon the aggressive boisterous energy of the unruly woman but fail to invest her with any genuine oppositional power, opting instead to conflate identities of gender, race, and weight by casting the "big mama" role as male actors wearing Latex fat suits. For the most part, then, film depictions of the outsize woman restrict her to the social margins, forcing us to wait for Hollywood to embrace a true body diversity, one that would "shrink" the monstrous big mama to a more human—and humanized—image on the cinema screen. Hopefully, the wait will not be too long.

Glossary of Terms

Several terms cited in this glossary are based on definitions provided in Keel, P. K. (2005) *Eating Disorders* (pp. 175–180). Upper Saddle River, NJ: Pearson Prentice-Hall.

Amenorrhea: The absence of menstrual periods for at least three consecutive months, without the aid of hormonal administration.

Anorexia Nervosa (AN): A condition characterized by a refusal to maintain normal body weight at or above 85 percent of normal weight for the given height and age, and although underweight, an extreme fear of becoming fat. Marked by body image disturbance as well as amenorrhea. Two subtypes of AN are recognized; Anorexia Nervosa restricting type (ANR) is characterized by severely limiting food intake to achieve weight loss; Anorexia Nervosa binge eating/purging type (ANBP) is characterized by intermittent binge eating and purging, in addition to the general AN diagnostic criteria.

Bariatric Surgery: A surgery performed on the stomach and/or intestines to restrict food intake and facilitate significant weight loss. The two most common methods are known as gastric bypass and gastric banding surgery.

Binge Eating: This behavior is characterized by eating an excessive amount of food, larger than most people would eat, in a limited time frame, accompanied with a sense of lack of control over what and how much one is eating. Binge eating appears in BN, BED, and SED.

Binge Eating Disorder (BED): A condition characterized by binge eating at least twice a week for at least six months, experiencing a lack of control during the binge episode, distress about bingeing, rapid eating, and eating alone. Unlike bulimia, no compensatory measures are performed in response to the binge episodes.

Body Dysmorphic Disorder (BDD): Extreme preoccupation with an imagined or exaggerated defect in appearance. The fixation is often the face, as well as skin, hips, breasts, and legs for women.

Bulimia Nervosa (BN): Characterized by repeated binge eating and repeated compensatory behaviors including self-induced vomiting and laxative abuse in order to prevent weight gain; episodes occur at least twice a week for at least three months. Self-evaluation is highly dependent on body shape and weight.

Cognitive Distortions: Patterns of thinking that fail to reflect objective reality. Some examples are dichotomous thinking (known commonly as black-and-white thinking), selective abstraction (imagining one part represents the whole), and rule-bound thinking, a highly rigid cognitive style.

Dietary Restraint: Eating and food choice behaviors organized around the intent to lose weight or prevent weight gain by strictly limiting food intake and avoiding high calorie foods.

Eating Disorder Not Otherwise Specified (EDNOS): A clinical diagnosis that includes all clinically significant disorders of eating that do not fully meet the diagnostic criteria for either AN or BN.

Emotional Eating: Using food to self-soothe uncomfortable affects or feelings or as distraction and anesthesia for anxiety or depression or anger.

Emotional Regulation: The ability to deny, intensify, weaken, curtail, or mask emotions in order to experience them without fluctuation that may interfere with the quality of life.

Enmeshment: A state in family dynamics when personal boundaries are overridden, most typically between parent and child.

Exercise Bulimia: A subtype of BN in which the compensatory behavior is a "non-purging" type, that is, excessive exercise is used to compensate for the binge episode in place of laxatives, purging, etc.

Menarche: The age at which girls experience their first menstrual period.

Muscle Dysmorphic Disorder (MDD): A body image disturbance characterized by perceiving one's own muscles as much smaller than they actually are, causing significant distress and efforts to increase muscle mass. It is often viewed as a type of Body Dysmorphic Disorder. It can also be referred to as Reverse Anorexia.

Obesity: Occurs when the Body Mass Index (BMI) is greater than or equal to 30. BMI is calculated based on height and weight.

Overweight degrees: The amount to which an individual is overweight, based on ranges of Body Mass Index. These are categorized as overweight (BMI of 25–29), obese class I (BMI of 30–35), obese class II (BMI of 35–40), and obese class III (BMI greater than 40).

Pro-ana: Short for pro-anorexia, these Web sites support anorexia as a lifestyle and not a disorder. They provide a community for those afflicted with AN to support their behaviors and share weight loss tips.

Psychoanalytic: The central assumption of this theory is that psychopathology arises from unconscious intrapsychic conflicts. This paradigm was originally developed by Sigmund Freud.

Psychodynamic Therapy: A therapy based on the theory that disorders arise from internal conflicts that the patient may not be aware of. The goal is for the therapist to facilitate insight by allowing the patient to explore symptoms and the possible meanings behind them.

Reverse Anorexia: Related to muscle dysmorphia, this typically occurs in males who believe that they cannot get "big" enough (usually in muscle size).

Socioeconomic Status: A combination of educational and professional attainment and income that determines a relative position in the community.

Sub-Clinical Eating Disorder (SED): On the spectrum of eating disorders, any practices of disordered eating that are significant but do not completely meet the diagnostic criteria of AN, BN, BED, or EDNOS.

Weightism: Prejudice or discrimination against people based on body weight.

Notes

Introduction

1. Schwartz, H. (1986). *Never satisfied: A cultural history of diets, fantasies and fat* (p. 26). New York: Free Press.

2. Many feminist cultural critics and historians have commented on this exchange of inner for outer value, including Jean Kilbourne's indictment of advertising's toxic effects on girls in *Deadly Persuasion*, in which she wryly noted "calories count more than character," and Joan Jacobs Brumberg who has traced how the measure of female character in Victorian America has been replaced by good looks. Kilbourne, J. (1999). *Deadly persuasion: Why women and girls must fight the addictive power of advertising.* New York: Free Press; Brumberg, J. J. (1997). *The body project: An intimate history of American girls.* New York: Random House.

3. Friedman, J., & Epstein, R. (Producers). (1996). *The celluloid closet* [Motion Picture]. United States: Telling Picture Productions.

4. Gates, P. (2006). Detecting men: Masculinity and the Hollywood detective film (p. 7). Albany: State University of New York Press.

5. See for example Griffiths, J. A., & McCabe, M. P. (2000). The influence of significant others on disordered eating and body dissatisfaction among early adolescent girls. *European Eating Disorders Review, 8*(4), 301–314; Rieder, S., & Ruderman, A. (2001). Cognitive factors associated with binge and purge eating behaviors: The interaction of body dissatisfaction and body image. *Cognitive Therapy and Research, 25*(6), 801–812; and Tylka, T. L. (2004). The relation between body dissatisfaction and eating disorder symptomatology: An analysis of moderating variables. *Journal of Counseling Psychology, 51*(2), 178–191, all of which found statistically significant correlations between reported body dissatisfaction and such behaviors as binge eating, purging, and food restriction among large samples of college women. Still more recently Trautmann et al. (2007) found body dissatisfaction to be a significant predictor of bulimia. Trautmann, J., Worthy, S. L., & Lokken, K. L. (2007). Body dissatisfaction, bulimic symptoms, and clothing practices among college women. *Journal of Psychology, 141*(5), 485–498.

6. Jean Kilbourne cites this statistic and other body size distribution studies in "Still Killing Us Softly: Advertising and the Obsession with Thinness," in Fallon, P. Katzman, M. & Wooley, S. C. (Eds.). (1994). *Feminist perspectives on eating disorders*. New York: The Guilford Press.

7. A similar phenomenon has long been observed in the fashion industry, where high fashion designers display clothes made for sizes as low as "double zero" while the average female consumer can only fit into sizes between size 8 and 16. This dissonance is driven by the fact, as one fashion magazine noted, that "much of fashion marketing is based on inspiring envy." Hall, A. (2008, October 19). The ultimate fashion faux pas. *The Boston Globe*, p. 8.

8. Writing about the literary tradition of the "Young Man from the Provinces Novel" critic Louis Menand offers a relevant description of the dangers of seductive illusions: "Although the world that glitters inside the gates is mostly a sham, you can lose your soul trying to get there. Something real is at stake in the pursuit of an illusion." Menand, L. (2008, September 29). Regrets only: Lionel Trilling and his discontents. *The New Yorker, 84*(30), 85.

9. Mulvey, L. (1975). Visual pleasure and narrative cinema. Reprinted in S. Thornham (Ed.) (1999). *Feminist film theory: A reader* (p. 62). New York: New York University Press.

10. For expanded discussion of the range of discourses about eating disorders, particularly the history of anorexia, see the work of cultural scholars Hepworth, J. (1999). *The social construction of anorexia nervosa*. London: Sage Publications, and Malson, H. (1998). *The thin woman: Feminism, post-structuralism and the social psychology of anorexia nervosa*. London: Routledge.

11. For recent genetic research see Klump, K. L. & Culbert, K. M. (2007). Molecular genetic studies of eating disorders: Current status and future directions. *Current Directions in Psychological Science, 16*(1), 37–41.

12. See the iconic work in this area by Bordo, S. (1993). *Unbearable weight: Feminism, western culture, and the body*. Berkeley: University of California Press; Orbach, S. (1979). *Fat is a feminist issue*. New York: Berkley Publishing; and Chernin, K. (1981). *The obsession: Reflections on the tyranny of slenderness*. New York: Harper & Row.

13. While early "media effects" research sought to blame mass media on a wide variety of social ills, especially violent behavior, subsequent cultural critics, sociologists, and communication theorists have shown that media interacts within a larger sociopolitical environment. See for example Barker, M., & Petley, J. (Eds.). (2001). *Ill effects: The media/violence debate* (2nd ed.). London: Routledge; and Weaver, C. K., & Carter, C. (Eds.). (2006). *Critical readings: Violence and the media*. Maidenhead: Open University Press, for various perspectives on this aspect of the media effects model in communications theory.

The controversy originated from mid-twentieth-century concerns about the possible dangerous audience effects of such "mass" media as radio and television in encouraging violence and copycat criminal behavior and consequent media censorship. As the debate extended to film it famously forced director Stanley Kubrick to withdraw his controversial film *A Clockwork Orange* (1971) from distribution to the public until his death in 2000. In his disavowal of his film's effects on viewers who claimed they had been inspired by the film, Kubrick declared: "To try to fasten any responsibility on art as the cause of life seems to me to put the case the wrong way around . . . to attribute powerful suggestive qualities to a film is at odds with the scientifically accepted view that . . . people cannot be made to do things which are at odds with their natures." Quoted in Duncan, P. (2008). *Stanley Kubrick: Visual poet* (p. 72). Los Angeles: Taschen. The media effects debate continues in today's age of Internet and videogames with many remaining unconvinced that violent media images have the kind of behavioral effects people initially feared. See Sonia Livingston, for example, in *Young people and new media: Childhood and the changing media environment* (2002). London: Sage; and the forthcoming *Children and the Internet: Great expectations and challenging realities.* Malden, MA: Polity Press.

14. Gauntlett, D. (2005). *Moving experiences: Media effects and beyond.* (2nd ed.) (p. 5). London: John Libbey.

15. Giles, D. (2003). *Media psychology* (p. 157). Mahwah, NJ: Lawrence Erlbaum. For an expanded discussion of this interaction between popular media and social environment in terms of cultivation theory see also chapter 2: "Theoretical Issues in Media Research."

16. The percentages cited here are "life-time prevalence" rates, referring to the percentage of women who at some point in their life had these diagnoses. While the rates increased in the second half of the twentieth century, they have not done so in the past decade. See Keel, P. K. (2005). *Eating disorders* (p. 4). Upper Saddle River, NJ: Pearson Prentice-Hall.

17. Bingeing and purging in one-third of college women, for example, is cited by Catherine Baker. (2003). *Fed up: College students and eating problems* (p.7). Carlsbad, CA: Gurze Books.

18. Croll, J., Neumark-Sztainer, D., Story, M., & Ireland, M. (2002). Prevalence and risk and protective factors related to disordered eating behaviors among adolescents: Relationship to gender and ethnicity. *The Journal of Adolescent Health: Official Publication of the Society for Adolescent Medicine, 31*(2), 166–175; and Neumark-Sztainer, D., Wall, M., Guo, J., Story, M., Haines, J., & Eisenberg, M. (2006). Obesity, disordered eating, and eating disorders in a longitudinal study of adolescents: How do dieters fare five years later? *Journal of the American Dietetic Association, 106*(4), 559–568.

19. Maine, M. (2000). *Body wars: Making peace with women's bodies* (p. 219). Carlsbad, CA: Gurze Books.

20. Robinson, T. N., Chang, J. Y., Haydel, K. F., & Killen, J. D. (2001). Overweight concerns and body dissatisfaction among third-grade children: The impacts of ethnicity and socioeconomic status. *The Journal of Pediatrics, 128*(2), 181–187.

21. Based on data from a nationally representative survey conducted in 2001–03, anorexia rates for males were .3 percent compared to .9 percent for females; bulimia rates were .5 percent for males and 1.5 percent for females. Hudson, J., Hiripi, E., Pope, H. G. Jr., & Kessler, R.C. (2007). The prevalence and correlates of eating disorders in the national comorbidity survey replication. *Biological Psychiatry, 6*(3), 348–350.

22. For a psychiatric description of these disorders see Pope, H. G. Jr., Gruber, A. J., Choi, P., Olivardia, R., & Phillips, K. A. (1997). Muscle dysmorphia: An underrecognized form of body dysmorphic disorder. *Psychosomatics, 38*, 548–557.

23. Neumark-Sztainer, D., Croll, J., Story, M., Hannan, P. J., French, S. A., & Perry, C. (2002). Ethnic/racial differences in weight-related concerns and behaviors among adolescent girls and boys: Findings from Project EAT. *Journal of Psychosomatic Research, 53*(5), 963–974.

24. Bojorquez, I., & Unikel, C. (2004). Presence of disordered eating among Mexican teenage women from a semi-urban area: Its relation to the cultural hypothesis. *European Eating Disorder Review, 12*(3), 197–202.

25. Eapen, V., Mabrouk, A. A., & Bin-Othman, S. (2006). Disordered eating attitudes and symptomatology among adolescent girls in the United Arab Emirates. *Eating Behaviors, 7*(1), 53–60.

26. Eddy, K. T., Hennessey, M., & Thompson-Brenner, H. (2007). Eating pathology in East African women: The role of media exposure and globalization. *The Journal of Nervous and Mental Disease, 195*(3), 196–202.

27. Goodman, E. (2004). *Paper trail: Common sense in uncommon times* (p. 204). New York: Simon & Schuster.

28. Becker, A. E., Burwell, R. A., Gilman, S. E., Herzog, D. B., & Hamburg, P. (2002). Eating behaviours and attitudes following prolonged exposure to television among ethnic Fijian adolescent girls. *The British Journal of Psychiatry: The Journal of Mental Science, 180*, 509–514.

29. Grabe, S., Hyde, J. S., & Ward, L. M. (2008). The role of the media in body image concerns among women: A meta-analysis of experimental and correlational studies. *Psychological Bulletin, 134*(3), 460–476. For additional reviews confirming validation of these findings see also *The media & body image* by Wykes, M., & Gunter, B. (2005). London: Sage Publications; and *Media psychology* by Giles, D. (2003). Mahwah, NJ: Lawrence Erlbaum.

30. For an overview of this particular research problem see Wykes, M., & Gunter, B. (2005) pp.168–170 and Grabe, et al. (2008).

31. Elizabeth Affuso, commenting on MTV's reality program *The Hills*, describes such "multitasking" by fans who watch the show while clicking on associated Web sites such as "Virtual Hills" where they can purchase products and dress their avatars in designer clothes from the show while listening to music on MTV. (2009). "Don't just watch it, live it"—technology, corporate

partnerships and *The Hills. Jump Cut, 51*. Retrieved June 24, 2009 from http://www.ejumpcut.org/currentissue/Hills-Affuso/index.html.

32. Wykes, M., & Gunter, B. (2005). p. 133.

33. See Wykes & Gunter chapters 7 and 9 for an expanded discussion of this heightened exposure response in clinical and subclinical subjects. They conclude: "At best, media images of the feminine body are politically oppressive and commercially exploitative. At worst, they may justify a young woman's efforts at self-annihilation." p. 219.

34. Tyler, P. (1999). Magic and myth of the movies. In Braudy, L., & Cohen, M. (Eds.), *Film theory and criticism* (p. 798). New York and Oxford: Oxford University Press.

35. *The Celluloid Closet* (1996).

36. One media analysis describes the role of this kind of "intertextuality" of images in the construction of the contemporary body ideal: "There are reinforcing body messages as the press prints stories about film stars, television follows up news in the morning papers, and the World Wide Web has sites for print news, broadcasting, and celebrities. So the media comprise an almost closed circle endlessly referring to the media. . . ." Wykes, M., & Gunter, B. (2005). p. 211.

37. For a fuller discussion of Marge's junk food consumption in the context of her unerotic domesticity see Kord, S., & Krimmer, E. (2005). *Hollywood divas, indie queens, & TV heroines* (pp. 135–138). Lanham, MD: Rowman & Littlefield.

38. Kales, E. (1991). Cognitive factors in eating behavior in bulimia. *Appetite, 17*, 209; Kales, E. (1989). A laboratory study of cognitive factors in bulimia: Abstinence violation effect. *Annals of the New York Academy of Sciences*, 535–537; Kales, E. (1987). Dieting to bulimia. *Psychology Today*, 21.

39. See the investigation into changes and effects of the male body ideal in a study of GI Joe action figure dolls and *Star Wars* characters in Pope, H. G., Olivardia, R., Gruber, A., & Borowiecki, J. (1999). Evolving ideals of male body image as seen through action toys. *International Journal of Eating Disorders, 26*, 65–72.

40. Readers will find such inquiry in Yvonne Tasker's well-known work *Spectacular bodies: Gender, genre, and the action cinema* (1993). London: Routledge, in which she examines the representations of masculinity as the muscle men "tough guys" of popular action movies.

41. Relevant to the notion of the female spectator as uncritical consumer of popular film, see the work of feminist scholar Mary Ann Doane in *The desire to desire*. (1987). Bloomington: Indiana University Press, on the "women's weepies," the precursor to Hollywood's "chick flix."

42. Tasker, Y., & Negra, D. (Eds.). (2005, Winter). In focus: Postfeminism and contemporary media studies. *Cinema Journal, 44*(2), 107.

Chapter 1. Body Identifications

1. U.S. Census data reported that only 20 percent of Americans were over age forty-five in the 1920s.

2. Cited in Addison, H. (2006). Must the players keep young?: Early Hollywood's cult of youth. *Cinema Journal, 45*(4), 17–19.

3. Addison, H. (2006). p. 19.

4. Kuhn, A. (1985). *The power of the image: Essays on representation and sexuality* (p. 13). London: Routledge.

5. See Moseley, R. (Ed.). (2005). *Fashioning film stars: Dress, culture, identity* (pp. 109–120). London: BFI Publishing.

6. Stacey, J. (1999). Feminine fascinations: Forms of identification in star-audience relations. In S. Thornham (Ed.), *Feminist film theory* (pp. 196–209). New York: New York University Press.

7. Stacey, J. (1999). p. 203.

8. Stacey, J. (1999). p. 206.

9. One major study, for example, found the degree of such internalization to be more predictive of body image disturbance than either the actual amount of media exposure or social awareness of the high status of slenderness. Cusamano, D., & Thompson, J. (1997). Body image and body shape ideals in magazines: Exposure, awareness, and internalization. *Sex Roles, 37,* 701–721.

10. See Mulvey, L. (1999). Visual pleasure and narrative cinema. In S. Thornham (Ed.), *Feminist film theory: A reader* (pp. 58–69). New York: New York University Press.

11. Mulvey, L. (1999). p. 63.

12. Mulvey, L. (1999). p. 61.

13. Wood, J. V. (1989). Theory and research concerning social comparisons of personal attributes. *Psychological Bulletin, 106,* 231–248. Cited in Giles, D. (2003). *Media psychology* (p. 157). Mahwah, NJ: Lawrence Erlbaum. Media exposure researchers using models from social comparison theory have found associations between individual susceptibility, particularly among adolescent girls, to sociocultural appearance conventions and pressures and higher degrees of body dissatisfaction following exposure to slender media images. For additional discussion of social comparison theory and media exposure studies see Wykes, M., & Gunter, B. (2005), pp. 142–145.

14. See Doane, M. D. (1999) Film and the masquerade: Theorising the female spectator. In S. Thornham (Ed.), *Feminist film theory: A reader* (pp. 131-145). New York: New York University Press; Silverman, K. (1980). Masochism and subjectivity. *Framework, 12,* 2–9; and Mayne, J. (1990). *The woman at the keyhole: Feminism and women's cinema.* Bloomington: University of Indiana Press.

15. For a review of these and other political applications of "gaze theory" see Manlove, C. T. (2007). Visual "drive" and cinematic narrative: Reading

gaze theory in Lacan, Hitchcock, and Mulvey. *Cinema Journal 46* (3), 83–108. And in more recent work Mulvey herself reconsiders how new technologies like DVDs, home viewing, and the ability to stop and start sections of a film at will—what she dubs the "cinema of delay"—affect her earlier models of spectatorship and identification. Cited in Chaudhuri, S. (2006). *Feminist film theorists.* London & New York: Routledge.

16. hooks, b. (1996). *Reel to real: Race, sex, and class at the movies.* London & New York: Routledge.

17. The scene's power extends beyond the film narrative to comment on the impact star images have historically exerted in *embodying* the dreams of romance and sexual desire upon their audiences. One of the earliest—and perhaps most moving—examples of this effect occurs at the conclusion of Buster Keaton's silent film *Sherlock Jr.* (1924), where following a now-famous dream sequence in which he is filmed literally stepping *into* the movie screen and becoming the hero of a series of exciting adventures, he returns to his "real" life as a painfully shy movie house projectionist and the forgiveness of his hometown girl. Before he kisses her in the movie theater he steals a glance at the screen to copy the technique of the actor making love to his leading lady in the film being projected above him. Many subsequent films, including Goddard's *Breathless* (1961) and Scorsese's *Taxi Driver* (1976), evoke this meditation on the relationship of film to fantasy and dreams of masculinity, femininity, and love, perhaps most memorably in Woody Allen's *Play It Again Sam* (1972) where a nervous and nerdy film critic is "coached" by a fantasized alter ego of Bogart's Sam Spade, another *film noir* tough guy, to overcome his anxiety with women and become an irresistible "ladies' man."

18. MTV Networks. (2007). *Famous face: Meet the patients.* Retrieved from http://www.mtv.com/onair/i_want_a_famous_face/meet_the_patients/index.jhtml?Patients=Mike%20and%20Matt.

19. D'Attoma, J. (Producer). (2006, October 5). Showbiz Tonight. [Television broadcast]. New York: Cable News Network.

20. Tasker, Y. (1998). *Working girls: Gender and sexuality in popular cinema* (p. 180). London: Routledge

21. Dyer, R. (1998). *Stars* (p. 35). London: BFI.

22. Wexman, V. W. (1993). *Creating the couple: Love, marriage, and Hollywood performance* (p. x). Princeton: Princeton University Press.

23. Marshall, P. D. (Ed.) (2006). *The celebrity culture reader* (p. 179). London: Routledge.

24. Tyra Banks, for example, who sees her media productions and image as empowering young girls to succeed as professional models, describes her personal brand as her trademark: "tough but still smiling." Hirschberg, L. (2008, June 1). Banksable. *The New York Times Magazine*, 38–45.

25. See McLeod, K. (2006). The private ownership of people. In P. D. Marshall (Ed.), *The celebrity culture reader* (pp. 649–665). London: Routledge.

26. Hedges, C. (2009). *Empire of illusion: The end of literacy and the triumph of spectacle* (p. 48). New York: Nation Books.

Chapter 2. Celebrity Bodies

1. In fact, more than two years later Smith's death was still listed among the top fifteen Internet news events of all time, along with President Obama's inauguration and several major airplane crashes, even superseding the demise of music star Michael Jackson. Bray, H. (2009, June 27). Pop icon's fans jam Internet sites. *The Boston Globe*, p. B5.

2. Shanahan, M. (2007, February 9). Life in the glare ends abruptly, in mystery: Anna Nicole Smith dies in Fla. at 39. *The Boston Globe*, p. A1.

3. Miller, F. (Ed.) (2006). *Leading ladies: The fifty most unforgettable actresses of the studio era* (p. 13). San Francisco: Chronicle Books.

4. Dyer, R. (1998). *Stars* (p. 43). London: BFI Publishing.

5. (2007, August 13). *In Touch Magazine*, p. 26.

6. Brumberg, J. J. (1997). *The body project: An intimate history of American girls* (p. xxiii). New York: Random House.

7. Quoted by cinematographer Harry Wolf in *Visions of Light: The Art of Cinematography*. Lawler, T., & Nishimuri, Y. (Producers), & Glassman, A., McCarthy, T., & Samuels, S. (Directors). (1992). [Motion picture]. United States, Japan: Image Entertainment.

8. Allis, S. (2008, March 9). She's more than that. *The Boston Globe*.

9. Grit to glam. (2008, March 10). *People, 69*(9).

10. Quoted in Jones, L. (2001, March 4). Me, myself, and Bridget Jones. *Sunday Times*.

11. Bayou, B. (2008). *The science of sexy*. New York: Gotham Books.

12. Bayou, (2008), p. 31.

13. Garner, D. M., & Garfinkel, P. E. (1979). The Eating Attitudes Test: An index of the symptoms of anorexia nervosa. *Psychological Medicine, 9*(2), 273–279.

14. Fox-Kales, E. (1991). Cognitive factors in eating behavior in bulimia. *Appetite, 17*, 209. The data reported here and elsewhere (see Bibliography) reports the results of my laboratory studies demonstrating the effects of abstinence violation on binge eating behavior in bulimic subjects.

15. My food diary. (2007, November). *In Style*, 426.

16. Tauber, M., Keith, A. E., Rizzo, M., McGee, T., Shelasky, A., Tan, M., et al. (2008, April 7). How to get a Hollywood body! *People, 69*(13), 54–61.

17. Since its 2004 introduction to Saudi Arabia, for example, *Oprah* has been rated the most popular English language TV show, in large part because Saudi women, many of whom suffer from obesity due to enforced inactivity and seclusion claim they are inspired by her weight loss efforts as well as her

message of personal empowerment. Zoepf, K. (2008, September 19). Veiled Saudi women find unlikely role model: Oprah. *The New York Times*, p. 1.

18. Cited in Weiss, J. (2006, March 23). Delivering the goods: Belly dancing lessons. Massage and yoga. Designer jeans. Pregnancy has spawned quite an industry. *The Boston Globe*. Retrieved from http://www.boston.com/.

19. Davis, K. (2006, May 14). Mothers superior: The high life of our modern mums. *Sunday Telegraph*, p. 87.

20. Abel, O., Adato, A., Adkins, G., Dubin, D., Gliatto, T., Green, M., et al. (2005, March 14). The Vanity Fair party. *People*, *63*(10), 100–106.

21. How they get their amazing after baby bodies! (2006, June 26). *Star*, p. 24. See also Saint Louis, C. (2009, November 12). Breast-feed the baby, love the calorie burn. *The New York Times*. Retrieved from http://www.nytimes.com/2009/11/12/fashion/12Skin.html?.

22. See, for example, Riley, L. (2006). *You and your baby: Pregnancy*. New York: Meredith Books.

23. Skurnick, L. (2006, December 23). What happens when "chick lit" grows up? *International Herald Tribune*, p. 7.

24. Cited in Wykes, M., & Gunter, B. (2005). *The media & body image: If looks could kill* (p. 213). London: Sage Publications. Several scholars have studied online pro-anorexia communities as a source of support for members who choose to resist mainstream medicalization and treatment of their condition. See for example Fox, N., Ward, K., & O'Rourke, A. (2005). Pro-anorexia, weight-loss drugs and the internet: An "anti-recovery" explanatory model of anorexia. *Sociology of Health & Illness*, *27*(7), 944–971. The majority of clinicians and media psychology researchers, however, have documented the negative effects of such sites, such as those reported recently in Bardone-Cone, A., & Cass, K. (2007). What does viewing of pro-anorexia websites do? An experimental examination of website exposure and moderating effects. *International Journal of Eating Disorders*, *40*(6), 537–548.

25. See for example Livingstone, S. (1999). New media, new audiences? *New Media & Society*, *1*(1), 59–66, and Livingstone, S. (2003). The changing nature of audiences: From the mass audience to the interactive media user. In A. Valdivia (Ed.), *The Blackwell companion to media research* (pp. 337–359). Oxford: Blackwell.

26. Marshall, P. D. (Ed.) (2006). *The celebrity culture reader* (p. 638). London: Routledge.

27. Zalis, E. (2003) At home in cyberspace: Staging autobiographical scenes. *Biography*, *26*(1), 84-119. As cited in Marshall, 2006, p. 638.

28. An example of the intersection between "real life" stars and self-created fan stardom was reported in the local press when actor Ben Affleck was filming *Gone Baby Gone* (2007) in a South Boston neighborhood. A fan who requested a photo with Affleck snuggled close to the star while her boyfriend loaded

the image onto her cell phone camera. After the shot, the young woman triumphantly thanked Affleck: 'Now I'm gonna be famous too!"

29. *Thinking YouTube fame, clerk fights off robber.* (2007, December 11). Retrieved from http://wcbstv.com/local/dunkin.donuts.youtube.2.608657.html.

30. MTV Networks. (2007). *Famous face: Meet the patients.* Retrieved from http://www.mtv.com/onair/i_want_a_famous_face/meet_the_patients/index.jhtml?Patients=Mike%20and%20Matt.

31. Voss, G. (2007, June 17). Desperately seeking stardom. *The Boston Globe Magazine,* 34.

32. Tabak, A. J. (2004, February 9). Hundreds register for new Facebook website. *Harvard Crimson.*

Chapter 3. Body Mastery and the Ideology of Fitness

1. Chabon, M. (2008, March 10). Secret skin: An essay in unitard theory. *The New Yorker, 84*(4), 66.

2. Markula, P. (2001). Firm but shapely, fit but sexy, strong but thin: The postmodern aerobicizing female bodies. In J. R. Johnston (Ed.), *American body in context* (p. 306). Wilmington, DE: Scholarly Resources, Inc.

3. Centers for Disease Control. (2004). Youth Risk Behavior Surveillance—United States, 2003. *Morbidity & Mortality Weekly Report, 53*(SS-02), 1–96.

4. Grossfeld, S. (2008, February 19). When cheers turn to depression. *The Boston Globe,* p. D1.

5. Adrienne Citrin, quoted in "A treadmill designed for kids? A debate over fitness takes shape," Teitell, B. (2008, September 4). *The Boston Globe,* p. E3.

6. (2008, July). *Marie Claire, 15*(7), 52.

7. See for example Hubbard, S. T., Gray, J. J., & Parker, S. (1998). Differences among women who exercise for "food related" and "non–food related" reasons. *European Eating Disorders Review, 6*(4), 255–265.

8. Zmijewski, C. F., & Howard, M. O. (2003). Exercise dependence and attitudes toward eating among young adults. *Eating Behaviors, 4*(2), 181–95.

9. One such study found as many as 83 percent of female dancers suffered from some variant of eating disorder pathology. Ringham, R., Klump, K., Kaye, W., Stone, D., Libman, S., Stowe, S., et al. (2006). Eating disorder symptomatology among ballet dancers. *The International Journal of Eating Disorders, 39*(6), 503–508.

10. Quentin Tarantino, as cited in Kord, S., & Krimmer, E. (2004). *Hollywood divas, indie queens, & TV heroines: Contemporary screen images of women* (note, p. 111). London: Rowman & Littlefield.

11. (2008, May). *Vanity Fair, 50*(5). She also models fashion accessories for Louis Vuitton and is company spokeswoman for Lancôme cosmetics.

12. A critique of beauty pageants in India comments on a similar contextualization of fashion as a kind of "beauty warfare to excel in the boxing ring of global contests," calling for the "soldier-like fortitude" of the beauty queen who is a "tenacious warrior." Parameswaran, R., (2004). Global queens, national celebrities: Tales of feminine triumph in post-liberalization India. *Critical Studies in Media Communication, 21*(4), 354.

13. The Making of Kill Bill Volume 2. *Kill Bill Volume 2.* (2004) Buena Vista Home Entertainment.

14. Denby, D. (2004, April 19). Chopping block; "Kill Bill Vol. 2." *The New Yorker, 80*(9), 202.

15. See Yvonne Tasker's ontogeny of the action heroine in *Spectacular bodies: Gender, genre and the action cinema* (pp. 18–20). London: Routledge, 1993.

16. Kord, S., & Krimmer, E. (p. 101).

17. See, for example, the Versace and Bebe advertisements depicted in *Beyond killing us softly: The strength to resist.* [Motion picture]. Lazarus, M., & Wunderlich, R. (Producers). (2000). Cambridge, MA: Cambridge Documentary Films.

Chapter 4. Body Transformation

1. Das, A. (2007, January 21). The search for beautiful. *The Boston Globe Magazine,* 33.

2. In a provocative reevaluation of the aesthetic surgery industry, Deborah Covino acknowledges its objectification and historical oppression of the woman's body but also suggests its progressive possibilities as a vehicle for personal agency and self-interest. See Covino, D. C. (2004). *Amending the abject body: Aesthetic makeovers in medicine and culture.* Albany: State University of New York Press.

3. Gunn, T. (Writer), & Verweyen, G. (Director). (2008, October 2). Meredith [Television series episode]. In Stone, S. A. & Cohen, S. J. (Producers) *Tim Gunn's guide to style.* Hollywood: Stone & Company Entertainment.

4. Hudson, D. A. (Producer). (2006, January 6). The Oprah Winfrey show [Television broadcast]. Chicago: Harpo Productions.

5. Duda, A., Redmann, J., Miskowiec, R., & Banks, T. (Producers). (2007, May 18). The Tyra Banks show [Television broadcast]. New York: Chelsea Television Studios.

6. Weed, K. (Director). (2004, April 7). Rachel and Kelly [Television series episode]. In A. Smith & N. Galan (Producers). *The swan.* Fox Television Distribution.

7. Brumberg, J. J. (1997). *The body project: An intimate history of American girls* (pp. 97–118). New York: Random House.

8. Bordo, S. (1993). *Unbearable weight: Feminism, western culture, and the body* (p. 245). Berkeley: University of California Press.

9. Featherstone, M. (2001). The body in consumer culture. In J. R. Johnston (Ed.), *American body in context* (p. 83). Wilmington, DE: Scholarly Resources.

10. Johnson, F., & Wardle, J. (2005). Dietary restraint, body dissatisfaction, and psychological distress: A prospective analysis. *Journal of Abnormal Psychology, 114*(1), 119–125.

11. Ohring, R., Graber, J. A., & Brooks-Gunn, J. (2002). Girls' recurrent and concurrent body dissatisfaction correlates and consequences over 8 years. *International Journal of Eating Disorders, 31*(4), 404–415.

12. Frank, J. B., & Thomas, C. D. (2003). Externalized self-perceptions, self-silencing, and the prediction of eating pathology. *Canadian Journal of Behavioural Science, 35*(3), 219–228.

13. See Appendix 2G: Items on the Body Dysmorphic Disorder Examination, in Thompson, J. K., Heinberg, L. J., Altabe, M., & Tantleff-Dunn, S. (1999). *Exacting beauty: Theory, assessment, and treatment of body image disturbance* (p. 82). Washington, DC: American Psychological Association.

14. American Society of Plastic Surgeons data, cited in Seigel, J. (2006, February 13). The cups runneth over. *The New York Times*.

15. Dufresne, R. G., Phillips, K. A., Vittoria, C. C., & Wilkel, C. S. (2001). A screening questionnaire for body dysmorphic disorder in a cosmetic dermatologic surgery practice. *Dermatologic Surgery: Official Publication for American Society for Dermatologic Surgery, 27*(5), 457–462.

16. Tasker, Y. (1998). Working girls: Gender and sexuality in popular cinema (p. 27). London: Routledge.

17. The spectacular financial success achieved by Lopez as the first Latina superstar is inseparable from her own "branding" of her body and designer line of clothes and accessories. Her famous rear end is known to be insured for $300 million and her entire body for $1 billion. Holmlund, C. (2005). Postfeminism from A to G. *Cinema Journal 44*(2), 117. For further discussion of J. Lo's now-iconic buttocks within the context of Latina bodies and sexuality see also Guzman, I. M. & Valdivia, A. N. (2010). Brain, brow, and booty: Latina iconicity in U.S. popular culture. In Weitz, R. (Ed.), *The politics of women's bodies: Sexuality, appearance, and behavior* (3rd ed.) (pp.155–162). New York: Oxford University Press.

18. See Kord, S., & Krimmer, E. (2004). *Hollywood divas, indie queens, and TV heroines: Contemporary screen images of women* (pp. 94–98). London: Rowman & Littlefield, for discussion of the film as a political apotheosis to American capitalism, which ignores these social and economic realities.

19. Actress Anne Hathaway had previous practice acting the part of an awkward fashion disaster who is transformed into a royal princess in the teen makeover movie *The Princess Diaries* (2001).

20. Nochimson, M. P. (2006). The Devil Wears Prada. *Cineaste, 32*(1), 50.

21. In its predictably stereotyped presentation of gender-bending, Hollywood casts its homosexuals as experts in femininity whose job it is to reform the unwomanly woman.

22. For another reading of the film which sees the both the pageant contestants and Gracie's role in raising their consciousness in more progressive terms see Kord, S. & Krimmer, E. pp. 48–49.

Chapter 5. Body Stigmatization

1. Cited in Goodman, C. (1995). *The invisible woman: Confronting weight prejudice in America* (p. 141). Carlsbad, CA: Gurze Books.

2. Would one thousand young American women rather increase the size of their income, political power, or breasts? (1994, February). *Esquire, 121*(2), 65–67.

3. Baum, C. L., & Ford, W. F. (2004). The wage effects of obesity: A longitudinal study. *Health Economics, 13*(9), 885–899.

4. Macartney, J. (2008, August 1). You're telling me to wear what? Chinese are ordered to smarten up for the Olympics. *The Times,* p.4. The edict also instructed women with thick legs to wear dark stockings.

5. In a lecture at the University of South Carolina, then Surgeon General Richard Cremona said: "Obesity is the terror within. Unless we do something about it, the magnitude of the dilemma will dwarf 9/11 or any other terrorist attempt." (2006, March 1). Obesity bigger threat than terrorism? *CBS News.* Retrieved from http://www.cbsnews.com/stories/2006/03/01/health/main1361849.shtml.

6. The bill, Mississippi House Bill 282, did not pass. H.R. 282 (2008).

7. Sturm, R. (2007). Increases in morbid obesity in the USA: 2000–2005. *Public Health, 121*(7), 492–496.

8. Wildman, R. P., Munter, P., Reynolds, K., McGinn, A. P., Rajpathak, S., Wylie-Rosett, J., et al. (2008). The obese without cardiometabolic risk factor clustering and the normal weight with cardiometabolic risk factor clustering. *Archives of Internal Medicine, 168*(15), 1617–1624. See also Parker-Pope, T. (2008, August 18). Better to be fat and fit than skinny and unfit. *The New York Times,* p. 5.

9. For a history of obesity see Gilman, S. (2004). *Fat boys: A slim book.* London: University of Nebraska Press; and Stearns, P. (2005). Fat in America. In C. E. Forth & A. Carden-Coyne (Eds.), *Cultures of the abdomen* (pp. 239–258). New York: Palgrave-Macmillan.

10. Steiner-Adair, C., & Vorenberg, A. P. (1999). Resisting weightism. In N. Piran, M. P. Levine, & C. Steiner-Adair (Eds.), *Preventing eating disorders: A handbook of interventions and special challenges* (p. 118). Philadelphia: Brunner/Mazel.

11. Rudd Center for Food Policy & Obesity (2008). *Weight bias: The need for public policy*. New Haven: Yale University Press.

12. Gregory, D. (2001). Heavy judgment: A sister talks about the pain of 'living large.' In J. R. Johnston (Ed.), *American body in context* (p. 313). Wilmington, DE: Scholarly Resources.

13. Gregory, D. (2001), (pp. 313–314).

14. Goodman, (1995), (p. 3).

15. For a discussion of weight and race discrimination see Braziel, J. E., & LeBesco, K. (Eds.). (2001). *Bodies out of bounds: Fatness and transgression* (p.3). Berkeley: University of California Press.

16. See Bordo, S. (1993). *Unbearable weight: Feminism, western culture, and the body.* Berkeley: University of California Press.; Orbach, S. (1979). *Fat is a feminist issue.* New York: Berkley Publishing; and Chernin, K. (1981). *The obsession: Reflections on the tyranny of slenderness.* New York: Harper & Row. See also Fox-Kales, E. (2003). Body double as body politic: Psychosocial myth and cultural binary in *Fatal Attraction. International Journal of Psychoanalysis, 84* (6), 1631–1637 on the "backlash" films of the 1980s and early '90s which demonize powerful and assertive women as monstrous predators.

17. Quote cited in Orenstein, C. (2005, Summer). The dialectic of fat: From Kirstie Alley to Broadway to Fiji. *Ms., 15*(2), 46–49.

18. Braziel, J. E., & LeBesco, K. (Eds.).(2001), (p.4).

19. Many studies documenting the effects of dietary restraint have reported this association. See for example Kales, E. (1991). Cognitive factors in eating behavior in bulimia. *Appetite, 17,* 209; and Kales, E. (1990). Macronutrient analysis of binge eating episodes in bulimia. *Physiology & Behavior, 48,* 837–841. See also a review of the research in dietary restraint theory in Polivy, J., & Herman, C. P. (1987). Diagnosis and treatment of normal eating. *Journal of Counseling and Clinical Psychology, 55*(5), 635–644.

20. In this sense these works represent what critic Richard Dyer has identified as the "fundamental ambivalence of popular cultural products [which have] both oppositional and hegemonic potential." Cited in Tasker, Y. (1998). *Working girls: Gender and sexuality in popular cinema* (p. 17). London: Routledge.

21. Wald, J. (2001, November 6). *Today* [Television broadcast]. New York: National Broadcasting Company.

22. Kuczynski, A. (2001, November 11). Charting the outer limits of inner beauty. *The New York Times*, p.1.

23. See Bell, K., & McNaughton, D. (2007). Feminism and the invisible fat man. *Body & Society, 13*(1), p. 128. for a discussion of this gendered body reversal.

24. See Mary Ann Doane's famous dissection of the "dirty joke" in "Film and the Masquerade: Theorizing the Female Spectator." In M. Merck, *The sexual subject: A screen reader in sexuality* (pp. 237–241). London: Routledge

(1982). Relevant here is the way the film follows Freud's prescriptive structure of the joke: the one who invents it, the person against whom it is told, and the third who is complicit with the teller and thus validates in his laughter the expression of the forbidden impulse released by the joker's wit. In *Jokes and their relation to the unconscious* (1905), Freud also describes the psychic processes by which pain is converted to laughter through empathy, the only extended investigation he made into the nature of empathy.

25. For a detailed, frame-by-frame exploration of this manipulation of the point of view shot in *Some Like It Hot*, see Kuhn, A. (1985). *The power of the image: Essays on representation and sexuality* (pp. 67–73). London: Routledge.

26. McCarthy, P. (2001, December 23). Playing the heavy. *The Sun Herald*, p. 1.

27. Sutherland, M. (2004, September). The comic visualised, or laughing at *Shallow Hal. Sense of Cinema*. Retrieved from http://www.senseofcinema.com/contents/04/33/shallow_hal.html.

28. *Shrek the Third* grossed more than $122 million at its opening weekend, surpassing *Shrek 2* and breaking animated film historic records. Chintan. (2007, September 10). Shrek the Third: Cinematography, editing, sound, mise-en-scene, S.H.E.P and other notes. Message posted to http://chintan-shrekthethird.blogspot.com/2007/09/shrek-thirs-cinematogprahy-editing.html.

29. Denby, D. (2007, May 28). Not kids' stuff. *The New Yorker, 83*(14), 86.

30. For two important discussions of the different significances embedded in the figure of Miss Piggy see Rowe, K. (1995). *The unruly woman: Gender and the genres of laughter* (pp. 25–49). Austin: University of Texas Press; and Stukator, A. (2001). "It's not over until the fat lady sings": Comedy, the carnivalesque, and body politics. In J. E. Braziel & K. LeBesco (Eds.), (2001), (pp. 197–213).

31. Steig, W. (2007). *The one and only Shrek! Plus five other stories* (pp. 37–38). New York: Square Fish Publishers.

32. The reference is cited by Bordo, S. (1993), (p. 116).

33. For a discussion of both these readings see Fox-Kales, E. (2001) Big mamas: The devouring feminine in contemporary cinema. *Proceedings of the 20th International Conference on Literature and Psychoanalysis*, ed. F. Pereira. Lisbon: Instituto Superior de Psicologia Aplicada, 105–107.

34. Rowe, K., (1995), (p.64).

35. Bordo, S., (1993), (p. 57).

Chapter 6. Teen Bodies

1. In 2007 the Walt Disney Company alone spent more than $1.3 billion on marketing their films and related entertainment products to young media consumers. Teens spend more than $153 billion on entertainment, with

girls devoting their expendable income primarily to shopping and moviegoing, usually in groups of three or more (Arbitron (2007). *The Arbitron cinema advertising study 2007: Making brands shine in the dark.* Retrieved from http://www.cinemaadcouncil.org/docs/cinema_study_2007.pdf). Teens also see the same films repeatedly. Gateward, F., & Pomerance, M. (Eds.). (2002). *Sugar, spice, and everything nice: Cinemas of girlhood* (p. 15). Detroit: Wayne State University Press. See also statistics citing teen girl consumer power in Fuchs, C. (2002). Too much of something is bad enough: Success and excess in *Spice World*. In F. Gateward & M. Pomerance (Eds.), (pp. 349–350).

2. Ackard, D. M., Fulkerson, J. A., & Neumark-Sztainer, D. (2007). Prevalence and utility of the DSM-IV eating disorder diagnostic criteria among youth. *The International Journal of Eating Disorders, 40*(5), 409–417.

3. Ward, G. (2002). Clueless in the neo-colonial world order. In F. Gateward, & M. Pomerance (Eds.), (p. 114). In this chapter Ward analyzes *Clueless* as an updated version of Austen's *Emma* within the contexts of American economic imperialism and traditional gender roles.

4. Hobson, L. B. (2004, April 25). Payback for the plastics. *London Free Press,* p. T2.

5. For an account of the suicide of one such MySpace victim see Collins, L. (2008, January 21). Friend game. *The New Yorker, 83*(44), 34–41. Reports of other such events have inspired calls for legislative action outlawing cyber-bullying. Cullen, K. (2010, February 2). No safe haven for bullies. *The Boston Globe,* p. B1.

6. See for example Jones, L. R., Fries, E., & Danish, S. J. (2007). Gender and ethnic differences in body image and opposite sex figure preferences of rural adolescents. *Body Image, 4*(1), 103–108.

7. From unpublished case notes and personal interviews with patients from my outpatient clinical practice and inpatient hospital eating disorder programs. After discharge from treatment programs many have recounted the competition during supervised meals to eat as little as possible of the prescribed caloric intake for weight recovery, as well as attempts to thwart the refeeding program by hiding food and laxatives.

8. For a historical account of both traditions see Brumberg, J. J. (1988). *Fasting girls: The emergence of anorexia nervosa as a modern disease.* Cambridge: Harvard University Press; and Bynum, C. W. (1987). *Holy feast and holy fast: The religious significance of food to medieval women.* Berkeley: University of California Press.

9. Neumark-Sztainer, D., Story, M., Resnick, M. D., & Blum, R. W. (1997). Adolescent vegetarians: A behavioral profile of a school-based population in Minnesota. *Archives of Pediatrics & Adolescent Medicine, 151*(8), 833–838. See also my own comments on the association between adolescent vegetarianism and eating disordered attitudes in "The Mystique of Meatless Cuisine," by Lawrence Lindner. (1999, November 2). *The Washington Post,* p. 20.

10. The film grossed more than $235 million at the box office, and spawned not just its own trilogy but three subsequent spinoff films. It is also ranks on the list of 50 Best High School Movies. (2006, September 15). The 50 best high school movies. *Entertainment Weekly*, *897*, 40.

11. In an interview about spring break at a Cancun beach one girl announced: "If I can be considered hot here, I'll be hot anywhere . . . I'm here to get confident." Daum, M. (2008, March 15). Raunch is rebranded as 'confidence.' *Los Angeles Times*.

12. American Psychological Association (2007). Report of the APA Task Force on the sexualization of girls executive summary. Washington, DC.

13. Kilbourne, J. (1999). Can't buy my love: How advertising changes the way we think and feel (p. 147). New York: Simon & Schuster.

14. For an examination of this trend see Hicks, M. (2008). *Bringing up geeks: How to protect your kid's childhood in a grow-up-too-fast world*. New York: Penguin Group.

15. Brumberg, J. J. (2002). Introduction. In L. Greenfield, *Girl Culture*. San Francisco: Chronicle Books.

16. Brooks-Gunn, J., & Donahue, E. H. (2008). Introducing the issue. *Children and Electronic Media*, *18*(1), p.7.

17. Sweeney, C. (2008, February 28). Never too young for that first pedicure. *The New York Times*, p. 3.

18. Thompson, J. K., Heinberg, L. J., Altabe, M., & Tantleff-Dunn, S. (1999). *Exacting beauty: Theory, assessment, and treatment of body image disturbance* (pp. 30–32). Washington, DC: American Psychological Association.

19. See for example Thompson et al. (pp. 175–180) which points to studies showing positive correlations between mother's and daughter's body dissatisfaction scores, weight concerns, dieting, and bulimic behaviors.

20. Kaplan, E. A. (1987). Mothering, feminism and representation: The maternal in melodrama and the woman's film 1910–1940. In Gledhill, C. (Ed.), *Home is where the heart is: Studies in melodrama and the woman's film* (p. 131). London: BFI Publishing.

Chapter 7. Alternative Visions

1. While the film included in its cast actors such as Dermot Mulroney and Jake Gyllenhaal, who went on to appear in mainstream Hollywood films, its reception was typical of the independent film: after premiering at the Telluride Film Festival it had only limited theatrical engagements in New York and Los Angeles and grossed a modest $91,910 during its opening weekend. Internet Movie Database. (n.d.) *Box office / business for Lovely & Amazing*. Retrieved from http://www.imdb.com/title/tt0258273/business.

2. Cooper, S. H., & Harris, A. (2005). Real women have curves (2002). *International Journal of Psychoanalysis, 86*(5), 1487.

3. Screenwriter Josefina Lopez in DVD commentary, LaVoo, G., & Brown, E. T. (Producers), & Cardoso, P. (Director). (2002). *Real women have curves* [Motion picture]. United States: Home Box Office.

4. An interesting variation on this theme takes place in the Hollywood family comedy *Spanglish*, which presents a devastating critique of the body obsession of an affluent L.A. mother (Tea Leoni) by juxtaposing her rejection of her overweight teenage daughter with the sympathetic and unconditional acceptance of the family's Mexican nanny Flor (Paz Vega). To drive the message home, the film relies on a voiceover from Flor's own daughter: "One particular cultural difference [is] that American women feel the same as Hispanic women a desire for the comfort of fullness but through dieting and exercising American women . . . become afraid of anything associated with curvaceousness—lust, sex, food, motherhood—all the best in life." Brooks, J. L. (Producer), & Haubegger, C., & Bradshaw, J. (Directors). (2004). *Spanglish* [Motion picture]. United States: Columbia Pictures Industries, Inc.

5. See Introduction, (pp. 9–10).

6. Claudia Milian, quoted in Diaz, J. (2006, November 8). Ugly beauty. *The Boston Globe*, p. D7.

7. See the preceding commentary in chapter 5 on the figure of the unruly woman.

8. See for example a study of Jo Brand, a British comedian whose orgiastic renditions of television cooking shows serve to upend the dictates of food denial and abstinence, in Kuppers, P. (2001). Fatties on stage: Feminist performances. In J. E. Braziel & K. LeBesco (Eds.), *Bodies out of bounds: Fatness and transgression* (pp. 277–291). Berkeley: University of California Press.

9. For an expanded discussion of Miss Piggy and other excessive female bodies as expressions of the grotesque and carnivalesque theatrical and aesthetic traditions see Stukator, A. (2001). "It's not over until the fat lady sings": Comedy, the carnivalesque, and body politics. In J. E. Braziel & K. LeBesco (Eds.), (pp. 197–213). For an extended discussion of the subversive cultural possibilities of obesity see Lebesco, K. (2004). *Revolting Bodies?: The struggle to redefine fat identity*. Amherst: University of Massachusetts Press.

10. Stukator, A. (p. 211).

11. Spainhour, A. A. (1999). *Effects of film on body image*. Unpublished manuscript.

12. Morris, W. (2007, July 29). Do the white thing. *The Boston Globe*, p. N9.

Bibliography

Ackard, D. M., Fulkerson, J. A., & Neumark-Sztainer, D. (2007). Prevalence and utility of the DSM-IV eating disorder diagnostic criteria among youth. *The International Journal of Eating Disorders, 40*(5), 409–417.

Addison, H. (2006). "Must the players keep young?": Early Hollywood's cult of youth. *Cinema Journal, 45*(4), 3–25.

Affuso, E. (2009). "Don't just watch it, live it"—technology, corporate partnerships and *The Hills*. *Jump Cut, 51.* June 24, 2009 <http://www.ejumpcut.org/currentissue/Hills-Affuso/index.html>.

Allis, S. (2008, March 9). She's more than that. *The Boston Globe.*

American Psychological Association (2007). Report of the APA Task Force on the sexualization of girls executive summary. Washington, DC.

Arbitron (2007). *The Arbitron cinema advertising study 2007: Making brands shine in the dark.* Retrieved from: <http://www.cinemaadcouncil.org/docs/cinema_study_2007.pdf>.

Baker, C. (2003). *Fed up: College students and eating problems.* Carlsbad, CA: Gurze Books.

Bardone-Cone, A., & Cass, K. (2007). What does viewing of pro-anorexia websites do? An experimental examination of website exposure and moderating effects. *International Journal of Eating Disorders, 40*(6), 537–548.

Barker, M., & Petley, J. (Eds.). (2001). *Ill effects: The media/violence debate* (2nd ed.). London: Routledge.

Baum, C. L., & Ford, W. F. (2004). The wage effects of obesity: A longitudinal study. *Health Economics, 13*(9), 885–899.

Bayou, B. (2008). *The science of sexy.* New York: Gotham Books.

Becker, A. E., Burwell, R. A., Gilman, S. E., Herzog, D. B., & Hamburg, P. (2002). Eating behaviours and attitudes following prolonged exposure to television among ethnic Fijian adolescent girls. *The British Journal of Psychiatry: The Journal of Mental Science, 180*, 509–514.

Bell, K., & McNaughton, D. (2007) Feminism and the invisible fat man. *Body & Society, 13*(1), 107–131.

Bojorquez, I., & Unikel, C. (2004). Presence of disordered eating among Mexican teenage women from a semi-urban area: Its relation to the cultural hypothesis. *European Eating Disorder Review, 12*(3), 197–202.

Bordo, S. (1993). *Unbearable weight: Feminism, western culture, and the body*. Berkeley: University of California Press.

Bray, H. (2009, June 27). Pop icon's fans jam Internet sites. *The Boston Globe*, p. B5.

Braziel, J. E., & LeBesco, K. (Eds.). (2001). *Bodies out of bounds: Fatness and transgression* Berkeley: University of California Press.

Brooks, J. L. (Producer), & Haubegger, C., & Bradshaw, J. (Directors). (2004). *Spanglish* [Motion picture]. United States: Columbia Pictures Industries, Inc.

Brooks-Gunn, J., & Donahue, E. H. (2008). Introducing the issue. *Children and Electronic Media, 18*(1), 7.

Brumberg, J. J. (1988). Fasting girls: The emergence of anorexia nervosa as a modern disease. Cambridge: Harvard University Press.

Brumberg, J. J. (1997). The body project: An intimate history of American girls. New York: Random House.

Brumberg, J. J. (2002). Introduction. In L. Greenfield, *Girl culture*. San Francisco: Chronicle Books.

Bynum, C. W. (1987). Holy feast and holy fast: The religious significance of food to medieval women. Berkeley: University of California Press.

Centers for Disease Control. (2004). Youth risk behavior surveillance—United States, 2003. *Morbidity & Mortality Weekly Report, 53*(SS-02), 1–96.

Chabon, M. (2008, March 10). Secret skin: An essay in unitard theory. *The New Yorker, 84*(4), 66.

Chaudhuri, S. (2006). *Feminist film theorists.* London & New York: Routledge.

Chernin, K. (1981). *The obsession: Reflections on the tyranny of slenderness*. New York: Harper & Row.

Collins, L. (2008, January 21). Friend game. *The New Yorker, 83*(44), 34–41.

Cooper, S. H., & Harris, A. (2005). Real women have curves (2002). *International Journal of Psychoanalysis, 86*(5), 1487.

Covino, D. C. (2004). *Amending the abject body: Aesthetic makeovers in medicine and culture*. Albany: State University of New York Press.

Croll, J., Neumark-Sztainer, D., Story, M., & Ireland, M. (2002). Prevalence and risk and protective factors related to disordered eating behaviors among adolescents: Relationship to gender and ethnicity. *The Journal of Adolescent Health: Official Publication of the Society for Adolescent Medicine, 31*(2), 166–175.

Cullen, K. (2010, February 2). No safe haven for bullies. *The Boston Globe*, p. B1.

Cusamano, D., & Thompson, J. (1997). Body image and body shape ideals in magazines: Exposure, awareness, and internalization. *Sex Roles, 37*, 701–721.

D'Attoma, J. (Producer). (2006, October 5). Showbiz Tonight. [Television broadcast]. New York: Cable News Network.

Das, A. (2007, January 21). The search for beautiful. *The Boston Globe Magazine*, 33.

Daum, M. (2008, March 15). Raunch is rebranded as "confidence." *Los Angeles Times*.

Davis, K. (2006, May 14). Mothers superior: The high life of our modern mums. *Sunday Telegraph*, p. 87.

Denby, D. (2004, April 19). Chopping block; "Kill Bill Vol. 2." *The New Yorker*, *80*(9), 202.

Denby, D. (2007, May 28). Not kids' stuff. *The New Yorker*, *83*(14), 86.

Diaz, J. (2006, November 8). Ugly beauty. *The Boston Globe*, p. D7.

Doane, M. D. (1987). *The desire to desire*. Bloomington: Indiana University Press.

Doane, M. D. (1999) Film and the masquerade: Theorising the female spectator. In S. Thornham (Ed.), *Feminist film theory: A reader* (pp. 131–145). New York: New York University Press.

Duda, A., Redmann, J., Miskowiec, R., & Banks, T. (Producers). (2007, May 18). *The Tyra Banks Show* [Television broadcast]. New York: Chelsea Television Studios.

Dufresne, R. G., Phillips, K. A., Vittoria, C. C., & Wilkel, C. S. (2001). A screening questionnaire for body dysmorphic disorder in a cosmetic dermatologic surgery practice. *Dermatologic Surgery: Official Publication for American Society for Dermatologic Surgery*, *27*(5), 457–462.

Duncan, P. (2008). *Stanley Kubrick: Visual poet*. Los Angeles: Taschen.

Dyer, R. (1998). *Stars*. London: BFI Publishing.

Eapen, V., Mabrouk, A. A., Bin-Othman, S. (2006). Disordered eating attitudes and symptomatology among adolescent girls in the United Arab Emirates. *Eating Behaviors*, *7*(1), 53–60.

Eddy, K. T., Hennessey, M., & Thompson-Brenner, H. (2007). Eating pathology in East African women: The role of media exposure and globalization. *The Journal of Nervous and Mental Disease*, *195*(3), 196–202.

Featherstone, M. (2001). The body in consumer culture. In J. R. Johnston (Ed.), *American body in context* (pp. 79–102). Wilmington, DE: Scholarly Resources.

Fox, N., Ward, K., & O'Rourke, A. (2005). Pro-anorexia, weight-loss drugs and the internet: An "anti-recovery" explanatory model of anorexia. *Sociology of Health & Illness*, *27*(7), 944–971.

Fox-Kales, E. (2001). Big mamas: The devouring feminine in contemporary cinema. *Proceedings of the 20th International Conference on Literature and Psychoanalysis*, ed. F. Pereira. Lisbon: Instituto Superior de Psicologia Aplicada, 105–107.

Fox-Kales, E. (2003). Body double as body politic: Psychosocial myth and cultural binary in *Fatal Attraction*. *International Journal of Psychoanalysis*, *84* (6), 1631–1637.

Frank, J. B., & Thomas, C. D. (2003). Externalized self-perceptions, self-silencing, and the prediction of eating pathology. *Canadian Journal of Behavioural Science, 35*(3), 219–228.

Freud, S., & Strachey, J. (1960). *Jokes and their relation to the unconscious.* New York: W. W. Norton.

Friedman, J., & Epstein, R. (Producers). (1996). *The celluloid closet* [Motion Picture]. United States: Telling Picture Productions.

Fuchs, C. (2002). Too much of something is bad enough: Success and excess in *Spice World.* In F. Gateward & M. Pomerance (Eds.), *Sugar, spice, and everything nice: Cinemas of girlhood* (pp. 343–360). Detroit: Wayne State University Press.

Garner, D. M., & Garfinkel, P. E. (1979). The Eating Attitudes Test: An index of the symptoms of anorexia nervosa. *Psychological Medicine, 9*(2), 273–279.

Gates, P. (2006). *Detecting men: Masculinity and the Hollywood detective film.* Albany: State University of New York Press.

Gateward, F., & Pomerance, M. (Eds.). (2002). *Sugar, spice, and everything nice: Cinemas of girlhood.* Detroit: Wayne State University Press.

Gauntlett, D. (2005). *Moving experiences: Media effects and beyond.* (2nd ed.). London: John Libbey.

Giles, D. (2003). *Media psychology.* Mahwah, NJ: Lawrence Erlbaum.

Gilman, S. (2004). *Fat boys: A slim book.* London: University of Nebraska Press.

Goodman, C. (1995). *The invisible woman: Confronting weight prejudice in America.* Carlsbad, CA: Gurze Books.

Goodman, E. (2004) *Paper trail: Common sense in uncommon times.* New York: Simon & Schuster.

Grabe, S., Hyde, J. S., & Ward, L. M. (2008). The role of the media in body image concerns among women: A meta-analysis of experimental and correlational studies. *Psychological Bulletin, 134*(3), 460–476.

Gregory, D. (2001). Heavy judgment: A sister talks about the pain of 'living large.' In J. R. Johnston (Ed.), *The American body in context* (pp. 311–318). Wilmington, DE: Scholarly Resources.

Griffiths, J. A., & McCabe, M. P. (2000). The influence of significant others on disordered eating and body dissatisfaction among early adolescent girls. *European Eating Disorders Review, 8*(4), 301–314.

Grit to glam. (2008, March 10). *People, 69* (9).

Grossfeld, S. (2008, February 19). When cheers turn to depression. *Boston Globe*, p. D1.

Gunn, T. (Writer), & Verweyen, G. (Director). (2008, October 2). Meredith [Television series episode]. In S. A. Stone & S. J. Cohen (Producers). *Tim Gunn's guide to style.* Hollywood: Stone & Company Entertainment.

Guzman, I. M., & Valdivia, A. N. (2010). Brain, brow, and booty: Latina iconicity in U.S. popular culture. In R. Weitz (Ed.), *The politics of women's bodies: Sexuality, appearance, and behavior* (3rd ed.) (pp.155–162). New York: Oxford University Press.

Hall, A. (2008, October 19). The ultimate fashion faux pas. *The Boston Globe*, p. 8.

Hamilton, B. E., Joyce, A. M., & Ventura, S. J. (2007). Births: Preliminary data for 2006. *National Vital Statistics Reports, 56*(7). Retrieved from <http://www.cdc.gov/nchs/data/nvsr/nvsr56/nvsr56_07.pdf>.

Hedges, C. (2009). *Empire of illusion: The end of literacy and the triumph of spectacle.* New York: Nation Books.

Hepworth, J. (1999). *The social construction of anorexia nervosa.* London: Sage Publications.

Hicks, M. (2008). *Bringing up geeks: How to protect your kid's childhood in a grow-up-too-fast world.* New York: Penguin Group.

Hirschberg, L. (2008, June 1). Banksable. *The New York Times Magazine*, 38–45.

Hobson, L. B. (2004, April 25). Payback for the plastics; Tina Fey says she was on the 'bottom rung' of the popular girls' ladder, but figures that's where her sense of humour was born. *London Free Press*, p. T2.

Holmlund, C. (2005). Postfeminism from A to G. *Cinema Journal, 44*(2), 117.

Hooks, B. (1996). *Reel to real: Race, sex, and class at the movies.* London & New York: Routledge.

Hubbard, S. T., Gray, J. J., & Parker, S. (1998). Differences among women who exercise for "food related" and "non–food related" reasons. *European Eating Disorders Review, 6*(4), 255–265.

Hudson, D. A. (Producer). (2006, January 6). *The Oprah Winfrey Show* [Television broadcast]. Chicago: Harpo Productions.

Hudson, J., Hiripi, E., Pope, H. G., Jr., & Kessler, R. C. (2007). The prevalence and correlates of eating disorders in the national comorbidity survey replication. *Biological Psychiatry, 6*(3), 348–350.

Johnson, F., & Wardle, J. (2005). Dietary restraint, body dissatisfaction, and psychological distress: A prospective analysis. *Journal of Abnormal Psychology, 114*(1), 119–125.

Jones, L. (2001, March 4). Me, myself, and Bridget Jones. *Sunday Times*.

Jones, L. R., Fries, E., & Danish, S.J. (2007). Gender and ethnic differences in body image and opposite sex figure preferences of rural adolescents. *Body Image, 4*(1), 103–108.

Kales, E. (1987). Dieting to bulimia. *Psychology Today, 21*.

Kales, E. (1989). A laboratory study of cognitive factors in bulimia: Abstinence violation effect. *Annals of the New York Academy of Sciences*, 535–537.

Kales, E. (1990). Macronutrient analysis of binge eating episodes in bulimia. *Physiology & Behavior, 48*, 837–841.

Kales, E. (1991). Cognitive factors in eating behavior in bulimia. *Appetite, 17*, 209.

Kaplan, E. A. (1987). Mothering, feminism and representation: The maternal in melodrama and the woman's film 1910–1940. In C. Gledhill (Ed.), *Home is where the heart is: Studies in melodrama and the woman's film.* London: BFI Publishing.

Keel, P. K. (2005). *Eating Disorders.* Upper Saddle River, NJ: Pearson Prentice-Hall.

Kilbourne, J. (1994). Still killing us softly: Advertising and the obsession with thinness. In P. Fallon, M. Katzman, & S. C. Wooley (Eds.), Feminist perspective on eating disorders (pp. 395–418). New York: The Guilford Press.

Kilbourne, J. (1999). *Can't buy my love: How advertising changes the way we think and feel*. New York: Simon & Schuster.

Kilbourne, J. (1999). *Deadly persuasion: Why women and girls must fight the addictive power of advertising*. New York: Free Press.

Klump, K. L. & Culbert, K. M. (2007). Molecular genetic studies of eating disorders: Current status and future directions. *Current Directions in Psychological Science, 16*(1), 37–41.

Kord, S., & Krimmer, E. (2004). *Hollywood divas, indie queens, and TV heroines: Contemporary screen images of women*. London: Rowman & Littlefield.

Kuczynski, A. (2001, November 11). Charting the outer limits of inner beauty. *The New York Times*, p.1.

Kuhn, A. (1985). *The power of the image: Essays on representation and sexuality*. London: Routledge.

Kuppers, P. (2001). Fatties on stage: Feminist performances. In J. E. Braziel & K. LeBesco (Eds.), *Bodies out of bounds: Fatness and transgression* (pp. 277–291). Berkeley: University of California Press.

LaVoo, G., & Brown, E. T. (Producers), & Cardoso, P. (Director). (2002). *Real women have curves* [Motion picture]. United States: Home Box Office.

Lawler, T., & Nishimuri, Y. (Producers), & Glassman, A., McCarthy, T., & Samuels, S. (Directors). (1992). *Visions of light: The art of cinematography* [Motion picture]. United States, Japan: Image Entertainment.

Lazarus, M., & Wunderlich, R. (Producers). (2000). *Beyond killing us softly: The Strength to Resist: The impact of media images on women and girls.* [Motion picture]. United States: Cambridge Documentary Films.

Lebesco, K. (2004). *Revolting bodies?: The struggle to redefine fat identity.* Amherst: University of Massachusetts Press.

Lindner, L. (1999, November 2). The mystique of meatless cuisine. *The Washington Post*, p.20.

Livingstone, S. (1999). New media, new audiences? *New Media & Society, 1*(1), 59–66.

Livingstone, S. (2002). *Young people and new media: Childhood and the changing media environment*. London: Sage.

Livingstone, S. (2003). The changing nature of audiences: From the mass audience to the interactive media user. In A. Valdivia (Ed.), *The Blackwell companion to media research* (pp. 337–359). Oxford: Blackwell.

Livingstone, S. (2009). Children and the internet: Great expectations and challenging realities. Malden, MA: Polity Press.

Macartney, J. (2008, August 1). You're telling me to wear what? Chinese are ordered to smarten up for the Olympics. *The Times*, p.4.

Maine, M. (2000). *Body wars: Making peace with women's bodies*. Carlsbad, CA: Gurze Books.

Malson, H. (1998). *The thin woman: Feminism, post-structuralism and the social psychology of anorexia nervosa*. London: Routledge.

Manlove, C. T. (2007). Visual "drive" and cinematic narrative: Reading gaze theory in Lacan, Hitchcock, and Mulvey. *Cinema Journal 46*(3), 83–108.

Markula, P. (2001). Firm but shapely, fit but sexy, strong but thin: The postmodern aerobicizing female bodies. In J. R. Johnston (Ed.), *The American body in context* (pp. 273–310). Wilmington, DE: Scholarly Resources, Inc.

Marshall, P. D. (Ed.) (2006). *The celebrity culture reader*. London: Routledge.

Mayne, J. (1990). *The woman at the keyhole: Feminism and women's cinema*. Bloomington: University of Indiana Press.

McCarthy, P. (2001, December 23). Playing the heavy. *The Sun Herald*, p. 1.

McLeod, K. (2006). The private ownership of people. In P. D. Marshall (Ed.), *The celebrity culture reader* (pp. 649–665). London: Routledge.

Menand, L. (2008, September 29). Regrets only: Lionel Trilling and his discontents. *The New Yorker, 84*(30), 85.

Miller, F. (Ed.) (2006). *Leading ladies: The fifty most unforgettable actresses of the studio era*. San Francisco: Chronicle Books.

Morris, W. (2007, July 29). Do the white thing. *The Boston Globe*, p. N9.

Moseley, R. (Ed.). (2005). *Fashioning film stars: Dress, culture, identity*. London: BFI Publishing.

MTV Networks. (2007). *Famous face: Meet the patients*. Retrieved from: <http://www.mtv.com/onair/i_want_a_famous_face/meet_the_patients/index.jhtml?Patients=Mike%20and%20Matt>.

Mulvey, L. (1999). Visual pleasure and narrative cinema. In S. Thornham (Ed.), *Feminist film theory: A reader* (p. 58–69). New York: New York University Press.

Neumark-Sztainer, D., Croll, J., Story, M., Hannan, P. J., French, S. A., & Perry, C. (2002). Ethnic/racial differences in weight-related concerns and behaviors among adolescent girls and boys: Finding from Project EAT. *Journal of Psychosomatic Research, 53*(5), 963–974.

Neumark-Sztainer, D., Story, M., Resnick, M. D., & Blum, R. W. (1997). Adolescent vegetarians: A behavioral profile of a school-based population in Minnesota. *Archives of Pediatrics & Adolescent Medicine, 151* (8), 833–838.

Neumark-Sztainer, D., Wall, M., Guo, J., Story, M., Haines, J., & Eisenberg, M. (2006). Obesity disordered eating, and eating disorders in a longitudinal study of adolescents: How do dieters fare five years later? *Journal of the American Dietetic Association, 106*(4), 559-568.

Nochimson, M. P. (2006). The Devil Wears Prada, *Cineaste, 32*(1), 50.

Obesity bigger threat than terrorism? (2006, March 1). *CBS News*. Retrieved from <http://www.cbsnews.com/stories/2006/03/01/health/main1361849.shtml>.

Ohring, R., Graber, J. A., & Brooks-Gunn, J. (2002). Girls' recurrent and concurrent body dissatisfaction correlates and consequences over 8 years. *International Journal of Eating Disorders, 31*(4), 404–415.

Orbach, S. (1979). *Fat is a feminist issue.* New York: Berkley Publishing.

Orenstein, C. (2005, Summer). The dialectic of fat: From Kirstie Alley to Broadway to Fiji. *Ms., 15*(2), 46–49.

Parameswaran, R., (2004). Global queens, national celebrities: Tales of feminine triumph in post-liberalization India. *Critical Studies in Media Communication, 21*(4), 354.

Parker-Pope, T. (2008, August 18). Better to be fat and fit than skinny and unfit. *The New York Times,* p. 5.

Polivy, J., & Herman, C. P. (1987). Diagnosis and treatment of normal eating. *Journal of Counseling and Clinical Psychology, 55*(5), 635–644.

Pope, H. G., Jr., Gruber, A. J., Choi, P., Olivardia, R., & Phillips, K. A. (1997). Muscle dysmorphia: An under recognized form of body dysmorphic disorder. *Psychosomatics, 38,* 548–557.

Pope, H. G., Olivardia, R., Gruber, A. & Borowiecki, J. (1999). Evolving ideals of male body image as seen through action toys. *International Journal of Eating Disorders, 26,* 65–72.

Rieder, S., & Ruderman, A. (2001). Cognitive factors associated with binge and purge eating behaviors: The interaction of body dissatisfaction and body image. *Cognitive Therapy and Research, 25*(6), 801–812.

Ringham, R., Klump, K., Kaye, W., Stone, D., Libman, S., Stowe, S., et al. (2006). Eating disorder symptomatology among ballet dancers. *The International Journal of Eating Disorders, 39*(6), 503–508.

Riley, L. (2006). *You and your baby: Pregnancy.* New York: Meredith Books.

Robinson, T. N., Chang, J. Y., Haydel, K. F., & Killen, J. D. (2001). Overweight concerns and body dissatisfaction among third-grade children: The impacts of ethnicity and socioeconomic status. *The Journal of Pediatrics, 128*(2), 181–187.

Rowe, K. (1995). *The unruly woman: Gender and the genres of laughter.* Austin: University of Texas Press.

Rudd Center for Food Policy & Obesity (2008). *Weight bias: The need for public policy.* New Haven: Yale University Press.

Schwartz, H. (1986). *Never satisfied: A cultural history of diets, fantasies and fat.* New York: Free Press.

Seigel, J. (2006, February 13). The cups runneth over. *The New York Times.*

Shanahan, M. (2007, February 9). Life in the glare ends abruptly, in mystery Anna Nicole Smith dies in Fla. at 39. *The Boston Globe,* p. A1.

Silverman, K. (1980). Masochism and subjectivity. *Framework, 12,* 2–9.

Skurnick, L. (2006, December 23). What happens when "chick lit" grows up? *International Herald Tribune,* p. 7.

Spainhour, A. A. (1999). *Effects of film on body image.* Unpublished manuscript.

Stacey, J. (1999). Feminine fascinations: Forms of identification in star-audience relations. In S. Thornham (Ed.), *Feminist film theory* (pp. 196–209). New York: New York University Press.

Stearns, P. (2005). Fat in America. In C. E. Forth & A. Carden-Coyne (Eds.), *Cultures of the abdomen* (pp. 239–258). New York: Palgrave-Macmillan.

Steig, W. (2007). *The one and only Shrek! Plus five other stories.* New York: Square Fish Publishers.

Steiner-Adair, C., & Vorenberg, A. P. (1999). Resisting weightism. In N. Piran, M. P. Levine, & C. Steiner-Adaire (Eds.), *Preventing eating disorders: A handbook of interventions and special challenges* (p. 105–121). Philadelphia: Brunner/Mazel.

Stukator, A. (2001). "It's not over until the fat lady sings": Comedy, the carnivalesque, and body politics. In J. E. Braziel & K. LeBesco (Eds.), *Bodies out of bounds: Fatness and transgression* (pp. 197–213). Berkeley: University of California Press.

Sturm, R. (2007) Increases in morbid obesity in the USA: 2000–2005. *Public Health, 121*(7), 492–496.

Sutherland, M. (2004, September). The comic visualised, or laughing at *Shallow Hal. Sense of Cinema.* Retrieved from <http://www.senseofcinema.com/contents/04/33/shallow_hal.html>.

Sweeney, C. (2008, February 28). Never too young for that first pedicure. *The New York Times*, p. 3.

Tabak, A. J. (2004, February 9). Hundreds register for new Facebook website. *Harvard Crimson.*

Tasker, Y. (1993). *Spectacular bodies: Gender, genre and the action cinema.* London: Routledge.

Tasker, Y. (1998). *Working girls: Gender and sexuality in popular cinema.* London: Routledge.

Tasker, Y., & Negra, D. (Eds.). (2005, Winter). In focus: Postfeminism and contemporary media studies. *Cinema Journal, 44*(2), 107.

Teitell, B. (2008, September 4). A treadmill designed for kids? A debate over fitness takes shape. *The Boston Globe*, p. E3.

Thinking YouTube fame, clerk fights off robber (2007, December 11). Retrieved from <http://wcbstv.com/local/dunkin.donuts.youtube.2.608657.html>.

Thompson, J. K., Heinberg, L. J., Altabe, M., & Tantleff-Dunn, S. (1999). *Exacting beauty: Theory assessment, and treatment of body image disturbance.* Washington, DC: American Psychological Association.

Trautmann, J., Worthy, S. L., & Lokken, K. L. (2007). Body dissatisfaction, bulimic symptoms, and clothing practices among college women. *Journal of Psychology, 141*(5), 485–498.

Tyler, P. (1999). Magic and myth of the movies. In L. Braudy & M. Cohen (Eds.), *Film theory and criticism.* New York and Oxford: Oxford University Press.

Tylka, T. L. (2004). The relation between body dissatisfaction and eating disorder symptomatology: An analysis of moderating variables. *Journal of Counseling Psychology, 51*(2), 178–191.

Voss, G. (2007, June 17). Desperately seeking stardom. *The Boston Globe Magazine,* 34.

Wald, J. (2001, November 6). *Today* [Television broadcast]. New York: National Broadcasting Company.

Ward, G. (2002). Clueless in the neo-colonial world order. In F. Gateward, & M. Pomerance (Eds.), *Sugar, spice, and everything nice: Cinemas of girlhood* (pp. 103–124). Detroit: Wayne State University Press.

Weaver, C. K., & Carter, C. (Eds.). (2006). *Critical readings: Violence and the media.* Maidenhead: Open University Press.

Weed, K. (Director). (2004, April 7). Rachel and Kelly [Television series episode]. In A. Smith & N. Galan (Producers). *The swan.* Fox Television Distribution.

Weiss, J. (2006, March 23). Delivering the goods: Belly dancing lessons. Massage and yoga. Designer jeans. Pregnancy has spawned quite an industry. *The Boston Globe.* Retrieved from: <http://www.boston.com>.

Wexman, V. W. (1993). *Creating the couple: Love, marriage, and Hollywood performance.* Princeton: Princeton University Press.

Wildman, R. P., Munter, P., Reynolds, K., McGinn, A. P., Rajpathak, S., Wylie-Rosett, J., et al. (2008). The obese without cardiometabolic risk factor clustering and the normal weight with cardio metabolic risk factor clustering. *Archives of Internal Medicine, 168*(15), 1617–1624.

Wykes, M., & Gunter, B. (2005). *The media & body image: If looks could kill.* London: Sage Publications.

Zalis, E. (2003) At home in cyberspace: Staging autobiographical scenes. *Biography, 26* (1), 84–119.

Zmijewski, C. F., & Howard, M. O. (2003). Exercise dependence and attitudes toward eating among young adults. *Eating Behaviors, 4*(2), 181.

Zoepf, K. (2008, September 19). Veiled Saudi women find unlikely role model: Oprah. *The New York Times,* p. 1.

Index

adolescence, 47, 119–22, 124, 126, 134, 136–37, 140, 142, 148
adolescent boys, 132
adolescent girls, 9, 15, 120, 136, 138, 140, 142, 162, 164, 179, 183
  Fijian, 162, 177
adolescent vegetarians, 174, 183
Alexander, Jason, 103
Alley, Kirstie, 45, 117
American Pie, 15, 125, 132–34, 138
Anderson, Pamela, 50
Aniston, Jennifer, 21–22, 43
Anna Nicole Show, 36
anorexia
  explanatory model of, 167, 179
  reverse, 8, 157
anorexia athletica, 57
anorexia nervosa, 5, 7–8, 25, 37, 42, 44, 58, 120, 127–28, 155, 160
  emergence of, 174, 178
  social construction of, 160, 181
  social psychology of, 160, 183
  symptoms of, 166, 180
appetites, 18, 43, 56, 96, 115, 141, 149, 152, 163, 166, 172, 181
  compulsive, 154
  dangerous undisciplined, 112
  denial of, 4, 111, 130
  destructive, 16
  female, 117, 126
  restrained, 104
  unrestrained, 97
Avatar, 12
Avengers, 63

Barbie dolls, 122, 135
Basinger, Kim, 30, 40
Bates, Kathy, 115
Bell, Kristin, 42
Berry, Halle, 43
Beyonce, 16, 43
Big Momma's House, 154
Biggest Loser, 14, 95–96, 111
binge eating, 7–8, 15–16, 100, 115, 137, 155, 159
Black, Jack, 103
Blass, Bill, 87
Blethyn, Brenda, 142
Blue Crush, 26
body dissatisfaction, 4, 8, 10, 12–13, 25, 27, 42, 74, 77, 125, 141, 152–53, 159, 161, 180–81, 184–86
  chronic, 14, 42
  interaction of, 159, 184
  reported, 159
body dysmorphic disorder (BDD), 14, 79, 156–57, 162, 170, 179, 184
Bollywood, 17
Bond, James, 61
Bordo, Susan, 76, 99, 118, 160, 169, 172–73, 178
Brand, Jo, 176
Bratt, Benjamin, 92
The Break Up, 21
Bridget Jones Diary, 37, *40*, 136
Bring It On, 54
Brumberg, Joan, 39, 159, 166, 169, 174–75, 178

bulimia nervosa (BN), 5–7, 13, 23, 37, 43, 48, 54, 58, 78, 100, 120, 127, 155–59, 163, 172, 181
Bullock, Sondra, 89
Bundchen, Giselle, 85

Caan, James, 115
Caine, Michael, 91
Cameron, James, 12
Cardoso, Patricia, 146–47, 176, 182
Carradine, David, 60
celebrities, 5, 16, 32–33, 35–37, 41–43, 45, 49–50, 55, 108, 118, 163
celebrity
    battles, 13
    beauty consumerism, 117
    body maintenance, 4
Celebrity Boot Camp, 43
celebrity confessions, 42
celebrity culture, 13, 33, 37, 39, 51, 125
celebrity mothers, 46
celebrity pregnancies, 45
Center Stage, 58–59
Chabon, Michael, 168, 178
Charlie's Angels, 63–64
Charming, Prince, 87–88, 112, 146
Chenoweth, Kristen, 43
Chernin, Kim, 99, 160, 172, 178
chic, anorectic, 99
Chicago, 41, 154, 169, 181
chick flicks, 12, 73, 94, 136, 141, 163
Child, Julia, 15
Chocolat, 15
Cinderella motifs, 80
Cinderellas, 79–81, 84–85
    transformed, 87
    workplace, 90
cinema, 3–4, 11, 22, 74, 108, 173, 185
    popular, 165, 170, 172, 185
    women's, 164, 183
cinema of delay, 165
cinema spectatorship, 11, 13, 28, 124
cinemas of girlhood, 174, 180, 186
cinematic conventions, 4, 23, 106
cinematic idealization, 13
cinematic structures, 141

cinematography, 14, 62, 108, 111, 166, 173, 182
Clinton, Bill, 97
Clockwork Orange, 161
Clueless, 15, 17, 120–21, 124–25, 174, 186
cognitive distortions, 156
cognitive factors, 159, 163, 166, 172, 181, 184
cognitive habit, 78
Cohen, Mickey, 29
Colbert, Claudette, 39
comedy, 28, 104–5, 110, 117, 173, 176, 185
commodification, 33, 46
consumer culture, 76, 120, 170, 179
    growing, 19
consumer marketing, 7
    domestic, 77
cosmetic surgeons, 79, 146
cosmetic surgery industry, 79
cosmetic surgery masquerade, 18
cosmetic surgical procedures, 51
Covino, Deborah, 169, 178
Crawford, Cindy, 125
Crawford, Joan, 20
Crowe, Russell, 30
Cruel Intentions, 23
cultural assimilation, 148
cultural erasure, 98
cultural expectations, 47, 104
cultural fears, 117–18
cultural hypothesis, 162, 178
cultural Zeitgeist, 12
culture, 3–4, 6–7, 17, 48, 56, 77, 98, 119, 135, 141, 145, 150, 164, 169, 171, 178
    eating-disordered, 13, 17–18
    western, 160, 169, 172, 178
Curtis, Tony, 3
Cyber-harassment, 126
Cyrus, Miley, 40

Dark Knight, 12
Demi Moore, 40, 46
Devil Wears Prada, 14, 80, 84–85, 92, 121, 143, 151, 170, 183
diagnoses, clinical, 156

diagnostic criteria, 7, 155–56, 158
diagnostic scale, standard, 10, 43
diagnostic tests, 119
Diary of a Mad Black Woman, 154
Diaz, Cameron, 41, 43, 112
diet culture, 1, 152
diet fatigue syndrome, 27
diet industry, 112, 154
diet infomercials, 110
diet pills, 36, 136
diet regimens, 16, 100
diet restrictions, 22, 115
dietary restraint theory, 172
dieting, 7, 9, 13, 44, 56, 110, 122, 163,
    175–76, 181
  destructive, 4
  stringent, 57
  yo-yo, 13, 101
dieting behaviors, 37, 47, 120, 138
dieting girls, 131
dieting mothers, 6
diets, 8, 27, 77, 88–89, 91–92, 100–1,
    129–30, 136–37, 139
  cultural history of, 159, 184
  semi-starvation, 4
discipline, 2, 4, 17, 51, 53, 56, 75–76,
    97, 115
  punishing, 63
Disney, Walt, 81, 83
disordered eating cognitions, 10
disordered eating practices, 13, 158
Divine, 153
Doane, Mary Ann, 27, 163–64, 172, 179
dreams, 12, 58, 74, 79–81, 84, 94, 114,
    165
  collective screen, 4, 12
  cultural, 14
Dreamworks, 102, 112
Drop Dead Gorgeous, 126, 128–29
Dunst, Kirsten, 33
Dyer, Richard, 3, 32, 37, 165–66, 172,
    179

Eating Attitudes Test, 166, 180
eating behavior, 4, 11, 21, 78, 80, 90,
    100, 118, 122, 136, 163, 166, 172,
    181

Eating Disorder Formula, 5
eating disorders, 1, 6–9, 15–17, 23, 33,
    38–39, 42–43, 47–48, 57–59, 61, 74,
    155–56, 160–61, 167–68, 177, 181–84
  celebrity, 41
  correlates of, 162, 181
  male, 8
  subclinical, 7
Edison, Thomas, 32
Ensler, Eve, 99
ethnic body diversities, 8
ethnic differences, 174, 181
ethnic overtones, 98
ethnic/racial differences, 162, 183
ethnicities, 7, 27, 161, 178, 184
exercise, 2, 47, 53–54, 56–57, 70, 101,
    168, 181
  excessive, 57, 157
  healthy, 53
exercise bulimia, 14, 57, 157
exercise dependence, 57, 168, 186
exercise rituals, 8, 58
exercisers, aerobic, 55, 57
Extreme Makeover, 14, 73, 75, 79

Facebook, 50, 168, 185
Facebook stardom, 50
fan magazines, 19, 37
fan subculture, 33
fans, 13, 32, 36, 39, 42, 44–46, 49,
    162, 167
  martial arts, 60
fantasies, 2, 32, 63–64, 76, 79, 111,
    159, 165, 184
  collective, 84
  contemporary cinema, 73
  cultural, 111
  hypersexualized, 150
  identificatory, 20
  male cultural, 63
  primitive childhood, 115
  sexual, 63, 108
  teen, 138
  undergraduate, 51
  urban Cinderella, 84
Fargo, 15
fashion accessory, 46, 60

fashion celebrities, 46
fashion crimes, 85
fashion experts, 54
fashion industry, 86, 160
fashion magazine, 11, 136, 143, 160
fashion marketing, 160
fashion moguls, 87
fashion statement bodies, 32, 67–68
fat
  dialectic of, 172, 184
  macronutrient, 131
Fat Actress, 102, 117
fat body, alien, 111
fat jokes, 110
  visual, 17
fat letter, 59
fat phobia, 100
fat woman
  filmic, 108
  stigmatized, 110
Fatal Attraction, 172, 179
fatness, 97, 101, 117–18, 152, 172, 176, 178, 182, 185
fatness anxiety, 57
female screen identification, 20
female spectator, 12, 16, 23, 163–64, 172, 179
female spectator's inspiration, 141
female viewers, 4–5, 13, 25, 63, 132
feminist film theory, 17, 145, 160, 164, 179, 183, 185
feminist perspectives, 99, 115, 160, 164, 169, 172, 175, 177–78, 181–83
Ferguson, Sarah, 45
Ferrara, America, 147, 152
Fey, Tina, 123, 181
Fiennes, Ralph, 81
A Fistful of Dollars, 62
fitness, 1, 3, 14, 32, 53, 55, 57, 97, 118, 168, 185
  ideology of, 70, 73, 76
fitness culture, 53
fitness regimens, 14, 56
Fonda, Jane, 55

food, 1–2, 4, 14–15, 17, 25, 39, 42–43, 51, 96, 101, 114–15, 129–31, 136–38, 149, 155–56, 174
  illegal, 139
  legal, 100
  soul, 154
food abstinence, 1, 16, 43, 129–30
food denial, 176
food preoccupation, 57
food restriction, 10, 127, 159
food sabotage, 126
Forgetting Sarah Marshall, 42
Foucault, Michel, 56
Frankel, David, 80
Freeman, Morgan, 67
Freud, Sigmund, 157, 173, 180

Gardner, Ava, 29
gastric bypass procedure, 45, 111, 155
Gauntlett, David, 161, 180
Gellar, Sarah Michelle, 23
gender, 6–7, 14, 22, 27, 91, 122, 154, 161, 163, 165, 169–70, 172–74, 178, 181, 184–85
gender constructs, 105, 153
gender reconstruction, 75
gender recuperation, 93
gender-bending, 171
gendered assumptions, 4
GI Joe action dolls, 163
Gilda, 21
girl culture, 175, 178
girlhood, 135, 174, 180, 186
girls
  developing, 137
  fasting, 130, 174, 178
  obese, 128
  pubescent, 136
  sexualization of, 175, 177
  teen, 8, 55, 119–20, 123, 125–26
  vulnerable, 26
girl's body, 15, 136, 149
Gone with the Wind, 15, 119
Goodman, John, 101
Graham, Sylvester, 1

Gyllenhaal, Jake, 175
gymorexia, 14, 57

Hairspray, 152–53
Hannah, Daryl, 59, 61, 64
Hardwicke, Catherine, 142
Harlow, Jean, 19
Haskell, Molly, 37
Hathaway, Anne, 38, 61, 84, 89,
    170
Hayworth, Rita, 21, 29
Heartbreak Kid, 91
Hefner, Hugh, 35
Hepburn, Audrey, 20
Hepburn, Katherine, 20
Hills, Beverly, 9, 20, 29, 121, 148
Hitchcock, Alfred, 165, 183
Holofcener, Nicole, 142
hooks, bell, 27
Hoskins, Bob, 83
Hudson, Kate, 43
Hustler magazine, 138
Hytner, Nicholas, 58

I Want a Famous Face, 32, 50
identification, 16, 21–22, 24, 28, 90,
    103, 142, 145, 164–65, 185
  encouraged fan, 19
  screen image, 31
identity, 20–21, 29–30, 44, 47, 51, 73,
    81, 120, 143, 164, 183
  corporeal, 32
  cultural, 6
  ethnic, 80, 83–84, 152
  new social, 82
  racial, 27, 30, 145
identity confusion, 140
identity politics, 12
identity restoration, 91
images
  aspirational, 141
  celebrity, 13, 33, 143
  cinematic, 120, 152
  fantasized, 17
  glamorized, 119

sexualized, 36, 39
star's, 32–33, 37
images of women eating, 16
internalization, 10, 12, 22, 28, 164, 178
Internet, 35, 38, 45, 48–49, 51, 125,
    142, 161, 166–67, 179, 182
internet saboteur, 126
intertextuality, 163
It's Complicated, 16

Jawbreakers, 16, 120, 126, 128, 130–31
Jenny Craig, 45, 118
Johansson, Scarlett, 40
Jolie, Angelina, 25, 46, 63
Julie and Julia, 15
Juno, 15

Keaton, Buster, 165
Keener, Catherine, 142
Kids Getting Older Younger, 15, 120
Kilbourne, Jean, 159–60, 175, 182
Kill Bill, 14, 54, 60–61, 63–64, 67–68,
    86, 127, 169, 179
King, Stephen, 115–16
Klein, Calvin, 44
Klum, Heidi, 87
Knightley, Keira, 40
Kubrick, Stanley, 161, 179

L.A. Confidential, 13, 28, 30, 36, 176
Lacan, Jacques, 13, 24, 165, 183
Lacanian mirror, 13
Ladd, Alan, 31
Lake, Ricky, 153
Lake, Veronica, 28–31
Lara Croft, 63, 67
Last Holiday, 154
Latina bodies, 170
Latina superstar, first, 170
Latina viewers, 152
Legally Blonde, 136
Leoni, Tea, 176
Like Water for Chocolate, 15
Livingstone, Sonia, 161, 167, 182
Lohan, Lindsay, 13, 36, 48, 122

Lombard, Carole, 39
Lopez, Jennifer, 16, 32, 43, 77, 80, 82
Lovely and Amazing, 15, 142–46, 150

Macpherson, Elle, 61
Madonna, 46–47, 61, 86
Maid in Manhattan, 14, 18, 80, 83–84,
     87, 92, 147
The Major and the Minor, 28–29
makeover beauty culture, 125
makeover movies, 7, 14, 18, 79, 94,
     142, 146
  teen, 170
makeover narratives, 92
makeovers, famous, 41
male bodies, 8, 153, 157, 162
male body image, 163, 184
male gaze, 27, 124, 144
Manheim, Camryn, 110
martial arts movies, 61, 64–65
Mayer, Louis B., 39
Mayne, Judith, 27, 164, 183
Mean Girls, 15, 120–27, 138–39
media, 6–7, 10–11, 35–36, 160,
     162–63, 167, 180, 186
  new, 17, 51, 161, 167, 182
  postfeminist, 18
  supportive celebrity, 7
  true confession, 41
media beauty culture, 77
media effects, 6, 10, 16, 161, 180
  model, 160
  research, 6, 160
media exposure, 11, 26, 162, 164, 179
  thin-ideal, 10
media exposure research, 12, 22, 25,
     164
media images, 6, 11, 13, 83, 163, 182
  eroticized, 134
media psychology research, 6, 9,
     161–62, 164, 167, 180
Meet Me in St. Louis, 119
Melrose Place, 9
Menand, Louis, 160, 183
Million Dollar Baby, 40, 67, 69
Mirren, Helen, 33, 38

The Mirror Has Two Faces, 15, 91
Misery, 14, 115–16
Miss Congeniality, 14–15, 18, 89–90,
     93–94, 126
Miss Piggy, 113, 152, 173, 176
Monroe, Marilyn, 29, 35–36
Montana, Hannah, 40, 50
Moore, Julianne, 40
Mortimer, Emily, 142
mother
  diet-conscious, 91
  divorced, 91
  expectant, 46
  monstrous, 116
  nursing, 47
  omnipotent, 115
  unnatural, 115
mothers, 8, 58, 70, 74, 101–2, 125,
     138–40, 145–46, 148, 150–52,
     167, 175–76, 179
movie spinoff products, 112
movie star bodies, 13, 32
movie stars, 3–4, 19–20, 22, 24, 32–33,
     48, 55, 79
movies
  boxing, 68
  porn, 132
  surfing, 26
Mr. and Mrs. Smith, 25
MTV, 32, 50, 162
MTV music videos, 137
MTV Networks, 165, 168, 183
Mulholland Drive, 21
Mulroney, Dermot, 144, 175
Mulvey, Laura, 5, 12–13, 22–24, 27,
     124, 160, 164–65, 183
Murphy, Eddie, 101
Murray, Bill, 64
muscle building, 53–55, 68, 157, 163
muscle dysmorphia, 8, 157, 162, 184
Myers, Nancy, 16

National Association to Advance Fat
     Acceptance, 102
Never Been Kissed, 120, 122, 129
Nollywood, 17

normative discontent, 94, 126
Novak, Kim, 80
The Nutty Professor, 101

obese heroines, 102
obesity, 45, 96–98, 115, 157, 161, 166, 171, 176, 183
  morbid, 45, 171, 185
  war on, 97
Olson, Mary Kate, 47–48
Olympics, 96, 171, 182
Ontiveros, Lupe, 148
Oprah's triumph, 41, 45
Orbach, Susie, 99, 160, 172, 184
Oscars, 38, 40, 46
Oscars Red Carpet show, 38

Paltrow, Gwyneth, 13, 18, 27, 43, 46, 102, 106, 108, 110–11, 154
parent free zone, 148
parental authority, 130
parental eye, 38
parents, 8, 50, 55–56, 101, 123, 128, 135, 138, 140, 150, 156
  anxious, 55
Parker, Tyler, 11
Patricia Cardoso, 146–47, 176, 182
Photoplay magazine, 19
Pitt, Brad, 32
Playboy magazine, 35–36, 40, 50, 132
postfeminism, 163, 170, 181, 185
Powell, William, 19
pregnancy, 45–46, 66, 104, 167, 184, 186
  celebrity teen, 135
  consumer, 46
pregnancy chic, 46
Pretty Woman, 79
Princess Diaries, 170
Production Code, 39
prostitution, 29, 32, 64
pro-anorexia, 48, 157, 167, 179
pro-anorexia websites, 167, 177
psychoanalytic theory, 27, 115, 157
puberty, 15, 129, 136, 142

publicists, 33, 38, 81
publicity, right of, 33

Queen Latifah, 16, 36, 45, 153–54

Real Women Have Curves, 15, 146, 148–49, 176, 178, 182
Richardson, Natasha, 81
Ritchie, Nicole, 48
Robbins, Tony, 103, 106
Rogen, Seth, 101
Rogers, Ginger, 28
romantic comedies, 12, 15, 28, 61, 91, 142
  popular, 21
romantic comedy genre, 106
Roseanne, 117, 152
Rowe, Kathleen, 117, 173, 184
Russell, Jane, 29

Sarandon, Susan, 12
Saturday Night Fever, 154
screen, split, 38
screen bodies, 3, 12–13, 19
  perfected, 4
screen idealization, 24
screen identification, 4, 12–13, 16, 21
screen persona, 20
screen representation, 24
self-scrutiny, 13, 19, 49–50, 55, 146
  obsessive, 42
sexuality, 27, 46, 136, 138, 147, 149, 164–65, 170, 172–73, 180, 182, 185
sexualization
  insistent, 65
  premature, 119
sexualized bodies, 5
sexualized female images, 68
Shallow Hal, 17, 98, 102–6, 110–12, 141, 153, 173, 185
Shrek films, 102, 112–14, 173, 185
Shrek franchise, 112
Silverman, Kaja, 27
Silverstone. Alicia, 121
Smith, Anna Nicole, 35–36, 166, 184

social comparisons, 26, 41, 164
social invisibility, 98, 111
social media networking, 7, 50
social power, 73, 125–26, 141
socioeconomic incentive, 76
socioeconomic status, 98, 158, 161, 184
Solondz, Todd, 142
Something about Mary, 102
Something's Gotta Give, 16
soundtracks, 14, 80, 86, 92, 94, 119, 151
Spanglish, 176, 178
Spears, Britney, 36, 50, 103, 135
spectators, 4, 12, 22, 24, 48, 105–6
  black woman, 27
  male, 22, 63
  transgendered, 27
spectatorship positions, 27
Stacey, Jackie, 12, 20, 164, 185
star identification, 13
star images, 20, 32–33, 37, 51, 165
star persona, 33
star power, 28
star system, 28
stars, 19–20, 33, 36–40, 42–43, 45–47,
  49–51, 58, 152, 165–67, 179
  crossover, 16
  rap, 49
  teen, 40, 147
star's body image, 39
star-audience relations, 164, 185
Stewart, James, 80
stigmatization, 125
  persistent, 98
  social, 14
Stompanato, Johnny, 29
Streep, Meryl, 85
Streisand, Barbra, 91
studio era, 166, 183
studio heads, 119
studio system, 37
sub-clinical eating disorders (SED), 155,
  158
supermodel actresses, 9
supermodel superwomen, 62, 89, 106
superwomen
  action movie, 53
  avenging, 64

superwomen assassins, 14
superwomen bodies, 61, 63
Surgeon General, 97, 171
surgeries, 32, 42, 50, 100, 111, 155
  aesthetic, 7, 29, 32, 41
  bariatric, 45, 155
  breast, 74, 135, 139
  cosmetic, 38, 76–77, 81, 92
  gastric banding, 155
  gastric bypass, 36
The Swan, 14, 75
Swank, Hillary, 40, 67–68

tabloid press, 33, 38–39, 41–42, 45–46,
  82, 118
Tarantino, Quentin, 59, 67, 168
Tasker, Yvonne, 18, 32, 163, 165,
  169–70, 172, 185
Taxi Driver, 165
Teen Vogue, 121
television, 7, 9, 11, 14, 37, 49–50, 63,
  75, 101, 123, 128, 134–35, 160,
  162–63, 169, 177
  celebrity gossip, 32
television makeover, 74, 76, 110
television market, 135
Terminator II, 63
theory
  communications, 160
  cultivation, 6, 11, 161
  social comparison, 26, 164
theory of cinema spectatorship, 13,
  124
Theron, Charlize, 40
Thin Commandments, 48
Thinspiration, 48
Thirteen, 142
13 Going on Thirty, 135
This Gun For Hire, 31
Thurman, Uma, 43, 60–61, 64
Timberlake, Justin, 113
transformation, 2, 18, 74–75, 80,
  83–84, 89, 94, 112, 125
  cosmetic, 134
  instantaneous, 148
  magical, 81, 85, 146
  social, 20, 92

transgression, 38, 172, 176, 182, 185
   dietary, 75
transgressive body challenges, 117
transgressive figure, 152
Travolta, John, 153–54
Trilling, Lionel, 160, 183
The Truth About Cats and Dogs, 61
Tucci, Stanley, 85
Turner, Lana, 29–30
tween consumer beauty market, 15
tweens, 2, 119–20
Twitter, 48, 50
Tyra Banks, 38, 165, 169, 179

Ugly Betty, 152

Vagina Monologues, 99
Vanity Fair, 40, 46, 61, 167–68
Vaughn, Vince, 22
vegetarianism, 130–31
Vertigo, 80
videogames, 38, 161
view from behind, 63
Vogue magazine, 86
Volver, 15

Wang, David, 80
Wanted, 63, 131
Waters, John, 152–53
website exposure, 167, 177
website images, 35, 46, 48, 50, 95
weight, 2, 4, 8–9, 27, 40–42, 56,
   58–59, 95–98, 117–18, 120, 125,
   136, 138, 147, 149–51, 156–57
   goal, 26, 86
   pre-partum, 47
weight bias, 172, 184
weight control measures, extreme, 8,
   127

weight discrimination, 97
weight loss ads, 108
weight loss tips, 157
weight obsessions, 92, 124
weight prejudices, 153, 171, 180
weight stigmatization, 100
weightism, 96–100, 102, 110, 118, 152,
   158
Welcome to the Dollhouse, 142
Wilder, Billy, 28
Wilson, Carnie, 36, 45
Winfrey, Oprah, 13, 36, 44, 166–67,
   169, 181, 186
Witherspoon, Reese, 23
Wizard of Oz, 119
woman
   obese, 106, 109–11, 152
   outsize, 14, 94, 98, 101, 117, 142,
      152, 154
   single professional, 136
   thin, 160, 183
   unruly, 117
woman motorcyclist, 75
women
   aging, 16
   medieval, 174, 178
   midlife, 44
women warriors, 53, 61, 64–65, 67, 86
women's weepies, 163
Wonder Woman, 63
Working Girl, 79
workout regimens, 38, 43, 55–57, 95
world cinemas, 17

youth, cult of, 19, 76, 86, 141, 164,
   174, 177
YouTube, 48–49

Zellweger, Renee, 36, 41